US–China Relations in the 21st Century

US–China Relations in the 21st Century addresses the bilateral relations of these two nations on international, domestic, societal, and individual levels between 1990 and 2005. Peaceful power shift remains a central problem in world politics, since historically power transition from a dominant nation to a challenger has been associated with international wars. This book examines whether China and the US can learn from history and manage a potential power transition peacefully. Grounding his research on contemporary US–China relations with thorough theoretical, historical, and policy exploration, Zhu selects two important cases of power transitions in history as the background for this study: power rivalry between Great Britain and Germany (1871–1914) that led to World War I, and the peaceful power transition from Great Britain to the United States (1865–1945).

US–China Relations in the 21st Century contributes to the current IR theory by proposing a new analytical model on global power transition and provides recommendations for peacefully handling a potential power transition from the US to China in the future. This original and comprehensive study is essential reading for scholars of US and Chinese foreign policy, world politics, and international relations.

Zhiqun Zhu, Ph.D., is Assistant Professor of International Political Economy and Diplomacy at the University of Bridgeport, USA.

Politics in Asia series
Formerly edited by Michael Leifer
London School of Economics

ASEAN and the Security of South-East Asia
Michael Leifer

China's Policy Towards Territorial Disputes
The case of the South China Sea Islands
Chi-kin Lo

India and Southeast Asia
Indian perceptions and policies
Mohammed Ayoob

Gorbachev and Southeast Asia
Leszek Buszynski

Indonesian Politics under Suharto
Order, development and pressure for change
Michael R. J. Vatikiotis

The State and Ethnic Politics in Southeast Asia
David Brown

The Politics of Nation Building and Citizenship in Singapore
Michael Hill and Lian Kwen Fee

Politics in Indonesia
Democracy, Islam and the ideology of tolerance
Douglas E. Ramage

Communitarian Ideology and Democracy in Singapore
Beng-Huat Chua

The Challenge of Democracy in Nepal
Louise Brown

Japan's Asia Policy
Wolf Mendl

The International Politics of the Asia-Pacific, 1945–1995
Michael Yahuda

Political Change in Southeast Asia
Trimming the Banyan Tree
Michael R. J. Vatikiotis

Hong Kong
China's challenge
Michael Yahuda

Korea Versus Korea
A case of contested legitimacy
B. K. Gills

Taiwan and Chinese Nationalism
National identity and status in international society
Christopher Hughes

Managing Political Change in Singapore
The elected presidency
Kevin Y. L. Tan and Lam Peng Er

US–China Relations in the 21st Century
Power transition and peace

Zhiqun Zhu

Foreword by Robert Sutter

Routledge
Taylor & Francis Group

LONDON AND NEW YORK

First published 2006 by Routledge
2 Park Square, Milton Park, Abingdon, Oxon OX14 4RN

Simultaneously published in the USA and Canada
by Routledge
270 Madison Avenue, New York, NY 10016

Transferred to Digital Printing 2006

Routledge is an imprint of the Taylor & Francis Group, an informa business

© 2006 Zhiqun Zhu

Typeset in Baskerville by Prepress Projects Ltd, Perth
Printed and bound in Great Britain by Biddles, King's Lynn

British Library Cataloguing in Publication Data
A catalogue record for this book is available from the British Library

Library of Congress Cataloging in Publication Data
Zhu, Zhiqun.
US–China relations in the 21st century : power transition and peace /
   by Zhiqun Zhu.
   p. cm. – (Politics in Asia series)
   Includes bibliographical references and index.
   1. United States–Foreign relations–China. 2. China–Foreign
   relations–United States. 3. United States–Foreign relations–
   1989–. 4. Great powers. 5. Peaceful change (International
   relations).
   I. Title. II. Series.
   E183.8.C5Z539 2006
   327.73051'09'051–dc22
   2005018104

ISBN10: 0–415–70208–9
ISBN13: 9–78–0–415–70208–9

Contents

Illustrations

Figures

Tables

Acknowledgments

It has been a long journey for me to finish this book. Over the years, I have accumulated enormous debts to many people. First and foremost, I dedicate this book to my parents in China. My father, Zhu Feng, and mother, Jiang Qiaodi, have had great expectations of me since my childhood. Their unconditional love and support have guided me through ups and downs in my life. It is they who taught me the true meaning of "where there is a will, there is a way." By traditional Chinese standards, I'm not a dutiful son for having lived so far away from my parents as they fight against aging and failing health. I can only repay their love with hard work and success in what I pursue.

The book is written on the basis of my doctoral dissertation finished at the University of South Carolina. Professor Donald J. Puchala, my academic advisor and dissertation director, is one of the most important and influential people in my life. He has the unique talent of identifying potential values in any research proposal and pointing one in the right direction. He is the major reason why I chose and stayed at the University of South Carolina for my doctoral research. I remain grateful to him for his sound advice and constant support. Other members of my dissertation committee, Professor Harvey Starr, Professor Charles W. Kegley, Professor John Hsieh, and Professor James Kuhlman, have all provided useful suggestions and comments to help my research in various ways, for which I wish to express my deep appreciation. Some ideas from this research were presented at the International Studies Association conferences in Chicago (2001), Hong Kong (2001), and New Orleans (2002). I thank the discussants and fellow panelists for their helpful comments.

In the course of research and writing, Professor Kenneth W. Thompson at the University of Virginia helped me win a fellowship from the Institute for the Study of World Politics in Washington, DC. Professor Thompson also kindly invited me to share my views on US–China relations at the Miller Center at the University of Virginia. He has continued to cheer me on as I embark on my college teaching career. I deeply appreciate his kindness and wish him well.

I spent a very fruitful year at Hamilton College in central New York as a visiting assistant professor of government in the 2003–4 academic year.

Colleagues at this fine liberal arts college set a very high standard for their teaching and research. I enjoyed chatting with them and wish to thank them for their encouragement.

It is at the University of Bridgeport that I eventually finished this book. I'm very excited to be able to teach here and contribute to the expanding political science and international relations programs. The University of Bridgeport is a diverse and thriving community, with a large percentage of international students and faculty. Colleagues at the International College are extremely supportive and have shown great interest in my research. Students here are hungry for knowledge about China, Asia, and US–China relations. I introduced some of the ideas in the book to my International Relations and US–China Relations classes at Hamilton College and World Politics and Political Economy of China classes at the University of Bridgeport. Questions and comments from students helped me clarify my points and sharpen my arguments.

Dr. Robert Sutter, a leading scholar on US–China relations and Visiting Professor of Asian Studies at the School of Foreign Service, Georgetown University, gladly viewed my manuscript and wrote a foreword for the book. I'm grateful for his generous support and help.

My good friend Fahrettin Sumer, Assistant Professor of Politics and Economics at Benedict College in South Carolina, and his wife, Sheima, volunteered to proofread the manuscript and helped improve the quality of the book. I wish to thank them for their friendship and kindness. Of course, any errors in the book remain my own responsibility.

Stephanie Rogers, Asian Studies editor at Routledge, first responded to my original book proposal positively and then encouraged me to revise the manuscript to make it more saleable. Along the way, Stephanie and her assistant Helen Baker have answered many of my questions very patiently. Production Editor Andrew R. Davidson and his team are extremely efficient and helpful. It's been a great experience to work with them. Without their help, this book could not have been published smoothly.

Last but not least, I want to express my special gratitude to my wife and best friend, Zhimin Xu. Over the past eight years, Zhimin has sacrificed a lot and has always stood firmly by me. She complements me in many aspects and makes me a better person. I started my dissertation research when Zhimin was pregnant with our first daughter, Julia. The birth of Julia on 6 May 2001 added much joy to our life. Julia is an intelligent, energetic, and lovely girl. I defended my dissertation just before Julia turned two. When I finished this book, Julia was already four and her sister Sophia will be born soon. I also wish to use this book as my personal welcoming gift to my second daughter, Sophia. Undoubtedly, Zhimin, Julia, and even Sophia have all left their indelible marks on this book. I'm confident that my family, as a strong team, will accomplish more projects in our life together.

Zhiqun Zhu
Bridgeport, Connecticut
May 2005

Foreword

Zhiqun Zhu's pathbreaking study goes far in helping us deal sensibly with what he rightfully identifies as one of the key issues in world politics in the twenty-first century – the rise of China and its implications for US leadership in Asian and world affairs. Employing relevant historical analysis involving Great Britain, Imperial Germany, and the United States, and using an impressive array of international relations theories, Dr. Zhu develops clear hypotheses and an overall theoretical framework that can guide our thinking in the years ahead regarding China's rising power, possible coexistence with the US superpower, and perhaps an eventual power transition between the two countries.

The organization of the study is admirably clear. The prose is direct, to the point, and easy to grasp. There are many contentious issues in US–China relations and in interpreting Chinese foreign policy objectives and goals. Dr. Zhu deals with these with balance and grace. The policy recommendations flow from the analysis, which highlights the importance of US and Chinese leadership, understanding, and accommodation in an international environment heavily influenced by forces of globalization and interdependence that is predicted to allow for a peaceful rise of Chinese influence relative to the United States.

While broadening our theoretical understanding and knowledge, Dr. Zhu's assessment has obvious practical policy implications as well. The debate over "the China threat" was at full throttle in the United States during the 1990s. It subsided following the election of George W. Bush and the 11 September 2001 terrorist attack on America. US strategists were diverted to an immediate global threat of uncertain proportions and duration. The wars in Afghanistan and Iraq placed US strategic interests squarely in the difficulties of southwest Asia, adding to the diversion from China. Nonetheless, US military planners and those who support them in the US intelligence community and in the Congress have remained vigilant over the rapid improvement and expansion of Chinese air and naval power. Much of the Chinese military buildup seems directed at coercing Taiwan and confronting US power if it were to intervene in a Taiwan contingency. In the post-Cold War world, China has remained the only large power building military forces to attack Americans – a reality that cannot be ignored by American officials.

Meanwhile, China's rapid economic growth of nearly 10 percent annually is accompanied by growth in trade almost double that amount. China has become the leading engine of growth in Asia, eclipsing Japan for regional leadership. China accompanies this rising economic importance with adroit and flexible diplomacy that appeals to regional governments and elite and popular opinion. China's rising "soft power" based on a geo-economic strategy that seeks common ground with Asian neighbors interested in mutual economic development and growth often outshines US policies that after 9/11 focus heavily on getting Asian governments to do more in the war on terrorism.

There is some debate among specialists about whether China will soon or ever become a peer with the United States in Asian and world leadership. Chinese leaders and people meanwhile have resentments and concerns over past and present US policies and behavior. US support for Taiwan heads the list of Chinese complaints about US global and regional dominance that have been muffled in recent years but continue to influence Chinese strategic thinking and behavior. How much influence is a matter of intense debate. Some see Chinese leaders increasingly accommodating to world conditions including US world leadership, while others interpret Deng Xiaoping's advice that Chinese leaders should "bide their time" in gradually building "comprehensive national power" as an implicit warning that a more powerful future China will pursue revisionist goals.

While it deals fairly with alternative outcomes, Zhiqun Zhu's assessment is relatively optimistic that China will continue to rise in power and influence, and that US and Chinese leaders can reach understandings that avoid conflict and war and allow for adjustments in their relative power in Asian and world affairs during the twenty-first century. Whether or not one subscribes to this perspective, anyone interested in China's rising power and its implications for US interests needs to consider the elements of Dr. Zhu's thoughtful and comprehensive framework of analysis. The alternative is half baked assessment and poorly informed policy that are almost certain to push the United States and China into the directions of needless confrontation and conflict that Dr. Zhu seeks to avoid.

Robert Sutter
Georgetown University
April 2005

1   Introduction

The big question: how can the United States and China manage a potential power transition peacefully?

In May and June 2005, *Newsweek* and the *Atlantic Monthly*, two major journals in the United States, both published cover stories about China. *Newsweek*'s special report, titled "Is China the World's Next Superpower?," somberly examined unprecedented new challenges – both opportunities and threats – for the United States in the years ahead. The *Atlantic Monthly*'s cover story, "How We Would Fight China," argued that China would become a more formidable adversary than Russia ever was.[1] What exactly is going to happen between a rising power and the world's sole superpower? This book is about the rise and fall of great powers. More specifically, it is about China's rise and US–China relations in the twenty-first century.

The reemergence of the People's Republic of China as a great economic, political, and military power and its consequences at the end of the twentieth century and in the early twenty-first century will probably become one of the most significant and most frequently written and read chapters in any future book of international politics and world history. Already, people around the world are watching China's growth with different reactions, which range from expectation and admiration to awe and apprehension.

On one hand, those who view China's rise in a positive light tend to think that China's time has come after more than a century of weakness, suffering, and humiliation. They see China's rapid modernization as an opportunity not just for China itself but also for the international community. China's vast market potential, its huge aggregate wealth, and its robust trade with other parts of the world, for example, provide enormous benefits to people both in and outside China. A more prosperous and more confident China is more likely to become a responsible, respectful, and democratic China, they argue. They also tend to agree with China's official pronouncement that China's rise has been and will continue to be peaceful and beneficial to the region and the world in general. China's modernization does not pose a threat to anybody or challenge any power in Asia, they would also argue.

On the other hand, those who view China's ascendancy in a less favorable light tend to believe that China's future is worrisome since its growth has already created so many problems for itself and others, including environmental degradation, a widening income gap, increasing unemployment, trade imbalances, and a regional arms race. Perhaps China's rise itself is not so disturbing, some point out, but because of the undemocratic nature of Chinese politics and its unpredictability, people have to worry about how China is going to use its growing wealth and power in the future. There are also others, particularly in some quarters of the United States, Japan, and Taiwan, who consider the ascendance of the People's Republic of China as the greatest threat to their security or economic interests. In fact, an analogy is often drawn between today's China and pre-World War I Germany. Some people assume that China, with growing economic and military might, will inevitably challenge the existing international system and the dominant global power violently and force a global confrontation just as pre-World War I Germany did. It is therefore interesting and important to study whether a potential power transition from the United States to China will lead to another major war in the international system. This is a very serious topic not just for international relations students and policy makers who are concerned about international security, but also for the general public who care about the future of mankind.

From a historical perspective, a power transition in the international system is truly disruptive. The rise and fall of great powers is one of the most intriguing phenomena in world history and international relations. Historically the cyclical power transitions from a dominant nation to a challenger used to be associated with large-scale systemic wars. As one leading realist international relations scholar observed, peaceful power transition in the international system had a very low probability.[2] The mechanism that regulated power transitions had been war, either because a rising nation would use violence to achieve the global power status that befitted its material resources and capabilities, or because the declining dominant power would attempt to prevent the inevitable defeat before it was too late. This makes it even more important to study history and international politics so that ways can be found to manage current US–China interactions judiciously and to help the relationship evolve peacefully in the future.

Students of international relations and world history have studied war and power transitions for generations and much progress has been made in understanding the causes, conduct, and consequences of war associated with power transitions. Nevertheless and somewhat surprisingly, little attention has been devoted to identifying the factors and conditions that might incline states toward peaceful coexistence and cooperation during a power transition; as a result, very little is actually known about whether and how a global power transition can be managed peacefully.

Indeed, the few cases of peaceful power transitions have not been seriously studied. The peaceful transatlantic global power transfer at the end of World War II and its significance for future global and regional power transitions, for example, are grossly under-researched. The existing literature on power transitions focuses on the origins, general causes, and timing of war between the competing powers; it is almost silent on the question of peaceful change and provides little policy options for the great powers before and during a power transition. Though some neoliberal international relations scholars have suggested that war is very unlikely between two democracies, this democratic peace proposition does not help much in dealing with a power transition in a non-democratic dyad, such as a potential regional and global power shift from the United States to China, especially in the Asia-Pacific region.

By understanding the conditions, factors, and circumstances that push states into rivalries and crises, we can take steps to mitigate them. Built upon comparative historical studies, this book searches for those conditions, factors, and circumstances that are most salient and critical during power transitions. The book is motivated by the following research and policy questions: What are the conditions and factors that caused violent systemic changes during power transitions in history? What are the conditions and factors that may be conducive to a peaceful power transition? How will globalization and deepening interdependence between states change the nature and dynamics of great power interactions and a potential power transition in the future? And most importantly, will China's rise to great power status be peaceful? And how can a potential power transition from the United States to China be managed successfully? Clearly, these are some of the important issues in international security and foreign policy studies that require more scholarly attention. This book addresses these questions and aims at enhancing the general understanding of great power politics, international and regional security, international conflict and conflict resolution, and US–China relations in the twenty-first century.

Why this book?

It is probably not an exaggeration to claim that US–China relations are the most complex and important bilateral relations in the twenty-first century. How the two powers handle their relations will determine their future and the peace of the world. Since this fragile relationship had been filled with so many twists and turns in the past, it becomes imperative to study the nature and trend of the relations between these two major powers of today. There is a huge collection of books on US–China relations, but this book offers a new and unique perspective. It studies US–China relations in the context of a potential global power transition, draws lessons from historical cases of power competition, and provides policy recommendations on how to peacefully manage US–China relations in the twenty-first century.

The objectives of this book are threefold: theoretical modification, methodological contribution, and policy recommendations. The book is intended not only for foreign policy makers and scholars who are concerned about great power relations, international security, and international conflicts, but also for international relations and political science students and those in the public who are interested in the rise and fall of great powers, international political economy in the twenty-first century, the prospect of peacefully managing a potential power transition in the future, and US–China relations in general.

Theoretically, this book modifies and expands the power transition research in international relations first proposed by the political scientist A. F. K. Organski (1958) and advances peace studies by clearly identifying conditions and factors that are pivotal during power transitions in the international system. The issue of peaceful systemic change is simply under-studied in international relations scholarship. This research pays more attention to conditions for peaceful systemic change, especially to conditions and factors that would help the rising power and the dominant power to manage their interactions constructively and conditions and factors that would discourage them from resorting to war as the solution to their differences. This book takes a comprehensive approach that involves elements of both realism and idealism in analyzing important issues in international politics. Different from the classic realist school that focuses on material power, state, military, and security issues, this research also studies economic, cultural, social, personnel, and other connections between states under certain international and domestic conditions. In addition, it brings globalization and interdependence into the discussion of state to state relations during the global power realignment.

Departing from the Organskian power transition model, which is basically a historical–structural interpretation, this book presents an agent–structure model that also emphasizes the role of decision-making and diplomacy in the study of power transition.[3] The research incorporates Kenneth Waltz's "three images" of the causes of war into the theoretical framework and links domestic factors and international developments in one perspective through analysis at global, domestic, societal, and individual levels.[4] The theoretical exploration suggests that, equipped with this multilevel analysis, the power transition theory will become a more forceful analytical tool in explaining and predicting great power relations.

Systematic comparative and historical study will be the major methodology in this book. Little research has been done to systematically compare and contrast major power transitions in history in order to come up with an analytical framework that can be used to account for other power transitions and to predict a future one. This book takes up this challenge. Methodologically, this research also attempts to bridge the gap between history and political science. There has been a poor link between the two disciplines. The two fields have been treated as distant subjects that employ divergent research methods, with one focusing on holistic interpretation and the other on empirical analysis. As political scientist Jack Levy commented, historians tend to describe and explain the connections between a series of events, whereas political scientists like to formulate and test general theoretical propositions about relationships between variables or classes of events.[5] However, both history and political science share a focus on people and the ways they organize their affairs in certain domestic and international environments. This book attempts to bring the two disciplines together by testing and expanding power transition theory through a detailed study of historical events from a multilevel analysis. And in doing so it applies international relations theory to the real world in both historical and contemporary settings. The book is interpretive, analytic, and predictive.

The policy recommendations developed from this research will be significant for managing great power relations and seeking international and regional security in the contemporary world. This book studies the important issue of how the nature and degree of interactions between two competing powers within certain international and domestic environments will affect the outcome of the power transition. Since the current literature on power transition lacks research on strategies for managing power transition peacefully, this research also attempts to fill the theoretical and policy gap in this regard. It explores strategies for peaceful coexistence and cooperation between two rival powers, such as ways to accommodate a challenging power without compromising the vital interests of the dominant power so as to avoid conflict when power discrepancy is narrowed and power parity is reached. If wars can be prevented before they start, then lasting peace will become more likely. Specific policy recommendations are particularly useful for the United States and China as they manage their difficult bilateral relations in the early decades of the twenty-first century.

Power transition takes place at both international and regional levels. How to manage relations between powers with conflicting interests, and how dominant powers can deal with rising powers more constructively in international political economy are serious challenges great powers have to face. The analytical framework developed from case studies in this research is also applicable to other cases and scenarios of power transitions at both international and regional levels.

Causes of war and conditions of peace have attracted and puzzled generations of international relations and foreign policy scholars. The next global power transition will surely take place under different conditions from previous ones, since it will occur in the era of nuclear weapons, globalization, growing interdependence, and revolutionary changes in information technology. It is very likely that we will witness the change of the mechanism of change itself. Power transition research could and should offer an explanation of international relations generally, rather than a more limited account of international war. It is hoped that the theoretical framework developed from this book will be helpful for managing relations between and among states that have diverse interests in the twenty-first century. And it is hoped that ways can be found to manage the next power transition in the international system (such as the one from the United States to China) peacefully.

Traditional, realist views of power transition tend to focus on conflict and war in the international system. This book analyzes why most power transitions led to war and why few ended in peace. As a contribution to the field of international relations, my book, through a multilevel analysis, proposes a modified theory that combines power transition with changed conditions associated with globalization, and explores the prospect of peaceful systemic transformation through multilateral engagement and cooperation in an era of deepening interdependence. It specifically develops strategies for peacefully managing systemic change in the future. This book will significantly advance the research of peace studies in international politics. The originality of the research lies not only in its critique and expansion of traditional international relations theories but also in its creative and practical proposal that power transitions can be managed in a peaceful way if both powers abide by certain rules of the game in their interactions. Changes in the international system since the end of the Cold War, such as deepening interdependence among major powers, have enhanced the likelihood of rule observation by these powers in their interactions with one another and multilateral cooperation, despite America's traditional preference for unilateralism.

The bloody record of past power transitions underscores the importance of new efforts to think through how to handle systemic change peacefully. The end of the Cold War has brought about a world in which the United States enjoys seemingly insurmountable supremacy as the only global power. Though America's military and economic preponderance, backed up by its impressive "soft power" stemming from the breadth and depth of its cultural and ideological reach, may continue for quite some time, it should not breed complacency that systemic change is necessarily far off. After all, America's share in world's total output has declined from about half at the end of World War II to less than a quarter today. More significantly, anti-Americanism is strong in many parts of the world, including in such traditional American allies as France, Germany, Great Britain, Japan, and South Korea. America's relative decline and increasingly unpopular foreign policy are accompanied by impressive growth and rise of other powers and players in the world. The key challenge for human beings today is to manage a potential power transition from the American supremacy to a different world order in the twenty-first century peacefully.

Anticipating the future of world politics is risky business, but it is prudent for decision makers to prepare for all future possibilities and make choices that have long-term impact. How power will be distributed in the twenty-first century remains an issue that invites debate. Generally speaking, the European Union (EU), China, Japan, Russia, and India are considered to have the potential capability to challenge America's world and regional leadership. Among all these potential rivals, however, a steadily rising China may present the most credible challenge for US foreign policy in the future. Japan and the EU, despite occasional trade and other frictions and policy disagreements, enjoy close security, political, economic, and social ties with the United States. For quite some time in the future Russia has to deal with enormous political and economic problems and challenges at home that have accumulated since the disintegration of the former Soviet Union before it will emerge as a leading power again; and India has to overcome the chronic problem of poor democratic performance and population explosion before its power potential can be fully materialized. Compared with China, these powers are less likely to directly challenge America's global and regional dominance in the near future.

If its economy, international influence, and military power continue to grow and expand in the next couple of decades, and if it becomes dissatisfied with the international and regional order imposed and maintained by the United States, the People's Republic of China stands very likely to challenge America's predominance in world affairs, especially in the Asia-Pacific region. On top of the various disagreements between the two countries lies the most explosive Taiwan issue, which is quickly spinning out of control as Taiwan's independence movement deepens and Beijing's resolve to keep the island within the "one China" framework hardens. The United States is already facing a policy dilemma over Taiwan's future. Lessons from history should not be ignored, and greater efforts are needed to manage US–China relations in the early decades of the twenty-first century to ensure a peaceful potential power transition in the international system.

This book is not just about US–China relations. Those who believe that a potential power transition is more likely to take place from the United States to the EU or to any other state or group of states will find that the theoretical framework and policy prescriptions developed from this book are not case-specific and can be applied to other scenarios.

The structure of the book

This book takes a historical and comparative approach to study power transitions and great power interactions in international relations, with the aim of providing policy prescriptions for managing a potential global or regional power transition in the twenty-first century. This first chapter is a general introduction to the book and research rationale, including research scope and research design, and the significance of the book. Chapter 2 constitutes the theoretical core of the book. I will critically survey international relations theories on the rise and fall of great powers, particularly on power transition and its linkage to war. Based on the survey and my criticism, I will develop a set of hypotheses and a new theoretical framework that incorporates Organski's original power transition proposition with the Waltzian "three images" as well as conditions of globalization and interdependence. I contend that traditional power transition theory treats power transition as a predetermined incident, with almost no consideration of how the decision environment will affect both the process and the outcome of a particular power transition. The decision environment includes various factors at all levels of bilateral interactions between the two competing powers, such as international structure, domestic politics, societal forces, and personalities of individual leaders. I argue that my new theoretical framework which provides an agent–structural interpretation of great power interactions can better explain and predict power transitions at both international and regional levels.

Chapters 3 and 4 are empirical historical case studies. To grasp the dynamics of power transitions, I will examine two cases from history: power rivalry between Germany and Great Britain (1871–1914), and power transition from Great Britain to the United States (1865–1945). Using my new power transition theoretical framework, I will analyze why the first case resulted in war and the second ended in peace between the competing powers. The first case is selected because the power rivalry between the two great nations and their failed management are considered to be one of the causes leading to World War I. The fact that both cases include Great Britain is interesting and informative. It is fascinating to study why the British mishandled their relations with Germany but succeeded in peacefully managing their interactions with the United States.

Drawing inferences from historical analysis, in Chapter 5 I will focus on contemporary US–China relations (1990–2005) and develop strategies for managing a potential power transition from the United States to China in the twenty-first century. The United States assumed global leadership at the end of World War II; if history repeats itself again, it is likely that some time in the twenty-first century the United States may relinquish, either willingly or unwillingly, its global and regional leadership. China is one of the few potential contenders that might accept the new leadership role, especially in Asia. This is also a policy-related section of the book. The policy prescriptions will have immediate implications for policy makers in the United States, China and elsewhere. Chapter 6 systematically compares and contrasts these three cases and revisits the hypotheses developed and tested in earlier chapters. Differences and similarities between the three cases will be elaborated and analyzed. The questions whether today's China resembles pre-World War I Germany and whether China's rise will be peaceful are to be answered in this chapter. Based on the comparisons and contrasts, I note the huge differences between today's China and pre-World War I Germany and remain optimistic that China will continue to be a stabilizing contributor to regional and global peace and prosperity.

Chapter 7 summarizes and concludes the book, with a brief discussion of theoretical development and policy recommendations for the United States and China. From reviewing interactions between the two powers at international, domestic, societal, and individual levels since 1990, I argue that China and the United States have gradually learned and are still learning how to manage their complicated relationship. Despite some vast differences between the two sides, the bilateral relations have moved forward over the past decade or so. Even on the most difficult issue of Taiwan's political relations with the People's Republic of China, the United States and China share the views that the current status quo across the Taiwan Strait cannot be changed unilaterally and that the dispute should be resolved peacefully. If such controversial issues as Taiwan are to be managed wisely, there is strong reason to believe that a potential power transition from the United States to China will be smooth and peaceful.

2 Rethinking theories of power transition

Are there theories that can be used to explain and predict US–China relations? This chapter looks at power transitions and US–China relations from a theoretical perspective. Theories and historical lessons are powerful tools that are, if applied properly, constructive for managing today's complicated bilateral relations between the world's fastest growing power and the world's only superpower in the course of a global power shift.

The rise and fall of great powers in history: a theoretical review

Great powers rise and fall.[1] Historically, power transitions used to be accompanied by major wars in the international system. The rise of the Iberian powers, the Ottoman Empire, the Hapsburg Empire, the United Provinces, Spain, France, Germany, and Japan during different historical periods from 1400 to 1900 all led to violent systemic changes. The cyclical wars associated with power transitions in the past prompted the historian E. H. Carr to identify the "problem of peaceful change" as the central dilemma of international relations.[2] "Great powers emerge from great wars," declared a renowned international relations scholar.[3] If peaceful change is impossible, the only pathway to greatness for states is through war.

Literature that accounts for power transition and its linkage to war abounds in international relations. Among others, Arnold Toynbee (1950), Quincy Wright (1965), Charles Doran (1971), Robert Gilpin (1981), George Modelski (1987), Immanuel Wallerstein (1987), Paul Kennedy (1987, 1993), and Torbjorn Knutsen (1999) all discerned a historical pattern or cycle of major wars associated with systemic changes in world politics. A. F. K. Organski (1958) more explicitly linked power transition to wars between great powers.

From a historical perspective, Toynbee (1950) observes that a phase of "general war" is usually followed by a "breathing space" which deteriorates into a conflictual era of "supplementary wars" until a power transition is completed and a new system is established.[4] One of the earliest scholars on war studies, Wright (1964) notes that "major wars" have occurred with great regularity throughout modern history, and have been followed, first, by a period of general peace, then by a cluster of "minor wars" and, finally, by another period of peace after a new world order is established.[5] Statesmen have been wrestling with peaceful solutions to the transformation in relative power of major nations in the international system throughout history.

In his first book, *The Politics of Assimilation: Hegemony and Its Aftermath* (1971), Charles F. Doran developed the "power cycle" theory of state rise and decline (shifting tides of history) as the cause of major war. A complete statement of the power cycle theory with strategic policy implications appeared in his *Systems in Crisis: New Imperatives of High Politics at Century's End* (1991). In his 1991 book, Doran presents a bold, original, and wide-ranging analysis of the present balance of power, of future prospects for the international system, and of the problems involved in this transformation. Doran demonstrates why such change has often been accompanied by world war, providing new insights into the causes of World War I. Further developing his theory of the power cycle, Doran reveals the structural bounds on statecraft and shows how the tides of history can suddenly and unexpectedly shift against the state. But, he asserts, the outcome of systems change is not predetermined and can be both peaceful and secure. Perhaps without sufficient empirical support, he stops short of elaborating on how a peaceful change can happen.

Taking a neo-realist approach, Robert Gilpin, in his *War and Change in World Politics* (1981), maintains that each power transition is resolved through "hegemonic war" which re-establishes an equilibrium in the international system. Hegemonic powers arrange the system to their advantage; however, because of diminishing returns, rising costs, diffusion of power to rivals, and decline in polity, it becomes more and more difficult to maintain the status quo. If the challenger is not accommodated, a hegemonic war ensues and the system is rearranged by the victor. The cycle of change is completed when a new status quo reflecting the redistribution of power is in place. The decline of a hegemon is virtually inevitable and is due to several factors: the costs of maintaining dominance in the system, the loss of economic and technological leadership, the erosion of the hegemon's resource base, the differential growth and distribution of power among states, and the tendency for power to shift from the center to the periphery as fighting among states in the central system weakens them all. Thus, for Gilpin, uneven economic, political, and technological developments lead to the cyclical power transitions and war.

Immanuel Wallerstein, a prominent proponent of the neo-Marxist world-systems theory, which focuses on international inequality and dependence, asserts that world wars have regularly broken out during the course of modern history, and that they have been followed by phases of hegemonic maturity, hegemonic decline, and the ascent of rival hegemonies. He sees power transition as "a regular happening." "The basic reason was the same: the overall productivity edge relative to that of the closest rival states ... had begun to fritter away."[6]

Paul Kennedy also brings political economy into the study of great power politics. In his *The Rise and Fall of the Great Powers: Economic Change and Military Conflict from 1500 to 2000* (1987), Kennedy states that technological advancement, demographic change, and economic growth are the driving forces of historical development. He argues that great powers will fall because eventually they all experience overspending as a result of expanded economic and military interests overseas. For Kennedy, "imperial overstretch" that has occurred throughout history is the reason that great powers fall one after another.

George Modelski's (1987) ambitious theory of long cycles seeks to explain international conflicts and patterns of leadership since 1494. He sees five "long cycles" of about 100 years each. In his view, a long cycle always begins with a major global war. A single state then emerges as the new world power and legitimizes its preponderance with postwar peace treaties. In time, though, the leader loses legitimacy, and deconcentration of power leads to another global war and a new world power.[7] Modelski's long cycle theory confirms the observation of other scholars, but his use of naval power as the sine qua non of global power may be an item for debate.

In the tradition of historical–structural analysis, Torbjorn Knutsen explains that world orders are introduced by an initial wave of great wars and, later, destroyed by a subsequent war wave. Once the initial war wave subsides, three phases of order ensue in sequence: a hegemonic phase manifests a clear hierarchy of power and, consequently, a high level of stability; in the second phase, the hegemon's lead falters, challengers emerge, and systemic instability increases; and the third phase is one of relative equality among the declining hegemon and its challengers. Lacking a hierarchy, who gets to define and enforce the rules is unclear. Conflicts increase and the order continues to erode until another wave of warfare demolishes what remains. In Knutsen's view, the hegemonic ability to lead is based on domestic consensus and legitimacy which is translated into systemic legitimacy. When the hegemon loses its domestic consensus, the reverberations are soon felt in the international system. In other words, the hegemon's soft power and its domestic politics will largely determine its foreign policy and international posture.

Economists also reported "long cycle" economic waves. In his study in the 1920s Nikolai Kondratieff claimed that there have been three major economic "waves" since the 1780s, each about 50 years long.[8] He observed that the greatest number of social upheavals (wars and revolutions) occurred during the periods of the rising wave of each long cycle. George Modelski and William Thompson, in their individual and joint efforts since the late 1970s, emphasize periodic succession struggles in world leadership among great powers. Their theory of long cycles posits that the succession to leadership is directly related to systemic bouts of warfare. In a more recent study, Modelski and Thompson argue that the rise and decline of leading sectors in the global economy (the Kondratieff process) coordinate with the rise and fall of world powers (the long cycle of global politics).[9] But they fall short of discussing which cycle (economic or political) comes first, or whether the two types of cycles are concurrent.

All these theories tell us much about the causes, conduct, and consequences of the cyclical wars between major powers, but little is known about whether and why states may choose to cooperate peacefully during systemic transformations. In contrast, the power transition theory not only accounts for why great powers go to war, it also allows us to anticipate how war can be avoided and how peace is likely to be achieved.

The Organskian power transition theory

It was A. F. K. Organski who, in his *World Politics* (1958), first and most explicitly linked power transition to wars between great powers and called attention to the danger that the probability of war may increase during a period of power transition. Power transition theory predates many competing or similar theories. For example, Doran's power cycle theory (1971), Keohane's hegemonic stability theory (1980), Gilpin's hegemonic leadership theory (1981), and Modelski's leadership long cycle theory (1987) were all developed later than Organski's power transition theory and may well have been informed by it. Like other theories on the rise and fall of great powers, the power transition theory holds differential rates of economic growth to be the motivating force that drives a simple but seemingly inescapable mechanism for change in the international system. As new nations develop, the old leader is challenged. Ordinarily, such challenges by newcomers result in war. The conclusion of one such war is the beginning of another cycle of growth, expansion, and eventual decline before the world moves toward a new round of hegemonic conflict.

A direct challenge to classic realism, which claims the international system is anarchical, Organski and other power transition theorists believe that the international system is hierarchical, and that in each historical era a single dominant state leads the international order as head of a coalition of satisfied powers. As long as the leader of this status quo coalition enjoys a preponderance of power, peace is maintained. But when power reaches parity, i.e., when a dissatisfied challenger begins to overtake the status quo power, wars are most likely to break out. The basic hypothesis is that the probability of war increases as the power gap narrows, especially as a rival *unsatisfied* challenger comes closer to equaling the capabilities of the once stronger guardian of the status quo.[10]

Power transition theorists emphasize "power parity" and "dissatisfaction with the status quo" as crucial elements contributing to the risk of system-transforming war. The theory is based primarily on changes in the distribution of power in the international system. "The cornerstone of power transition theory is that *parity* is the necessary condition for major war."[11] They define "parity" as the phase in which a potential challenger develops more than 80 percent of the resources of the dominant power. Parity ends when the challenger exceeds the resources of the dominant nation by 20 percent.[12] When a major war is waged, the relative resources among the great powers are redistributed. And when the war is over, the power pyramid will be rearranged.

Though they generally believe that war is most likely during power transfer, power transition scholars disagree on exactly when war will erupt or who will initiate it. Will wars be fought before or after the transition? Will the speed of the transition affect the start of war? Who is more likely to initiate such a war? Organski originally argued that the dissatisfied challenger initiates conflict prior to the actual takeover, but in a later study, he and Kugler reported that the dissatisfied challenger initiates war after the transition.[13] But both logically and empirically, the dominant power may initiate a preemptive war before a challenger becomes too powerful.

"The fundamental elements uniting all power transition research are concerns with the importance of *internal* growth for *international* politics, a focus on international *hierarchy* rather than *anarchy*, and the importance of *relative power* and *evaluations of the international status quo* in anticipation of interstate war."[14] National power and capabilities can be augmented through internal growth such as industrialization and external connections such as alliance formation, but power transition theory emphasizes domestic growth as the most important source of national power. Domestic growth is so central that initially the term "power transition" referred to the process by which a country develops domestically (it undergoes a transition from underdeveloped to developed).[15] It is assumed that the internal development of other states cannot be stopped by the dominant power. If the international status quo does not help a country to develop, it can still develop in isolation. Indeed, many rising powers became rich and powerful in spite of the status quo that was economically, politically, and militarily contrary to their interests. This was exactly the situation faced by Germany between the two world wars and the Soviet Union in the 1930s through 1950s.[15]

Aside from power parity, another important aspect of power transition theory is the status quo evaluation by the challenging power. It is very rare that a dominant power will be dissatisfied with the existing international order since that order is established and/or maintained by the dominant power itself.[16] It is therefore important to look at whether the challenging power is satisfied or not. If a rising power is dissatisfied with the status quo, like the pre-WWI Germany, then a violent power transition is expected. If the challenging power is satisfied with the status quo, it is not expected to challenge the established order violently when its strength reaches parity with the dominant power. When the challenger is considered a benign power and when both powers are satisfied with the international status quo, the actual overtaking is most likely to be peaceful. This was the case of the United States and Great Britain in the early twentieth century. The United States' overtaking of Great Britain did not threaten the structure of the existing international order. It simply reinforced existing rules.

To determine whether a challenging power is satisfied with the status quo, scholars have suggested some indicators of a challenger's status quo evaluations such as money market discount rate, arms buildup, domestic attributes, and international behavior. For example, if the purchasing power of a country's money were in decline, the people of that country would be able to buy less with their money, and consequently would be dissatisfied. And if a rising state increases its military expenditure at a rate greater than it has in the past or faster than the dominant power, it indicates dissatisfaction with the status quo.[17] According to power transition theory, a dissatisfied challenger is most likely to become an aggressive power. But how to accommodate the challenger without sacrificing the vital interests of the status quo power is an interesting yet scarcely studied question. Does the challenger have legitimate reasons to assert its power? If so, how can the dominant power help to make it a satisfied power but not an aggressive one? These questions remain unanswered.

Competitor theory: balance of power

In general, there have been two schools of thought on the relationship between power distribution and the onset of war: the balance-of-power (power parity) theory and the power transition (power preponderance or hegemonic stability) theory.

Power transition theory was originally advanced as a competitor to the balance-of-power theory. The idea that power parity leads to war is in sharp contrast to the classical realist theory of Hans Morgenthau, Henry Kissinger, and Kenneth Waltz, which argues that major war is likely when one state is preponderant and unlikely when great powers are relatively equal. A balance of power keeps the peace by convincing potential aggressors that war will have both high costs and a low probability of success. A direct challenge to classic realism and the balance-of-power theory, power transition theory views the international system not as anarchic but as a hierarchically organized order in which actors accept their positions based on relative power distribution. Turning classical realism on its head, the power transition theory argues that a hegemonic system with one powerful actor will be stable because it is in the hegemon's self-interest to maintain the political and military order. The objective of nations is not to maximize power, but to maximize net gains and maintain a dominant position in the system. The balance-of-power theory implies that state actions are dictated by a universal preference and insatiable national appetite for power, while the power transition theory contemplates that states vie for control over the rules and norms of international intercourse and for control over the values by which nations live and interact. In other words, for balance of power theory, power is an end itself; for power transition theory, power is both a means and an end.

Nevertheless, power transition and balance of power theories are similar in that each posits that states confronted with an external threat will engage in balancing or counterbalancing behavior. For those involved in a balance-of-power situation, this means acting, such as through alliance formation, to prevent any state or coalition of states from upsetting the existing equilibrium by becoming too strong. For the hegemon in a power transition, it means acting, such as initiating preemptive war, to prevent a challenger from surpassing it and assuming its position of dominance. And for the challenger in a power transition, it means acting, such as through consolidating military and industrial modernization, to prevent the hegemon from blocking its rise to ascendancy.

The scholarly debate between the two major theories in international relations is inconclusive and obscure, and history may provide cases to support both theories. But power transition theory seems to have an empirical and logical edge over balance-of-power theory. Power transition theorists point out limitations of the balance-of-power theory and believe that, at a minimum, power transition theory should be considered a major contender for explanations of international phenomena by any serious researcher.[18]

Both power transition theory and balance-of-power theory emphasize dissatisfaction with the status quo as a crucial element contributing to systemic war. However, some scholars, using the rational actor model, claim that dissatisfaction with the status quo is unrelated to the likelihood of war. The anticipated gains must be larger than the expected domestic costs, or else a rational actor will not wage war. The decision for wars that transform the international system is the result of a domestic strategic calculation of benefits and costs that may not involve dissatisfaction with the status quo.[19] International interactions follow a path of reasoned judgment. Even war is waged with reason rather than without it.

Criticism

Power transition theory identifies one possible cause of wars between great powers, but there are multilevel factors that contribute to the outbreak of wars.[21] Even theorists of power transition themselves reject the deterministic claim that power transition alone causes wars.[22] Power transition provides an opportunity for war, but for a war to occur, there must exist other factors, particularly the international and domestic constraints and the political will of decision makers on each side. It is assumed that if power transition is managed properly, or if there is no incentive for war on both sides, a systemic change may evolve peacefully.

Power transition theory describes a phenomenon in international relations that is predetermined and automatic. But power parity doesn't always lead to war between rivals. Power transition theory fails to acknowledge the uncertainties associated with power differentials and the dynamic interdependent relationship between the status quo power and the challenging power. It leaves out such vital variables as decision-making, statesmanship, and diplomacy. Even from the much-used rational choice perspective, great powers may choose to cooperate during a systemic change in an interdependent world if cooperation yields more benefits. Or as the expected utility model suggests, if the expected gains outweigh costs, a decision maker will probably strive for the expected benefits.[23] Power transition theory reduces a policy maker to the status of a prisoner of the international structure rather than an agent capable of influencing the outcome of power transition.

Decisions to go to war are constrained by, among other considerations, foreign policies, domestic political structure, perceptions of individual leaders, public opinion, and acceptance by the international community. To study whether a power transition will lead to war, political, economic, military, cultural, and social dimensions of great power relations have to be examined. Power transition theory emphasizes domestic growth as the source of national power. It only vaguely links domestic and international politics in one single perspective. In this respect, the logic of two-level games on international negotiations could provide a better explanation for war or peace decisions as a result of the interactions between international and domestic environments.[24] Power transition theory also fails to acknowledge the importance of the international regime. How globalization, interdependence, and multilateral cooperation will affect power transition is a question largely evaded by power transition scholars.

A multilevel analysis is needed to identify multiple causes of international conflict and war. In his *Man, the State, and War* (1959), Kenneth N. Waltz explicitly explored the causes of international conflict at individual, domestic, and systemic levels. The three images, i.e., international conflict caused by flawed human behavior, international conflict caused by domestic structure of states, and international conflict caused by international anarchy, as a whole form a more powerful explanatory tool than any one image alone. "The third image describes the framework of world politics, but without the first and second images there can be no knowledge of the forces that determine policy; the first and second images describe the forces in world politics, but without the third image it is impossible to assess their importance or predict their results," explains Waltz.[25] We may borrow Waltz's "three images" and develop them into four levels of analysis: international, domestic, societal, and individual. Robert Putnam's two-level games theory may also help explain the decision-making process associated with power transition.[26] Aided with the explanatory strength of the multilevel analysis, the power transition theory will offer a more forceful theoretical framework regarding great power interactions.

Power transition theory, like other historical–structural analyses in international relations, treats power transitions in an ideal vacuum without considering the dynamic interactions between great powers and the constraints each power faces in an interdependent structure. Little is said about the impact of the interdependent structure on power transition and the role of other players in the international system during power transition. International relations are not static; the dynamic relations between and among different players at different levels may well change the process and outcome of power transitions. Power parity may provide an opportunity for initiating wars, but the final decisions for war have to be made by political leaders, who are constrained by both domestic and international environments.

The power transition proposition sounds deterministic and pessimistic. In fact, power parity doesn't always lead to war between rivals, and power transitions don't always eventuate in war. Power transition theory fails to acknowledge the uncertainties associated with power transfer and the dynamic interdependent relationship between the status quo power and the challenging power. It does not discuss the impact of the interactions among decision-makers, domestic structure, and international environment on the process of power transition. And most importantly, little attention has been devoted to identifying the factors that would incline both powers toward cooperation and a peaceful change.

Power transition theorists believe that their theory is superior to competing realist theories such as the balance-of-power theory. Indeed, the balance-of-power theory confronts major empirical and logical problems. For example, it cannot explain how a multipolar system with tight and roughly equal alliances, such as the one that existed before 1914, could still fall into major war. Also, it cannot explain why, in the key bipolar cases in history (Sparta–Athens, Carthage–Rome, and France–Hapsburgs), wars ensued when the two great powers were essentially equal. However, the power transition theory itself is not without problems. For example, it cannot explain satisfactorily why the Cold War did not develop into a hot war when the two superpowers were roughly equal in military strength. Perhaps the deterrence theory and the invention of nuclear weapons (e.g. mutual assured destruction) could provide some of the explanations here.[27] Furthermore, power transition theory does not offer a deductively consistent explanation of when war starts and who initiates war.

This brief theoretical review indicates that, while much progress has been made in the study of war, little is known about the dynamic process of power transition and the factors and conditions that may contribute to a peaceful power transition. The current literature on power transitions is surprisingly silent on the issue of whether and how a peaceful change can take place. An obvious reason for the dearth of such research lies in the fact that peaceful power transitions are very rare in history. Also, the very few instances of peaceful power transitions have not attracted the attention of scholars precisely because war did not break out. They may have been treated and studied for other theoretical purposes. Though the liberal democratic peace theory claims that democracies rarely fight each other, it does not help much in dealing with a power transition in a non-democratic dyad.

In a recent and rare study on peaceful power transition, some scholars contend that a peaceful systemic change depends on three core variables – benign images of one another, agreement on the arrangement of the international order, and the legitimacy of the order.[28] But unfortunately this is proposed as a hypothesis without solid empirical testing by the authors.

The relative paucity of studies of peaceful power transition requires that more research should be done in peace studies and the gap in the scholarship on peaceful power transitions needs to be filled. The relationship between deep interdependence and power transition has not been seriously studied. For example, how does globalization affect the process of power transition? How will the interactions among individuals, states, and the interdependent international structure under conditions of globalization and multilateralism change the course and dynamics of power transition? This research will engage in such theoretical and empirical exploration based on historical study.

A new model of power transition theory

The central argument of this book is that, although power parity and dissatisfaction of the challenging power with the status quo may be necessary conditions for wars associated with power transition, the process and outcome of a power transition are determined by the interactions of the international environment, domestic politics, societal links, and individual leaders (Figure 2.1). Power transition provides a window for war, but war or peace decisions are made by political leaders, who base their decisions on evaluations of the overall relationship between the two competing powers under certain international and domestic conditions. This new theoretical framework is superior to traditional realist theories such as power transition and balance-of-power in that it treats power transition as a dynamic process and places it in a broader international and domestic context to study. It looks for other possible causes of war (and thus potential conditions of peace) in addition to power parity and dissatisfaction. In doing so it develops and expands the Organskian power transition theory.

The original power transition theory does not look at the power transition process from different levels of analysis. The new framework emphasizes the importance of non-systemic factors that have largely been ignored by structural realism such as societal links, personalities of leaders, domestic politics, and statesmanship. The non-systemic factors are critical variables to be reckoned with in understanding state behavior. This contextual, interactive, and integrative perspective is more nuanced and more persuasive. Unlike Organski's original historical–structural interpretation, this new model offers an agent–structural interpretation and incorporates decision-making and status quo evaluations into power transition studies.

Power transition theory asserts that the joint condition of power parity and dissatisfaction with the status quo is most likely to lead to war between great powers. I assume that the historical cycle of the rise and fall of powers will continue, and that a rising power's internal development can hardly be blocked by the dominant power (though the dominant power may launch a preemptive war to blunt or temporarily slow the challenger's internal growth). In other words, power parity will be reached between two contending states sooner or later. What warrants more attention is the rising power's

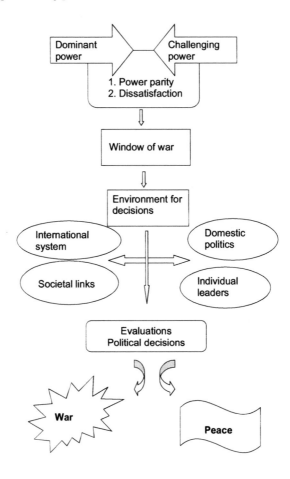

Figure 2.1 The dynamics of power transition: a multilevel analysis.

evaluation of the status quo. And this evaluation needs to be analyzed from multiple levels.

According to power transition theory, most challengers would be dissatis-fied with the status quo because they "have grown to full power after the existing international order was fully established and the benefits already al-located."[29] Like power transition theory, status inconsistency may also cause dissatisfaction by the challenger.[30] The status inconsistency argument claims that actors in any social and political system can be ranked according to their achieved or objective status (such as the amount of power they have accumu-lated) as well as according to their ascribed or subjective status (such as the amount of respect they are shown by other members of the system). Actors high on achieved status but low on ascribed status are "status inconsistent." States suffering from such inconsistency are frustrated and may engage in aggressive behavior, directed at achieving the respect they feel they deserve. Therefore, if conditions and factors exist or are created that make the challenger satisfied with the status quo, then a peaceful power transition is more likely. Of course, to make a challenger satisfactory with the international order does not mean appeasement of all its policies and intentions. How to accommodate a rising power's legitimate vital interests without harming the interests of the dominant power and violently disrupting the international system is a classic and crucial issue facing policy makers.

When the power differential between the existing hegemon and the rising challenger narrows, windows for war are open. But the existence of an underlying cause of war does not mean war will always be the result. As the rising power closes in on the declining power, the rising power expects its ideas about how the system ought to be organized and governed to be taken seriously. If these notions about order are fundamentally at odds with those of the declining power and if neither side is willing to give way, the proximate cause of war will emerge, and a conflict is very likely. So, if agreement on the principles of order is successfully negotiated and the rising power's legitimate concerns are addressed, an important proximate cause of war will be removed, and the chances of a peaceful transition will be increased.

The elements of order may include the hierarchy of prestige, rules about trade and defense, and mutual recognition of the sphere of influence. For example, during Japan's rise as an Asian power in the late nineteenth century, it failed to move up in the international hierarchy of prestige, nor was its sphere of influence or attempt at territorial change recognized by other powers. Japan's victory over China in the Sino-Japanese War of 1894–5 marked its debut as a great power in Asia. Russia, Germany, and France subsequently threatened collective military action if Japan did not return the Liaodong Peninsula to China. Japanese humiliation and anger were further exacerbated when these powers proceeded to claim ports in the very territory that Japan had been forced to return. This drove home Japan's inferior status among great powers. Some writers contend that Japan's frustration and humiliation by the Western powers during its rise to international society contributed to greater subsequent Japanese aggression.[31]

In contrast, Britain was quick to recognize the United States' great power status in 1895 and to reaffirm America's sphere of influence in the western hemisphere. Both countries also had common understandings on trade and the role of arbitration in disputes. To a great extent, the British and Americans succeeded in establishing a Deutschian "security community".[32] These common understandings and mutual responsiveness facilitated the peaceful overtake. In this sense, it is encouraging that China and the United States have reached agreement on trade and China's entry into the World Trade Organization (WTO) and cooperated closely on certain issues at both global and regional levels from anti-terrorism to peace on the Korean peninsula. If the two countries further cooperate and enhance their mutual trust, the creation of a cross-Pacific security community is not inconceivable.

Multilateralism in international relations offers a new and unique perspective for the study of power transition and great power relations. The material incentives of cooperation are too rewarding to be rejected. Thick webs of international institutions are beginning to reduce anarchy, at least in some parts of the world. Gradually people have learned not to expect violent conflict as a solution to problems across national borders. Increasingly, international problems are being handled by multilateral diplomacy. A general assumption is that, if a challenging power were engaged in the international community and became a founding member of the new status quo, it would be less likely to challenge it violently. Multilateral engagement in an interweaving international community that involves both the dominant power and the challenger makes a peaceful power transition more likely. A sustained process of strategic restraint and mutual accommodation will enable two rivals to view one another as benign polities.

It is also generally assumed that economic interdependence increases the stake in a stable and peaceful world. But having extensive ties in international economy alone may not prevent the outbreak of war between two states. The type of trade also matters a lot. The type of trade can reflect the quality of the bilateral relationship. For example, there are extensive trade and economic relations between China and the United States, but since 1989 the United States has cut off high-tech military exports to China. Bilateral trade focuses on agricultural products, food, footwear, clothing, and other non-sensitive items. The absence of trade in military hardware and software indicates a relationship that is not so close politically. Investment is also an important part of the commercial relationship, especially in today's interdependent world. When a country has investment in other countries like today's United States, Japan, China, and members of the EU, they literally own part of the economies of other countries. Much more is at stake if a bilateral relationship between great powers goes sour. As a result, they are more likely to attempt to preserve their beneficial relationship.

During Germany's rise at the end of nineteenth century and the beginning of the twentieth century, Germany's economic relations with other powers were impressive, but Germany's political structure gave prominence to the coalition of iron, rye, military, and Kaiser – actors with expansionist goals who saw economic ties entailing pernicious effects that could be mitigated only by transforming the nature of economic links with aggressive policies.[33] Obviously, as the two-level games logic suggests, how domestic institutions and constituencies respond to foreign relations has a greater impact than trade on the interactions between great powers.

Hypotheses and research design

To elaborate on the new theoretical framework, the following hypotheses are proposed and tested in this book:

General hypothesis: If the government, the public, and top leaders in both the dominant power and the challenging power have positive evaluations of the bilateral relationship in a friendly international system, power transition will end in peace.

This general hypothesis can be divided into five sub-hypotheses in order to analyze power transition from four different levels:

H1: The further a rising power is incorporated into the international system, the less likely it is to challenge the status quo violently.

H2: The more a rising power respects the dominant power's vital interests, the less likely it is to be perceived and treated as a threat by the dominant power.

H3: The more the dominant power respects a challenger's vital interests, the less likely the challenger is to become dissatisfied with the international order and its relations with the dominant power.

H4: The more extensive and strong links the two societies have, the less likely there is to be war between them.

H5: The more committed national leaders are to a stable and constructive relationship, the less likely there is to be war between the two powers.

The dependent variable in this research is the dichotomized outcome of power transition: war or peace. Specifically, the process and outcome of a power transition are determined and influenced by a set of conditions at various levels of bilateral interactions. The independent variables are conditions, factors and circumstances at the global, domestic, societal, and individual levels that have direct impact on the process and consequence of power transition as well as on the political decisions for war or peace.

Hypothesis 1 looks at the bilateral relationship at the international level. For example, does the dominant power welcome the rise of a challenger? To what extent has the challenger been incorporated into the international political and economic system? Are both powers participants and defenders of the current international regimes? Are they comfortable with each other in the international system? Hypotheses 2 and 3 study how perceptions and evaluations and corresponding foreign and domestic policies of each power affect relations between the two competitors. The "vital" interests include those that are considered the "core" of each country's domestic and foreign policies. For example, in the case of the United States, enhancing national security and promoting democracy and human rights are generally believed to be some of these vital interests. In the case of China, maintaining economic development and national unity such as preventing Taiwan or Tibet from becoming independent are some of those core interests. Hypothesis 4 looks at the relationship from the societal level. A close bilateral relationship cannot be maintained by political leaders alone without solid grassroots support. Hypothesis 5 studies the impact of the perceptions and evaluations of national leaders (through their words and deeds) on foreign policies. In short, this research studies great power relations from interactions and mutual responsiveness at individual, societal, governmental, and global levels. This decision-making environment is crucial when analyzing and predicting power transitions in the international system.

Case selection and methodology

An analogy is sometimes drawn between today's China and pre-World War I Germany: a growing economic and military power that will inevitably challenge the existing international system and the dominant power. Another parallel has been made between the current US effort to manage the rise of China and the British failure to accommodate or divert the ambitions of Germany in the late nineteenth century. If these analogies have some validity, then lessons from power transitions in history that involved Great Britain, Germany, and the United States may be very useful for managing US–China relations in the years ahead.

To test the hypotheses, I have selected two significant cases from history: the power rivalry between Great Britain and Germany (1871–1914) and the power transition from Great Britain to the United States (1865–1945). The first case is chosen because it is an outstanding example of how and why power transition led to a major war. Instances of peaceful power transition are rare in history, but the second case reveals how a peaceful change of global leadership could take place. Even though the Anglo-American relationship is considered "special" by many accounts, the successful power transition itself still warrants more study.

The facts that both power transitions occurred during roughly the same period of history and that both involved Great Britain provide remarkable insight as to why the then dominant power succeeded in peacefully dealing with one challenger but failed to do so with another. The past provides a guide to the future. The study of the power transition from Great Britain to the United States also serves as a natural bridge to the study of a potential power transition from the United States to China in the future. Though the American supremacy in economic, military, and "soft" power may continue for a while, many power transition scholars tend to believe that China is the most likely rising power that will challenge US predominance in world affairs, especially in the Asia-Pacific region. It is therefore significant to explore how the United States and China can manage a potential power transition in the twenty-first century.

To identify the factors and conditions that either caused violent systemic changes or contributed to peace between great powers, systematic comparative study is the major methodology in this research. Through systematic and comparative study, I will analyze why some power transitions ended in war and why some ended in peace.

Power transition theory emphasizes domestic growth as the most important source of national power. It links domestic development and foreign policy within a single perspective. In the case of the challenging power, its foreign policy derives from its rapid domestic economic and military growth and its desire to expand overseas; in the case of the dominant power, its foreign policy results from the potential national security threat its leadership and the public perceive from the rival power. Unfortunately, power transition theory does not explore how major domestic factors such as culture, political institutions, interest groups, and public opinion affect the interactions of the two powers as well as the nature and dynamics of power transition. This research studies how the process and outcome of the power transition are determined by interactions at the global, state, societal, and individual levels between the two competing powers.

Both qualitative and quantitative evidence will be assessed to determine and measure the state of great power relations. Together with systematic comparative case studies, quantitative indicators will be used to measure interactions between states. For my research, I will single out the volume and type of trade and investment, frequency of personnel exchange, mutual perceptions, mutual responsiveness, elite relations, public opinions, military strategies, domestic institutions, and cultural affinity as key variables that are significant in this study. These variables are operationalized with examples or data for the analysis of great power interactions during power transitions.

This book also studies the nature of the current international system for explaining and predicting changes in great power relations in the twenty-first century. Future power transitions will occur under different circumstances in an age of globalization and nuclear weapons. In fact, the concept "power" itself has become more complex and more difficult to define or measure in an interdependent world. An economically and militarily less powerful nation or even individuals can cause a great stir in the international system today. Also, what is the role of the international regime during power transition? Combining the historical findings with the conditions of the current international system, I will explore how a potential power transition from the United States to China is to be managed in the twenty-first century. Placing this third case in historical perspective, I will make an assessment of whether this dyad resembles any of the two cases studied, and how this potential power transition may evolve under different international and domestic environments. Any conclusion drawn from the third case study will only be tentative, but it may provide useful implications for policy makers and the public in the United States and China as well as the international community in general. Policy recommendations will also be suggested for both sides in order to peacefully manage this complex bilateral relationship in anticipation of a potential power transition. The multilevel analytical framework and policy implications are also significant in that they are applicable to other scenarios of potential power transition at both global and regional levels.

3 British–German relations, 1871–1914

Is today's China similar to pre-World War I Germany? Will China challenge the international system and US supremacy violently after it becomes powerful? This chapter, through examining British–German interactions at international, domestic, societal, and individual levels during the years between Germany's unification and the outbreak of World War I, attempts to shed light on what went wrong in the European power transition and what the United States and China can learn from the tragedy.

Great Britain's decline and Germany's rise

The period from 1871 to 1914 was one of peace for Germany and most of Europe, but it was also the time when tensions accumulated which produced the conflict in 1914. The complex international and domestic situations during the period covered in this study make it difficult to pinpoint any single state or factor as being responsible for the outbreak of World War I.[1] This book will not engage in the search for specific or direct causes of World War I, nor is it a historiographical study of the period; instead, it focuses on British–German interactions prior to the war and attempts to highlight some obvious problems in their relationship at the global, domestic, societal, and individual levels. I argue that though windows of conflict and war were open as a result of power rivalry between Great Britain and Germany, it was the negative interactions and unfavorable mutual responses at global, domestic, societal, and individual levels that led the two countries to war.

The new German state emerged from three local wars against Denmark, Austria, and France (1864, 1866, 1870–1). The dramatic victory of Prussia over France and the creation of the German Empire in 1870–1 marked a turning point in European history. The astonishing speed with which France, hitherto regarded as the greatest of continental European powers, was soundly defeated by Prussia heralded a new era in Europe in which the new German state would soon be in a dominant position.

Before 1870 probably only Great Britain could be described as a highly industrialized nation. Drawing on the rest of the world for raw materials and food, the nation as a whole could fabricate and export low-cost, high-quality machinery and consumer goods. Britain dominated global commerce and accumulated wealth more rapidly than any other country. In 1860 Britain was the "workshop of the world," producing at least two-thirds of its coal, about half its iron, five-sevenths of its steel, two-fifths of its hardware, and about half its commercial cotton cloth.[2] However, in the last decades of the nineteenth century, Britain had been declining as a world power. Germany's economic expansion was based on the development of the iron, steel, and mining industries. Coal production in Germany increased eightfold between 1870 and 1914, while in Britain it merely doubled (Table 3.1).

By 1900 Germany, the United States, and to a lesser extent France, Russia, and Japan were all embarked on a course of sustained, modern economic development. With the passage of time the vast gap that had once separated Britain from all its competitors narrowed and, in the cases of Germany and the United States, disappeared altogether. Meanwhile the growth of foreign navies and the extension of vast railroad networks across Europe and North America as well as into Asia had combined to eat away at the bases of Britain's traditional maritime strategy. The proliferation of rail lines lessened the vulnerability of Britain's enemies to blockades and small amphibious operations and rendered many of its own possessions more susceptible than they had ever been to attack over land.

Determined to catch up with the British, the Germans started out by buying British machinery and steel rails, the "high technologies" of the time.[3] Once Germany's industrialization had taken off, competition between British and German companies became increasingly fierce. And as Germany took technological leadership in new industries such as chemicals, the British felt increasingly threatened both economically and militarily. Between 1875–7 and 1884–5, British exports had increased by 8 percent. During the same period, those of Germany had risen 16 percent and those of the United States 35 percent.[4] From 1870 to 1913, Britain's predominant position in world

Table 3.1 Major industrial statistics (in million tons)

	Year	Great Britain	Germany
Coal	1870	112	34
	1900	228	149
	1914	292	277
Pig-iron	1870	6	1.3
	1900	9	7.5
	1914	11	14.7
Steel	1870	0.7	0.3
	1900	5	6.7
	1914	6.5	14

Source: A. J. P. Taylor, *The Struggle for Mastery in Europe: 1848–1918* (London: Oxford University Press, 1957), pp. xxix–xxx.

trade had dropped from 38 to 27 percent of the world total. Her economic, financial, and sea powers all declined. Britain's decline was accompanied by Germany's growth. The German share of the world trade had increased from 17 to 22 percent during the same period of time. German trade was gaining ground in many places at the expense of English exports. In the critical years between 1885 and 1913, British industrial production increased at the annual rate of 2.1 percent, Germany at 4.5 percent. In 1860 Britain had 25 percent of the world's industrial production; in 1913 less than 10 percent. Germany had raised her share from 15 percent to 17 percent between 1890 and 1900.[5] After 1890 Germany gradually became the greatest military and industrial power in Europe. The battle fleet, built from 1898 onwards, was the most imposing expression of Germany's new industrial power. A power transition was under way in Europe at the end of the nineteenth century and the beginning of the twentieth.

A later modernizer, Germany quickly caught up and eventually surpassed Great Britain in major industrial indices (see Table 3.1). At the beginning of the twentieth century, Germany's future prospects in the international system looked brighter than Britain's. In industrial productivity, economic growth, and foreign commerce, in literate population, technology, and military weight, Germany had a decisive advantage not only over Britain but over all its European rivals. The reasons for this difference in growth rates may still be a topic of lively debate among economic historians, but its consequences are no longer in dispute.

From "natural" allies to competitors

Britons and Germans were friendly cousins historically and had never fought each other before. Two chief Protestant states of Europe, Britain and Germany possessed a natural affinity for each other. The connections between the royal families, the many cultural and economic interactions, and the shared bonds of race closely linked the two peoples. Relations at the highest level had been cordial and high-level visits had been frequent.

Having been concerned for more than a century with the threats from the French and the Russians – their traditional enemies – the British were initially inclined to welcome the rise of Prussia and even the creation of the German Empire. A strong Germany seemed to be just what Britain needed, situated as it was between France and Russia. Germany's perfect geographical location might alleviate Russian and French pressures on Britain.

However, Prussia's stunning victory over France alarmed the British about the potential German threat. In the past, as long as the balance of power was maintained and Bismarck was satisfied with the post-1871 status quo in Europe, Germany was regarded as a "natural ally." But Wilhelm II, the new Kaiser, initiated his "new course" in foreign policy. Now Germany also appeared to have an interest in overseas expansion, and a series of minor Anglo-German disputes arose over places like Samoa, Togoland, and the

Cameroons. The Kaiser's support for the Boers in South Africa, along with the German decision in 1898 to build a fleet, began to stimulate opposition in Britain to the policy of cooperation with Germany.

Hegemonic stability theorists would argue that Great Britain had been the principal factor in the maintenance of a European balance of power. Indeed, she was determined to maintain the status quo. To prevent the rise of a challenger, England (and subsequently the United Kingdom) successfully waged wars against the Spain of Charles V and Philip II, the Holland of De Witt, and the France of Louis XIV and Napoleon. But developed as a result of industrialization and equipped with modern weaponry, the Germany of Bismarck and the Kaiser was stronger than all previous rivals. As German power grew after 1871, its appetite for trade, markets, and colonies naturally increased. While other European powers had divided colonies in Africa, the Middle East, and Asia, Germany possessed almost no colonies suitable for settlement and few territories worthy of exploitation. An ambitious Germany was bound to expand and challenge the status quo. A fierce competition started.

Germany was shut within its boundaries, the Baltic, the Danube, and the Rhine. The development of an ocean-going fleet seemed indispensable for Germany's expansion. However, Great Britain was adamant in maintaining a supreme navy and became the great obstacle to the realization of Germany's ambitions. Naval superiority was "a cardinal principle of British policy."[6] The naval rivalry set on foot by Germany was sure to provoke suspicions as to its ultimate intentions, and thus to embitter relations between the two otherwise friendly countries. Every stage in the development of the German fleet was followed by still larger additions to that of Britain. Mistress of the seas for 200 years and guarantor as well as beneficiary of the balance of power in Europe, Britain was not prepared for the advent of a power that demanded recognition as an equal. The British determination to keep the heritage of the past and to maintain the status quo was difficult for Germany to accept. Refusing to accept British hegemony as a law of the universe, Germany wanted to play a much larger role on the world's political stage than she found allotted to her under the status quo. A major cause of Anglo-German colonial estrangement was the fact that "from the first days of German colonial policy, England has sought to bar German progress in the most petty ways."[7] Even when territory had little value for England, as in the case of Samoa, German expansion was blocked. A denial of its "place in the sun" became intolerable to Germany. If the sun never set in the British Empire, where was the place for the proud German nation? A violent power transition was to be expected.

It must be pointed out that relations between Britain and Germany improved considerably during the Balkan crisis of 1912 and 1913 when they cooperated to preserve the peace of Europe. On the very eve of the war, a treaty had been drafted which established a harmony of views with regard to the Baghdad railway and African colonial questions. The argument that

Britain made no effort to accommodate Germany is not supported by the evidence of some sort of Anglo-German détente before the war.[8] However, Britain and Germany only cooperated on peripheral issues; they failed to reach a comprehensive political understanding, or a formal agreement on naval armaments, and especially on the role Germany should and could play in European and world politics – the core issues of dispute and issues vital to both Britain and Germany.

The international environment

By 1900, the Triple Alliance of Austria, Germany, and Italy, and the Dual Alliance of France and Russia had divided Europe into two armed camps, with Great Britain standing on the periphery. There were discussions in 1898 and again in 1901 about the possibility of an Anglo-German alliance, but the interests of the sides were too far apart to bring them together. The British wanted diplomatic support against Russia in the Far East; the Germans wanted British help, or at least benevolent neutrality, in a possible war in Europe.[9] In April 1904, Great Britain settled her African disputes with France – France giving Britain a free hand in Egypt, and Britain giving France a free hand in Morocco. In 1907 Great Britain concluded an agreement with Russia settling outstanding differences with regard to Persia, Afghanistan and Tibet. The Triple Entente of Russia, France, and Britain was complete. Now it was Triple Alliance against Triple Entente. Unfortunately, political and military camps hostile to each other could only escalate tensions.

As the most powerful nation, Britain could afford to act alone; but as it declined, it departed from the long-standing policy of "splendid isolation" during which Britain remained aloof from the continental alliances. A turning point was reached in 1902 when Britain formed an alliance with Japan. The outbreak of the Russo-Japanese war in February 1904, by threatening to drag in their respective partners, the British and the French, led directly to the Anglo-French entente in April 1904. Russia's defeat forced her to give up some of her expansionist designs in the Far East and Central Asia, thus making possible the entente with Britain in August 1907. Whether these changes in British policies were an imperialist plot designed to encircle Germany or a defensive response to the threat of German expansionism in Africa, the Middle East, and Asia, they were certainly not well received by the Germans, who were determined to challenge the British and become a world power.

By the beginning of the twentieth century, the British had begun to be engaged with almost all other great powers. The major premise of the diplomacy of Sir Edward Grey, the British Foreign Secretary who took office in 1906, had been to avoid a situation in which Britain might face a German menace without allies.[10] Hence the appeasement of the United States and the ententes with France and Russia; hence, too, the reinforcement of ties, especially to France, including recurring staff talks since late 1905 and the import naval arrangements of 1912. These were weighty moves, which nudged Britain away from isolation and toward alliance relationships. But

Britain settled for a dangerous halfway adjustment which stopped short of a full-fledged alliance that might have created both an effective control over French policy and an effective deterrent to German belligerence.[11] So far as Britain was concerned, the Triple Entente was a friendly relationship, not a formal alliance. Britain was under no obligation to support either France or Russia.[12] France was meant to provide a counterweight to German ambition. Insufficiently supported, it acted in the end more as an anchor, pulling the British irresistibly over the edge into an enervating European war.[13] Most significantly, the British did not engage with Germany sufficiently. Germany was thus not incorporated into the British-dominated international system during the early days of its growth. While British policy was hesitant and wavering, German policy became rash and aggressive.

Germany presumed that the imperial rivalries since the 1890s between Britain and France and between Britain and Russia were so deep that they could never be overcome, and so Britain would sooner or later be obliged to seek an alliance with Germany on Germany's terms. Throughout the 1890s, Germany had attempted to draw Britain into the Triple Alliance, but Britain had consistently refused. Britain's aloofness led to Germany's promotion of the idea of a "continental league" aimed at the British Empire when the war broke out in South Africa.[14]

The Germans became gradually convinced that the British would be persuaded to join only if the consequence of remaining aloof became too dangerous. Herein lies the diplomatic origin of the "risk fleet": Germany could build a naval force strong enough to ensure that Britain would not dare run the risk of war with her. Britain's refusal to enter an alliance also aroused suspicion in Germany. The Kaiser commented in 1904 that "this refusal to make an alliance was a plain sign of the English policy of encirclement." But British Prime Minister Herbert Henry Asquith insisted in 1908 that the British objectives had been "to maintain the public law of Europe" and "(to) prevent a disturbance of the peace."[15]

Before 1914 Germany's readiness to risk war for its own ends – either a local Balkan war fought by its ally in Vienna or a larger, continental war in which it, France, and Russia participated – seemed unshakably established. By either one of these wars the German government thought its interests would be served: at a minimum, a successful localized war – kept limited by Russia's backing off in fear – would probably break up the Franco-Russian alliance, shore up the tottering Austro-Hungarian Empire, and clear the way in Central Europe for an eventual German breakthrough to successful *Weltpolitik*. On a more ambitious level, the German government was convinced it could also secure these aims even more emphatically in a triumphant continental war. What Germany hoped was that Britain would remain neutral or at least nonbelligerent at the outset.

Germany's ambitions and its policies were closely monitored in Great Britain. In 1905 British planners began to construct contingency plans for war with Germany. The plans were designed to provide France with assistance in the event of a German attack. These plans and the possible Anglo-French alliance caused Germany to believe that it was being encircled and that other European states resented its growing power and prosperity and would do everything they could to prevent it from assuming its rightful place as a world power. Mutual distrust grew between Britain and Germany. No power was so trusted by both sides that it could serve as a mediator between the two.

The translation of *Weltpolitik* into practice was the main task of Germany diplomacy until 1907, when the Triple Entente was formed. The inauguration of *Weltpolitik* was the seizure of Jiaozhou in China in 1897. A demonstration of German naval power together with a landing by the naval infantry forced China's imperial government to "lease" the German Empire the Bay of Jiaozhou for 99 years. The seizure of Jiaozhou by Germany made Russia and Britain press for compensation. Russia received Port Arthur (Lushun) to the south, and Britain Weihaiwei between Jiaozhou and Port Arthur. The partition of China appeared to be imminent. Another consequence of Germany's territorial conquest on the Chinese mainland was closer cooperation between Japan and Britain against the Russo-German cooperation in the Far East, leading to the Anglo-Japanese Alliance in 1902. It marked the end of Britain's "splendid isolation" and preceded the Triple Entente of 1904–7.[16] The very first attempt by Germany to implement its *Weltpolitik* thus provoked other powers into a policy of containing Germany, even if only in the Far East. The objective of German imperialism was to achieve equality with Britain and eventually to deprive Britain of its supremacy, a status Britain was not willing to surrender.

A prominent feature of the international system at the end of nineteenth century and the beginning of the twentieth century was the lack of any international organization that could significantly play the role of an arbitrator or mediator. Britain and Germany could only keep their grievances to themselves and eventually confront each other openly. No country or international organization could stop Germany and its allies' aggressive actions.

In 1908 Austria-Hungary, in violation of the Treaty of Berlin, annexed Bosnia and Herzegovina. The German Emperor stood, as he said, "in shining armor," beside his ally to support this breach of the public law of Europe.[17] Russia protested against the annexation but was given to understand that opposition on its part would be met by force, and the annexation was not further challenged by Russia. Unfortunately, Austria-Hungary's aggression and Germany's support for this violation of international law were not challenged by Great Britain either. Sir Edward Grey told the Russian government at the time that this being "a Balkan affair," in which England had "no direct interest or concern," nothing more than diplomatic support would be given by it.[18] By not upholding international law and intervening in time, Britain did not behave like a responsible and reliable world power; it based its policy on its own interests. This could only embolden a challenging power's aggressiveness.

On 4 August 1914, when the German troops, violating Belgian neutrality, marched through Belgium in response to the alleged French intention of invading Belgium, the British, who had determined to keep Belgium a free and independent state since the Congress of Vienna in 1815, finally decided to enter the war against Germany. If England had bargained away its obligation to defend Belgium, it would have lost its credibility and would one day have had to withstand unaided the attack of a Germany that would have become more powerful and more aggressive than the Germany of 1914.

In bilateral commercial relations, Britain and Germany had maintained large volumes of trade during all these years. At the height of the Anglo-German naval race in 1907, Britain imported some £5,000,000 worth of iron and steel from Germany and Germany imported over £3,000,000 worth from England. Between 1904 and 1914, Britain became Germany's best customer and Germany was Britain's second-best market.[19] By 1914 Britain had lost its strength in technological sophistication. Britain was almost entirely dependent on Germany for ball bearings, magnetos, optical glass, and many of the chemicals used in manufacturing dyes, drugs, poison gas, and high explosives. A heavy importer of German clocks and toys, England lacked the precision machinery needed to produce shell casings.[20] Meanwhile, Germany leaped forward in industrial revolution and technological revolution. As a result, Germany was less dependent on Britain for trade. Although trade between Germany and Britain was extensive, it did not help to deflect conflict between the two powers.

Domestic politics

Domestic politics looms large in any analysis of foreign policy. The domestic situation does not make a war necessary, but it is an additional factor making one seem desirable, especially in the German case.

Britain pioneered the industrial revolution. By international standards, the modernization of its economic structure proceeded at a fairly modest pace. Germany, on the other hand, was largely agrarian even in 1871. Thereafter, however, industrial growth exploded, and by the turn of the century Germany had been propelled to the rank of an industrial power in the world. The slower British growth enabled British society to absorb the inevitable dislocations and turmoil much more effectively than was possible in Germany. The compressed pressure of German urbanization explains in large part the social and political tensions in Germany. Rapid social changes as a result of modernization had a direct impact on the stability of the political system and foreign policy.

Germany

The breathtaking rise of German industry had serious political, social, and psychological consequences. One of the immediate consequences of industrialization was the rapid increase in population. The German population rose from 41 million in 1871 to 64 million before the war. Germany by far surpassed France, traditionally the largest nation in Europe since the Middle Ages. Historically the lateral pressure from population often pushed nations toward expansionist policies. Indeed, in the last few years before the war the German population increase became an additional justification of the political expansion, both in Europe and overseas, sought by the Empire.

Industrialization and urbanization also created other social pressures. From the 1870s onwards Germans could no longer be fed by agricultural products from their own soil. Food had to be imported for rising population in the rapidly growing industrial and urban centers. The massive imports from Russia, America, and later Australia produced a permanent and sharpening crisis in German agriculture.

Colonial expansion was not only made possible by industrialization, but from the standpoint of Germany's ruling classes, it even became necessary. Industrial expansion created increasing demands for raw materials and markets for industrial goods. A feeling of power and pride after the founding of the Empire made for increased self-confidence. Finally, the necessity was felt to divert the attention of the emerging working class from domestic tensions and problems by a spectacular foreign policy abroad. These economic, political, and psychological factors were used to justify German *Weltpolitik* after 1896. Between April 1884 and May 1885, Germany took over its most important colonial possessions in Africa and Asia. These colonies served as an additional pretext for building a strong fleet and the acquisition of naval bases all over the world. However, *Weltpolitik* ran the risk of uniting the other imperialist powers against it, because Germany's claim to a "place in the sun" could be satisfied only at their expense.

Before 1914, both Germany and Britain experienced an alarming wave of unsettling events, resulting in social strife, economic dislocation, and left–right polarization. In Germany, industrialization upset the traditional balance of power in German society and produced dangerous instabilities and tensions. The situation heated up in proportion as the enemies of the existing system – *Reichsfeinde* as Bismarck had branded them – advanced in numbers and organizational strength. The advance of the Catholic center and then the Social Democrats and the trade unions seemed irresistible. The more the nation industrialized and modernized, the more the social structure that underpinned the Empire at its founding in 1871 inevitably altered in their favor. The Bismarckian system, fabricated for a traditional social order, could hardly accommodate strong bourgeois participation. Following the Social Democrats' advances in the 1912 Reichstag elections, a precarious domestic situation was pushing to the surface. The more the forces of change pressed for reforms, the more the forces of order took fright. Hence the alarming wave of fanatical chauvinism, mass demagogy, and crude racism that enveloped the nation from the right in the years before the war. The political system was moving toward crisis and probably breakdown. The German mood before 1914, the strange mixture of ideological despair, political bankruptcy, and overwhelming economic and military power became the propellants behind Germany's "preventive war" policy.[21]

The German Empire was founded on a complex of tensions and potential conflicts, which included the discrepancy between a modern economic structure through industrialization and the continuing leadership of the more traditional agrarian elites, and the tension between the divergent economic interests and foreign policy objectives of the industrial and agrarian wings of Germany's ruling class.

The elites in Wilhelmine Germany lived in an ambivalent and anxiety-ridden condition regarding modernism. On one hand, the industrial advance was welcomed as a means to national aggrandizement, a step toward successful *Weltpolitik*. On the other hand, few were optimistic about the future of an industrial society, and the social and political changes it created. The existing ruling groups lacked a political system with built-in mechanisms of political adjustment. In addition, Germany was still, for all its advanced industry, predominantly pre-industrial in social structure, which means that millions of threatened peasants in the countryside and more millions of old *Mittelstaende* within the cities were available for political mobilization from extremists. The social base for powerful reactionary or counter-reactionary mass movements was built into the very structures of Imperial Germany; in Britain, by contrast, it was almost wholly lacking. The German state was authoritarian, bent on preserving the privileges of Junkers, the military, the bureaucratic elites, and the industrial barons in the west. A strong state but a weak and inflexible regime reinforced the prospects for extremist aggressive policies in Germany.[22]

Imperial Germany was a nation internally fragmented among a host of competing antagonisms. Not only did no common political system unite the Germans for hundreds of years before the Empire was established in 1871, there was no large mass basis for the nation-state that emerged. The German political system was founded in a relatively non-industrialized society. It was a marriage between German nationalism and Prussian autocracy. It was inherently unstable. Imperialism proved an especially effective means of solidifying the allegiance of different sections of the German population. The international implications were enormous. German governments, in struggling with the terrific centrifugal forces at home, were constantly tempted to fall back on their ultimate stratagem – the diversion of the domestic conflict outward.[23] The German political elites had an overwhelming incentive to use foreign policy as a method of domestic control. The German tariff policies, by cutting off the national economy from international competition, hastened the growth of monopolies and cartels, strengthened the impulse to economic expansion abroad, and added to the frictions and tensions shooting up within the international system at the time.

As German statecraft failed to coordinate the divergent forces pulling the Empire in opposite directions, it was impossible to work out a concept of constructive and peaceful foreign policy. The birth of *Weltpolitik* brought a key weakness of German foreign policy to light: the uncertainty of German society regarding its status in the world. The *Weltpolitik* made clear that the aim of German foreign policy was to achieve the status of a world power. Yet right from the beginning German society was not sure whether prewar Germany was already a world power or not. This uncertainty itself produced a dangerous emotional and political instability.[24]

Great Britain

By the eve of World War I, Britain's preeminent position in the world was under assault, both from within and from without. The classic home of political stability, Britain was undergoing a cycle of internal unrest and tensions. Class conflict was spiraling, unions were growing militant, women suffragettes resorted to violence. Worse, the prospect of civil war loomed ever likelier in Ireland. Divided between Whigs and Radicals over domestic affairs, and between Imperialists and Internationalists over foreign policy, and faced with an emerging Labour Party on its left, the Liberal Party could not spawn a coherent vision of a new society to replace the one currently under attack. Amid these circumstances, the cabinet itself tended more and more to postpone and to wobble – Prime Minister Asquith was something of a master at inaction.[25] A sense of disaster in both foreign and domestic policies lurked in the air.

At the close of the nineteenth century when British power was declining, Britain's leaders shared a belief in the importance of sustaining "national economic power," but they lacked agreement on exactly what that concept meant or how it should be measured. In the 1880s and 1890s there was a tense debate between the so-called free-traders led by the Liberal Unionist Duke of Devonshire and the fair-traders represented by Joseph Chamberlain, the Colonial Secretary. Everyone wanted Britain to stay rich and get richer. Beyond this, however, there was little common ground. As a result, the British efforts to understand and respond to changes in Britain's position in the world economy were "confused, inconclusive, and ultimately inadequate."[26]

The free-traders often talked as if all that mattered was that the country's overall wealth expand more rapidly than its population. The composition and distribution of that wealth, as well as its magnitude in comparison with the wealth of other countries, was paid far less attention. Chamberlain, by contrast, believed that Britain's world standing depended on its relative wealth. He warned repeatedly that the country could become richer but weaker if it allowed itself to be surpassed by the efforts of other states, and he cautioned that a nation whose economy was based on industrial production would retain its international power and domestic stability longer than one that emphasized the mere provision of services.[27]

Chamberlain approached the available evidence with a firm conviction that Britain was declining. According to his calculation, between 1872 and

1902 the population of the United Kingdom had grown by 30 percent while its export trade had increased only 7.5 percent. "Our export trade has been practically stagnant for thirty years," claimed Chamberlain.[28] By the time he reached the Colonial Office in 1895, Chamberlain was already convinced that dramatic steps would have to be taken if Britain was to retain its economic position in the world. One of Chamberlain's first acts on taking over as Colonial Secretary was to seek evidence with which to persuade his colleagues and his countrymen of the need for commercial unification. He was fascinated by the potential of a united and perhaps even an enlarged British Empire. Without its colonies and the markets, money, and manpower they could provide, the UK would soon be displaced as the world's greatest power. Imperial federation and, in particular, economic unification were thus essential for national survival. In order to shake the prevailing belief in laissez-faire, Chamberlain had to prove that it was no longer operating to Britain's benefit.

On the other hand, the free-traders at the Treasury approached the question of Britain's economic and commercial performance differently. Comparing 1882 with 1902, they concluded that the value of Britain's imports had gone up 28 percent, twice as much as the value of its exports over the same period. Though they had to admit that the nation's exports were "not as buoyant as they might be," they contended that whether this could be taken as "a sign of lack of prosperity ... much less of national decadence" was an entirely separate question. By manipulating price indexes the Treasury was able to show that a more wholesome situation existed than appeared at first glance. If trade was measured in constant 1882 prices, for example, imports could be shown to have risen in total value by 56.6 percent while exports would jump a healthy 39.4 percent. Wherever they looked, the Treasury Department's analysis could find few signs of the problems that so troubled Chamberlain.[29]

In the absence of any more sophisticated measurement tools, the trade returns emerged as the accepted indicator of economic advancement. But it was perfectly possible that exports could grow while in other respects the British economy languished. British businessmen had become too concerned with the mere volume of their trade and too little interested in the kinds of innovations that could increase productivity and preserve their qualitative lead over foreign competitors. In the free-trade vs. fair-trade debate and the tariff reform controversy that followed, many free traders simply clung to laissez-faire and refused to admit that any problems existed, while most tariff reformers blamed foreign governments for all of Britain's woes. Little was done to address the serious economic and commercial problems. As a result, Britain lost its competitive edge in technological sophistication and became an "untended engine."[30]

The 1902 agreement with Japan alleviated British anxieties in the Far East and, together with an informal but no less important policy of appeasing the United States, freed naval resources for concentration in European waters. Russia's defeat by Japan and the improvement of relations with France made the task of preserving military superiority in Europe and facing the German challenge seem easier. Yet there was no master plan to deal with the difficulties. Various agencies of the government often did not cooperate and at times did not even communicate with one another. Even the nation's diplomacy was largely ad hoc and opportunistic. Although Foreign Secretary Lansdowne inaugurated the "new course," he had no clear conception of what the final outcome of his policy would be. "The great change of British policy was the consequence not of one but of a number of piece-meal decisions."[31] Great Britain failed to develop a sustainable policy toward Germany before the two nations headed toward conflict.

While British industry became less innovative and British foreign policies fell far short of lasting success at the turn of the century, the British society also became less confident of itself. A spiral of apprehension shook British life in repeated waves after 1900; invasion scares, scares about imperial disintegration, scares even about the quality of the British race, abounded.[32]

Nevertheless, Britain is an old democracy in which a pattern of conciliation and compromise was institutionalized. A complex of effective and flexible governmental institutions helped dampen the struggle for power by diverting it toward the parliamentary arena. The liberal political system helped to reconcile the working class with the ruling elites and enabled Britain to weather political crises. After 1815 the state played only a minor role in British economic life. The combination of an effective and flexible government but a weak state produced a situation that enormously influenced the resolution of socioeconomic conflict that industrialization heaped up without respite. Social conflict was largely diverted into political channels. Unlike their German counterparts, British policy makers did not succumb to any temptations to manipulate foreign policy for domestic purposes.

Domestic conflict had a contrary impact in the two nations. In Britain, for all the turmoil that erupted before 1914, foreign policy remained moderate and largely defensive. But internal conflict did take its toll. It added to the defensiveness of Britain's posture, indeed its increasing reactiveness, by leaving the nation stuck at a dangerous point halfway between isolation and full-fledged alliances. The result was an ambivalent policy which reinforced the German hope that Britain would stand aside. In Germany, domestic conflict was more politically far reaching, and its repercussions on foreign policy were pronouncedly of an aggressive sort. The fears and grudges that German elites nurtured in domestic politics were turned outward. The result was the policy of the calculated gamble in favor of war.

Societal links and public mood

Friendly relations between two countries can only be sustained by extensive ties between the two societies. Without popular support, foreign policy objectives cannot be realized. There were no opinion polls for the period studied here, but the public mood can be discerned from publications at the time.

Despite warm relations and family ties at the highest level, animosity toward each other could be felt at the societal level.

The fears and expectations of war, as always in times of a growing arms race and protracted international tension, led to the construction of fictional and speculative scenarios about war. At each level of the society there was a willingness to risk or to accept war as a solution to a whole range of problems, political, social, and international, to say nothing of war as apparently the only way of resisting a direct physical threat.[33] Reflecting some of the anxieties and expectations of the public, novels about invasions and wars became popular. British readers were alarmed by the translation in 1904 of a novel by August Niemann, *Der Weltkrieg: Deutsche Träume*, under the title *The Coming Conquest of England*, which sketched a frightening picture of a continental league against Britain, with a German landing in Scotland and a Russian landing in England.

In the first decade of the twentieth century, British and French novelists concentrated on the German threat and gave up the theme of an Anglo-French war. In England, novelist William Le Queux published in 1906 his most successful novel, *The Invasion of 1910,* with a letter of commendation by Field Marshal Earl Roberts, reflecting the popular fears of Germany.[34] The spread of the invasion novel was accompanied by the spread of the spy story. By 1914 the idea, if not the reality, of war became familiar in both Britain and Germany. It was these public sentiments that sharpened the Anglo-German conflict and made war possible.

Once Germany had embarked on a course of expansion abroad, conflict with Britain became inevitable. Ever since, Britain had loomed almost obsessively in German political thinking. It was aggravated by mixed subjective feelings in Germany toward Britain. On one hand, there was the traditional admiration for Britain, the mother country of the industrial revolution, and for the British Empire. On the other hand, public opinion in Germany became increasingly governed by resentment and an "inferiority complex." By the end of the nineteenth century, public opinion in Germany was decidedly more anti-British than British public opinion was anti-German. Bulow, then Secretary of State, admitted this state of affairs in a memorandum to the Kaiser in November 1899, adding with a sigh of relief: "How good that nobody in Britain really knows how anti-British German public opinion is."[35] Because German leaders could not be violently and openly anti-British for tactical reasons, they pursued a policy of formal restraint.

The press of both countries was largely to blame for the public hostility toward each other. Publicists and journalists engaged in the pleasing business of dissecting Anglo-German relations from every conceivable point of view, and the more irresponsible of them delighted to exaggerate differences and minimize points of common interests. In an article in the *Saturday Review*, a weekly journal representing the military and upper-class world of London, the author claimed "were Germany destroyed tomorrow there is not an Englishman in the world who would not be the richer."[36] London's other newspapers, notably the *Daily Mail, The Times*, and the *Morning Post* carried inflammatory articles and were pessimistic about Anglo-German relations.

As Anglo-German competition and antagonism intensified, anti-English feelings ran deep in Germany. Britain was believed to have denied Germany its rightful place in the world. German writers, propagandists, and cartoonists redefined Britain as the number one enemy (*Hauptfeind*) of the German people and their cultural heritage.[37] There was the general indictment of British Imperialism. "You acquired your empire," these critics said, "by measureless treachery, violence, the perfidious fomenting of strife."[38] Britain was called the "unblushing representative of barbarism in international law" and depicted as a "great robber state" which clamored vainly for peace, although it had waged more wars than any nation in Europe. Britain's possessions, Britain's arrogance on the seas, and its claim to world-wide empire were to Germany an insult not less humiliating than any it had met with in the past. What were these English pretensions? And upon what were they based? Many young soldiers, students, professors, politicians, and writers in Germany asked, "Are we to acquiesce to England's possession of one-fifth of the globe, with no title-deeds, no claim, except priority in robbery?"[39]

A German scholar explained his countrymen's bitter attitude toward Britain as "an emotional reaction against the high-and-mighty condescending air with which Englishmen were formerly accustomed to treat us socially, commercially, and politically as poor relations."[40] Ignorance spelled suspicion. On both sides facts were garbled, motives imputed, official statements belittled, and a most outrageous lack of perspective revealed. The British and Germans were extraordinarily ill-informed about one another's affairs and intentions. It was hard to imagine the two formerly friendly countries becoming so bitter toward each other. The inflamed state of public opinion on both sides made reconciliation extremely difficult.

The forces which determine the actions of empires and great powers are deeply hidden and not easily affected by words or even by feelings of hostility or friendship, remarked the British historian Professor J. A. Cramb.[41] Behind the rivalries of commerce, sea power, and colonies there loomed the challenge of culture. In the German race the instinct for empire was as ancient and deeply rooted as it was in the English race. "Is the world to become English?" was a question frequently raised in German discussions of international politics. There was an incentive for challenging the English domination and for proving the equality of the German spirit.[42] "We have to choose between loss of rank among the imperial peoples and a struggle for a place beside the Anglo-Saxons," General Friedrich von Bernhardi declared, "world dominion or downfall (*Weltmacht oder Niedergang*)!"[43] Some German extremists advocated the superiority of German *Kultur* and the German race. "We are morally and intellectually superior to all: without peers," said Professor Adolf Lasson of Berlin in 1914. "It is this quality which specially fits us for the leadership of the intellectual world," said General Bernhardi. And what stood in the way of those desires and aspirations? Germany might have other enemies such as Russia and France, but only one nation blocked the way. That nation was Britain, the enemy of enemies.

The biggest impact on the intellectual life of Wilhelmine Germany was made, apart from historians like Heinrich von Treitschke and Heinrich von Sybel, by Houston Stewart Chamberlain in particular with his *Die Grundlagen des 19 Jahrhunderts (The Foundations of the Nineteenth Century)* which appeared in 1899 and by 1912 had gone into ten editions. His great influence was due to the fact that into his system he incorporated the prevailing ideas of the age, above all the race theory. Race for Chamberlain was the dominating principle of history. From the third century onwards he saw the Germanic race emerge as the only culturally creative race from the "chaos of too many nations" which had been the result of the Roman domination of the world and had been preserved by the Catholic Church. Of all Germanic peoples it was the Germans in particular who were destined to rule the world. If the Germans failed to assert themselves they were doomed. "If Germany does not rule the world . . . it will disappear from the map; it is a question of either or."[44]

All the economic, demographic, political, and military factors converged in the last few years of the nineteenth century in Germany. They resulted in the irresistible claim that Germany should also enter a period of imperialist expansion. The chief exponents in public opinion were once again German university professors, from the Pan-German historian Heinrich von Treitschke to the originally Pan-German, later liberal sociologist Max Weber. They drew on German history in order to give their arguments added plausibility. Just as little Brandenburg had expanded to become Prussia in the eighteenth century, and Prussia had created the German Empire in the nineteenth century, the German Empire as a world power appeared possible in the twentieth century. After the founding of the Pan-German movement in 1891, Max Weber began a phase of imperialist agitation in public with his famous Inaugural lecture at Freiburg University in 1895. In it he pleaded for a new policy of striving for the status of a world power: "We have to grasp that the unification of Germany was a youthful prank which the nation committed in its olden days and which would have been better dispensed with because of its cost, if it were the end and not the beginning of a German *'Weltmacht-politik.'* "[45]

Long ago Prussia had established intellectual dominion over the whole of Germany, the influence of which extended among all nations. In this intellectual progress Germany had maintained a leadership in religion, art, poetry, science, politics, and social endeavor. Step by step with this wonderful development, Germany had cherished a dream of world dominion, not simply of a material dominion, but of a spiritual one, which should make the German mind, the German genius, and the German character prevail over the world.[46] The conviction that the world badly needed German *Kultur* to reach the highest plane of development had become firmly rooted in Germany.[47]

What was a fair share for Germany in the world? There was no answer to this crucial question. German nationalism oriented itself toward *Weltpolitik*.

The demands of the German nation for power and prestige, not only in Europe, but throughout the world, increased rapidly. But there was one insuperable obstacle in the way of this magnificent dream of a future world empire for Germany, and that was the accomplished, existing, actual world empire of Great Britain. Unless this obstacle was removed, the grand ideal of Germany's ambition could never be realized.

The general aim of British imperialism was no less ambitious. Britain intended "to give all men within its bounds an English mind; to give all who come within its sway the power to look at the things of man's life, at the past, at the future, from the standpoint of an Englishman . . ." Like an immortal energy the English spirit linked age to age. "This undying spirit is the true England, the true Britain, for which men strive and suffer in every zone and in every era, which silently controls their actions and shapes their character like an inward fate – 'England.' It is this which gives hope in hopeless times, imparting its immortal vigor to the statesman in his cabinet and to the soldier in the field."[48] The two proud cultures did not learn to appreciate and benefit from each other. The cultural superiority was drilled into the minds and hearts of many on both sides.

Naval race and decision makers

With the rise of German power, German society and statecraft were unable to define Germany's proper role in the world. Competing economic interests and foreign policy objectives made the German Empire look like a coach "where the horses are harnessed in opposite directions," or less charitably, like "the famous two asses bound together in opposite directions and each being offered a bundle of hay."[49] Germany's political leadership could not make up its mind and was condemned to muddle through to a catastrophe based on the very structure of the Reich.

Back in 1836 Clausewitz, a Prussian general, claimed that war was the continuation of politics by other means. This Prussian tradition of militarism was manifest in the unified Germany. Professor Heinrich von Treitschke of the University of Berlin claimed "only in war will a nation truly become a nation."[50] General Bernhardi argued that Germany's "place in the sun" could be acquired only by a war of aggression.[51] Wilhelm II himself was the greatest champion of militarism. He had labored to make the army the most important national institution.[52] In 1911 Chancellor Bethmann-Hollweg, repeating the truth enunciated by Treitschke in 1890, claimed that a nation's armed force is the expression of a nation's will to power, of a nation's will to life, and must advance with that life.[53]

Since 1871 Bismarck had followed a policy of restraint. Using diplomacy to achieve the balance of power, his motive was always fear, not conquest. So long as Wilhelm I lived, Bismarck could keep a hold on the reins. But his policy was doomed once an emperor representative of the new Germany was on the throne.[54] In June 1888 Wilhelm II succeeded the throne. In May 1888, then only Crown Prince, he had already made it clear that he would give greater emphasis to military considerations.[55]

The period between Bismarck's resignation in March 1890 and the inauguration of German *Weltpolitik* in 1897–8 was one of transition and full of discrepancies. Bismarck's policy of concentrating on Europe was carried on by his successor Caprivi, but was abandoned by Caprivi's successor Hohenlohe. The result was a policy of open imperialism. Under Wilhelm II, Germany adopted a policy which reflected its determination to break out from the difficult position of being located in Central Europe at a time of world-wide expansion on the part of other great powers – a determination that was symbolized by her decision to build an ocean-going battle fleet. The challenge confronting it in those years, declared the Chancellor, Prince Bernhard von Bulow, was whether Germany was going to be "the hammer" or "the anvil" of world politics.[56] The Moroccan crisis of 1905 was the direct result of this line of thinking within Germany. When Germany failed to secure the diplomatic victory it sought at the Algeciras Conference in 1906, it concentrated on challenging Britain at sea by escalating her naval building program. German leaders concluded that they must rely less on diplomacy and more on military and naval strength in order to compete with the British.

When Germany entered the period of imperialism in earnest, one of the most far-reaching decisions was to seek additional military power not on land – Prussia's and Germany's traditional domain – but at sea. The Naval Laws of 1898 and 1900 provided for the construction of a powerful German fleet. The German fleet was conceived for domestic and foreign political reasons. At home it was intended to rally the ruling and middle classes around the throne of the Hohenzollern and to weaken Parliament by giving the Crown a powerful instrument outside the control of the Reichstag. On the other hand the battle fleet was designed to challenge Britain, once it was completed.[57] However, the political and military calculations of German leaders failed because they did not sufficiently take into account what would happen if the world's strongest power on land wanted to become the second strongest power at sea as well.

Rear-Admiral Alfred von Tirpitz was put in charge of the task of creating a first-class fleet. His sole ambition for Germany was to build a "monster" fleet, and when it was ready "we will talk seriously to England!"[58] In March 1903 the British decided to create a North Sea fleet and to construct a base for it on the east coast of Scotland in response to German armaments. In 1905 the British decided to begin constructing the huge new "dreadnought" class of battleship (Table 3.2).

Britain had had full warning of what the nature of the coming contest with Germany would be. At that great meeting in Albert Hall in 1900, Lord Salisbury, then the greatest of British statesmen, gave the solemn warning to his people in his appeal to Englishmen to arm and prepare themselves for war, for a war which might be on them at any hour, a war for their very existence as a nation and as a race. But not all statesmen had his profound insight, and his warnings went unheeded.

Table 3.2 Comparison of military forces

	Britain	Germany
Population		
1871	32,000,000	41,000,000
1913	46,000,000	67,000,000
Army		
1872	197,000	407,000
1914	247,000	790,000
Navy		
1872	60,000	6,500
1914	146,000	73,000

Source: John Mander, *Our German Cousins: Anglo-German Relations in the 19th and 20th Centuries* (London: John Murray Publishers, 1974), pp. 198–9.

The British had little to fear in 1871 so far as their security was concerned. Germany was primarily a land power. Though the German army was, relative to Britain, over three times as strong in 1914 as in 1872, the menace was still unreal if the army could not rely on the navy to ferry it across the English Channel. But over the same period of time, the German navy had improved its ratio from 1:10 to a startling 1:2. It was the German naval growth that started to alarm the British. "The feature in modern German policy which caused political apprehension in the minds of English statesmen was neither the growth of Germany's commerce nor her desire for a place in the sun, but the continual development of her navy," remarked Sir Edward Cook.[59]

Whatever else may have separated them, most nineteenth-century Englishmen could have agreed on one thing: "command of the seas" was essential to their commerce, their empire, and their very survival. It was therefore a prime responsibility of the Admiralty and of the nation's political leadership to guarantee that the navy would always have ample forces with which to carry out its vital mission. As the naval powers of France, Russia, Germany, Japan, and the United States grew in the last decades of the nineteenth century, British supremacy on the seas were being challenged. As a response, the British officially adopted the "two-power standard" in 1889 as a way of ensuring continued control of the "narrow seas" around the Continent and the open seas beyond. British statesmen were used to thinking about sea power in terms of the following simple equation:

Two-power standard = equality with two next largest fleets
= superiority over France + Russia
= control of European waters
= command of the seas
= security of empire[60]

As the French and the Russians stepped up their naval preparations and moved into closer political and military alignment, there were persistent fears that they would somehow be able to defeat Britain at sea. From the beginning of the 1890s Britain was forced to run harder and harder just to stay even with its two main competitors. By the early twentieth century, three new navies had sprung into existence – those of the United States, Germany, and Japan. Germany was considered to be the likely third partner in an anti-British alliance, but it was not until after the turn of the century that it would begin to emerge in its own right as Britain's single most dangerous maritime competitor. The defeat of Russia by Japan in the Russo-Japanese War and the improvement of relations between England and France did not give Britain much breathing space. By 1905, the German navy had come to be perceived as the most threatening challenger for the continued control of Continental waters. The emergence of a strong German fleet raised the possibility that a two-power standard might not be enough to ensure British control of the narrow seas around the Continent.

From Germany's perspective, it was absolutely her legitimate right to develop an advanced navy to assert her place in the world as a great power. But from Britain's perspective, against whom could the new German fleet be used, if not against Britain? The frontiers of Germany are in the main on land; those of Britain are on the sea. The British Empire is "a worldwide Venice with the sea for streets."[61] In the matter of food supply Germany was in large measure self-supporting or fed overland. Great Britain might speedily starve if it lost command of the seas. There is thus no comparison "between the importance of the Germany Navy to Germany, and the importance of our Navy to us. Our Navy is to us what their Army is to them. To have a strong navy would increase their prestige, their diplomatic influence, their power of protecting their commerce; but it is not the matter of life and death to them that it is to us," as Sir Edward Grey said in Parliament on 29 March 1909.[62]

Germany already had by far the strongest army in the world. To appreciate the legitimate apprehension which her naval ambitions caused in Britain, it may be helpful to consider the situation by reversing the case. If Great Britain, already the first Naval Power, had set to work to build up a vast standing army comparable to that of Germany, what would have been felt and thought in Britain and elsewhere?

After Herr von Bethmann-Hollweg became Chancellor in July 1909, he made a naval proposal to the British. There could be no question, it was explained, of any departure from the German Navy Law as a whole, as that would meet with insuperable opposition in the Reichstag; but the German government was willing to discuss the questions of "retarding the rate" of building new ships. The German proposal also included two conditions: first, neither country should attack the other; second, in the event of an attack made on either power by a third power or group of powers, the power not attacked should stand aside. Britain had no problem with the first condition, but it seriously objected to the second condition. The German proposal involved a repudiation in certain events of England's treaty obligations. If Britain accepted the German condition and if France was attacked, Britain would be prevented from coming to France's aid. Supposing that Germany in a war with France were to invade Belgium, England would have been prevented from vindicating Belgium's neutrality.[63] The British government, unwilling to turn her back on her friendships with France and Russia and give up her treaty obligation to Belgium, declined the German Chancellor's proposal in the fall of 1909. Subsequent events showed how dishonorable Britain's acceptance of the proposal would in fact have been. Such acceptance would, moreover, have led to Britain's immediate isolation and a deserved and total loss of confidence in British loyalty and friendship in the future.

Without a general political agreement there could be no naval agreement. In 1912 and 1913 the First Lord of the Admiralty, Mr. Churchill, made his proposal for a "naval holiday." He pledged himself that any retardation or reduction in German construction should be followed by Britain in full proportion. If Germany decided to take a holiday and build no ships in any given year, Britain would follow suit and drop her program for the year likewise. Germany did not adopt the suggestion.

Geographical proximity caused Germany's maritime expansion to become a substantial infringement of what was held to be British national security. If Germany had been located at some safe distance away – say, in the Far East (like Japan) or the western hemisphere (like the USA), its expansionism would have caused far less agitation in Britain.[64] On the other hand, Germany's sense of insecurity due to its geographical location and its ambition to become a world power were not recognized by the British. The British insisted that their fleet was a vital necessity, but the German fleet was a luxury. They even rejected the German proposal of the 3:2 ratio of capital ships in Britain's favor.

In 1898 the Emperor of Russia proposed an international conference for the purpose of devising means of reducing expenditure on naval and military armaments. The proposal was received with some sympathy in Britain. The British views were defined in Parliament by the First Lord of the Admiralty, Mr. Goschen, who declared that, while it was not possible to alter the *relative* position of Great Britain, "if the other great naval powers would be prepared to diminish their program of ship-building, we should be prepared on our side to meet such a procedure by modifying ours."[65] Britain was not ready to give up its naval superiority no matter what.

In 1870–1 Britain had taken a neutral position. Once the German aim became clear, the British leadership realized that Germany's ambitions could only be satisfied at the expense of the British Empire. To the British, the German naval buildup constituted an unacceptable threat to their security. To Germans, the British policy seemed a hypocritical refusal to allow any other country the privilege long enjoyed by Britain. A spiral of distrust developed between policy makers on both sides. If the legitimate security concerns of either side had been taken seriously by the other, the naval race would not have become so intense.

It should be pointed out that diplomatic relations between Britain and Germany had been relatively friendly and stable over the years and contacts at the highest level had been frequent. For example, in the fall of 1907 the German Emperor paid a visit to England and in a speech at the Guildhall professed emphatically sentiments of amity toward Britain. The Kaiser was a frequent visitor to the country homes of his cousin, the British King. King Edward personally traveled to Berlin to visit the German Emperor in August 1908 to open the naval negotiations. In 1911 the German Emperor went to London to attend the unveiling of Queen Victoria's memorial and was received enthusiastically by the populace. Shortly afterwards, the German Crown Prince attended the coronation of King George, and was similarly received. British feeling at the time, it was reported in Berlin, was "decidedly friendly to Germany."[66] But warm relations at the highest level were not enough to deflect conflict if the relationship was supported by the public and not sustained by each power's foreign policy objectives and perceptions.

It may be helpful here to compare Britain's sensitivity to German naval growth with Britain's treatment of rising American naval power. While the Royal Navy was facing challenges from the Continent, the United States and Great Britain had been involved in sporadic efforts to renegotiate the Clayton–Bulwer Treaty of 1850, under whose terms neither party was permitted to build and exert exclusive control over a Central American sea canal. The US government was anxious to remove this restriction on its freedom of action, particularly since it had acquired possessions in the Caribbean and the Pacific whose defense might require the rapid shuttling of naval forces. It was precisely to prevent this enhanced American flexibility that the British had resisted any change in the status quo.

After the beginning of 1900, and especially after Lord Salisbury handed over his duties as head of the Foreign Office to Lord Lansdowne, circumstances changed considerably. With all their troubles in South Africa, Europe, and the Far East, the British were only too willing to reach some sort of agreement with the United States. Since 1899 Naval Intelligence had been warning that there was a high probability that an Isthmian canal would be built and that such a project would benefit the United States at the expense of Great Britain. In the opinion of the naval experts, control of any waterway across the Isthmus would reside with the nation that was able to place superior forces at its approaches. A canal would hurt British interests because it would virtually ensure American supremacy off American coasts in wartime. But by all indications the Admiralty had previously reached the conclusion that a canal was inevitable. Whatever its official, technical objections to an Isthmian waterway, the Admiralty seemed by the beginning of 1901 to have accepted this fact. Indeed, with or without a canal, the buildup of the US fleet made American regional supremacy increasingly likely with each passing year. A new treaty was signed in November 1901. In a tacit recognition of American supremacy in the western hemisphere , the British acquiesced to an American-built and -controlled canal. The new treaty committed Great

Britain to naval inferiority in American waters and therefore to friendship with the United States.[67] Similar treatment was not accorded to Germany; instead a fierce naval race ensued.

The battle fleet was the pride of most of the German middle class and the rest of society and was a substantial economic investment for German heavy industry. The need to protect growing German commerce overseas and the establishment of German colonies were additional reasons put forward by the naval propagandists. Armaments bred armaments, and an armament program once started was not easy to stop, for its reversal would have wide social and economic consequences. The arms race created vested interests in both countries. There were enough built-in forces in the armaments and shipbuilding industries to make any slowing down in the rate of construction difficult.

On 30 July 1914, when all hope of peace had not yet disappeared, Sir Edward Grey made a last appeal to the German Chancellor to maintain the good relations between England and Germany. "If the peace of Europe can be preserved, and the present crisis safely passed, my own endeavor will be to promote some arrangement to which Germany could be a party, by which she could be assured that no aggressive or hostile policy would be pursued against her or her allies by France, Russia, and ourselves, jointly or severally."[68] But it was too late.

Inferences and summary

In summary, the Anglo-German antagonism basically arose from the facts that Germany grew out of its position as "a cluster of insignificant States under insignificant princelings," and that this growth gradually threatened to infringe perceived British interests and increased the nervousness of British decision-makers already concerned about "saving the Empire."[69] Tensions accumulated between the two powers as a result of the interplay of factors at the international, domestic, societal, and individual levels.

Since the days of Frederick the Great, Britain had been extending its imperial power all over the world. Germany, on the other hand, had remained cooped up within its narrow boundaries, with inadequate access to the sea, and without room for its rapidly increasingly population. "England's mere existence as an Empire has become a continuous aggression" to Germany, and "her proud claim to be mistress of the seas a perpetual affront."[70] It was a confrontation of two great and proud nations, each endowed from the past with memories of ancient valor, of heroism in art and poetry as in war and politics, and each possessing that attribute which can be described as innate capacity or genius for empire.

Germany's challenge manifested itself in three ways: a sense of entitlement to more influence in the world, rising economic power, and increasing military might. In many respects, Germany looked up to Britain as a worthy role model for development and governance. And the British, whose royalty were of German origin, admired German science and culture. What could Britain have done differently? Maybe the British could have done a better job of helping an insecure Germany find its place in the world economy and global power structure, rather than feeding these insecurities by allying themselves with Germany's "mortal enemy" at the time: France. The British may have also adopted a more engaging commercial policy toward Germany by opening up the vast markets of the British Empire.

The rivalry became a life and death struggle between two mighty powers, each entitled to the respect and admiration of the other and the onlooking world. In retrospect, if Britain and Germany had realized that, despite their rivalries, the world was large enough for them both, their traditional friendship would have become a bulwark for peace in Europe. And if France and Germany also reconciled, an alliance of three powers would have inaugurated a new era in the history of Europe and of mankind.

Competitions between great powers are inevitable. A lesson from the pre-WWI German–British rivalry is that great powers should funnel effort into economic competition and cooperation and promote exchanges at all levels with one another instead of allowing the competition to spill over into the military arena. Unfortunately great powers failed to learn that lesson after WWI. Before too long, a resurgent and revengeful Germany haunted the European continent again.

Some inferences can be made from this historical survey:

An arms race only escalates tensions and is not the solution to problems between states.
With an arms race going on, distrust deepens and animosity increases because both sides understand they are the very target of the other's military buildup. While each tries to enhance its security, the other feels more threatened and in turn further enhances its own security. Pre-World War I Germany and Great Britain were trapped in a classic security dilemma and failed to bring themselves out of it.

Friendly relations at both the high level and the grassroots level are important to avoid wars between two countries.
High-level contacts are significant. The frequency of high-level exchanges reflects the general status of the bilateral relationship. However, public sentiment influences foreign policy. It is hard to imagine that a close relationship could be maintained between two states without solid popular support. As in the case of German–British interactions, if the friendly contacts at the highest level are not supported at the public level, then bilateral relations cannot be sustained.

Public hatred toward a rival and militant rhetoric from both sides are harmful to normal relations between the two countries.
This is obvious. The enemy image may be self-fulfilling. Perceptions and misperceptions can fundamentally change the psychology of a nation and its

leaders. Nationalistic and warlike rhetoric is particularly dangerous in bilateral relations. Media inform the public but also shape public opinion. The media should also take some responsibility for perpetuating hatred between peoples through constantly presenting negative, often biased, images of a rival country.

Despite extensive trade and high-level exchanges between Germany and Britain, their fundamental interests were conflictual. They failed to eliminate war from their menu of choice.

Bilateral relations are multifaceted. In some dimensions, relations may be warm and close; in others, they may be tense and adversary. What determines the nature of the bilateral relationship are the fundamental interests of the two countries. In the German–British case, strong economic ties failed to prevent them from resorting to military options. Unfortunately, the fundamental interests of the two countries were the preservation or pursuit of global dominance. And for Germany and Britain, this could be achieved only through the elimination of its rival power. This confirms the argument that economic interdependence alone may not be able to prevent war; war decisions are made after political leaders have evaluated conditions at international, domestic, societal, and individual levels of interactions.

Britain wanted to preserve the status quo whereas Germany was taking steps to alter it. The high-profile German challenge and the aggressive German policy were perceived as the greatest threat to Britain's dominance in the Continent and on the seas. Germany was not fully accepted by and incorporated into the British-dominated international system.

Perhaps this is the tragedy of power transition and security dilemma. The status quo was maintained by Britain as the dominant power. If the international order were to be altered, Britain's fundamental interests would be affected. For a new power, how can it rise without causing concern and creating an image as a threat to the international system? What should the rising power do or not do so that it is perceived as a benign power by the international community, especially the dominant power? And what can the dominant power do to satisfy the challenger's legitimate demands and help to make it a peaceful power? Clearly these are difficult questions, and compromise seems to be the only option if the two rivals want to avoid conflict.

Some form of compromise such as Britain's accommodation of Germany's legitimate rights as a new power and Germany's sensitivity to the British pride as an established power might have reduced Anglo-German antagonism.

Unfortunately, no such compromises were ever reached. It takes two to tango; both sides need to make some concessions in order to peacefully coexist. Since deep mistrust had developed between them, no confidence-building measure existed. Will future powers learn to coexist and co-prosper in an era of interdependence?

No third country or any international organizations trusted by both sides was available for any meaningful mediation between the two rivals.

There was no regulating mechanism. Both belonged to adversary military alliances. There were no such international organizations as the United Nations or North Atlantic Treaty Organization (NATO) at the time. No other powers or individuals attempted to be a go-between either. Will economic globalization and increasing multilateralism change the dynamics of future power transitions?

A revisit of hypotheses

The above survey and inferences from pre-World War I Anglo-German inter-actions point to the validity of the following hypotheses:

H1: The further a rising power is incorporated into the international system, the less likely it is to challenge the status quo violently.

Germany started its imperial expansion when Britain and other powers already possessed overseas colonies, markets, and raw materials. By the beginning of the twentieth century, Britain had begun to be engaged with all major powers except Germany. Britain appeased the United States, formed an alliance with Japan, and reached the ententes with France and Russia. But Germany was considered the largest threat and was not incorporated into the British-dominated system. Left outside and felt unwelcome, Germany went its own way. If Britain had engaged Germany in a timely fashion during the latter's growth, the bilateral relations might have evolved differently.

H2: The more the rising power respects the dominant power's vital interests, the less likely it is to be perceived and treated as a threat by the dominant power.

As a dominant power, Great Britain had its established interests both in Europe and further afield. By ignoring the existing power's interests and attempting to break the status quo unilaterally, Germany was perceived as the greatest threat, not just by the British but also by other powers. Since Germany attempted to challenge British interests through military prepara-tion, it was naturally perceived and treated as the number one enemy. How to accommodate each power's vital interests remains a dilemma in power transition.

H3: The more the dominant power respects and accommodates a challenger's vital interests, the less likely the challenger is to become dissatisfied with the international order and its relations with the dominant power.

A proud and great nation, Germany felt it was her absolute right to assert her place in the world. Surrounded by historically hostile powers on the continent, Germany felt it had every reason to upgrade its military power. As the unified young nation grew, it became natural that Germany wanted respect and recognition of its new power status and interests. It is understandable that Germany's rising economic and military power caused serious concern in Britain, but how would the British explain to Germans that only they, not the Germans or anyone else, could maintain the predominant power and expand overseas?

H4: The more extensive and strong links the two societies have, the less likely there is to be war between them.

In the case of German–British relations, although high-level contacts were relatively frequent and generally friendly, deep in the society animosity existed. In both countries nationalism was strong, each believing that it alone was entitled to the greatest power status in the world. At the societal level, the public mood was antagonistic toward each other. The general state of the bilateral relations was unfavorable for peace.

H5: The more committed national leaders are to a stable bilateral relationship, the less likely there is to be war between the two powers.

The royal families in Great Britain and Germany were related by historical and family ties. The monarchs often visited each other, but it was unclear how committed they were to consolidating the traditional friendly relations between the two countries. Little evidence can be found to show that top leaders were fully committed, through their words and deeds, to strengthening the bilateral relationship and preventing it from falling to the point of inevitable conflict.

> *General hypothesis: If the government, the public, and top leaders in both the dominant power and the challenging power have positive evaluations of the bilateral relationship in a friendly international system, power transition will end in peace.*

Economically speaking, Germany and Britain were sufficiently interdependent. But they belonged to opposite military alliances. Trapped in a security dilemma, the two governments perceived one another as the greatest threat to their respective interests. The two societies' negative evaluations of interactions and dissatisfaction with each other were evident from their policies toward each other and the public mood in each society. Clearly the conditions and decision environments at international, domestic, societal, and individual levels were all negative for peaceful coexistence and cooperation between Great Britain and Germany during the years before World War I. It is not surprising that this power transition ended tragically.

These inferences and summary are illuminating as they suggest ways to avoid conflict and improve bilateral relations during a future power transition. These historical lessons will be juxtaposed with new international and domestic conditions as we focus on US–China relations later in the book. The next chapter will discuss Anglo-American relations from 1865 to 1945 and the hypotheses will be further tested in a different international and domestic context, providing more inferences and historical lessons.

4 Anglo-American relations, 1865–1945

> Lord Palmerston once said that Britain has no permanent friends – she has only permanent interests. With due respect to that illustrious British statesman, I must disagree. For Americans, Britain is a permanent friend, and the unbreakable link between our two nations is our permanent interest.
>
> Lyndon Johnson (1966)

> There is a union of mind and purpose between our peoples which is remarkable and which makes our relationship truly a remarkable one. It is special. It just is, and that's that.
>
> Margaret Thatcher (1985)

How did Great Britain and the United States peacefully manage their relations during the global power transition in the late nineteenth century and the early twentieth century? Conventional wisdom tells us that the two powers had common interests and their relations were special. But why did they share interests and how did the relationship become special?

By certain standards, the United States and China already share many interests at the beginning of the twenty-first century such as fighting against terror, maintaining peace on the Korean peninsula, and promoting international trade. But the two countries are far from enjoying a "special" relationship. Does this mean that the United States and China are doomed to a conflict course ahead? What can the United States and China learn from the special Anglo-American relationship in order to deal with today's transpacific relations smoothly? This chapter looks at the most successful power transition in history and provides further inferences and lessons for today's China and the United States as they manage their complicated relations in the twenty-first century in the context of a potential global power transition.

Britain's decline and America's rise

The British state emerged from a succession of wars. The overseas expansion was both evidence of its power and a means to augment it. The *Pax*

Britannica ultimately depended on the inability of rivals to challenge the British hegemony. During the first half of the nineteenth century, the chief contenders lagged behind industrially and were preoccupied with nation-building or beset by internal social conflicts. These states never accepted the British doctrine of free trade under the protection of the Royal Navy. At the beginning of the twentieth century, Britain faced two principal rivals to its supremacy: Germany and the United States. With both it was locked in industrial competition and in a series of diplomatic disputes. Both were building fleets that threatened its traditional supremacy at sea. Britain figured that America's challenge was remote. Germany, on the other hand, was much closer to home, a potential menace to the Low Countries, the North Sea, and the English Channel. Britain's response to these two new powers was very different. With the United States it began to cultivate what would later be called a "special relationship." With Germany it drifted into a deep antagonism that led to two world wars.

Great Britain once ruled the largest empire ever seen, with nearly one-fourth of the globe under its control, including such large areas as India, Canada, and Australia. The greatest sea power in history, Great Britain in the 1870s possessed more battleships than the rest of the world combined. The first industrialized nation, it had been the world's largest economy and trading nation during much of the eighteenth and nineteenth centuries. The sensation of national power was probably most palpable during the celebrations for Queen Victoria's Diamond Jubilee in June 1897. A week of festivities ended with a vast naval pageant off the Isle of Wight. A Canadian poet penned his own tribute to the celebrations:

> Here's to Queen Victoria
> Dressed in all her regalia
> With one foot in Canada
> And the other in Australia[1]

But the decline of Great Britain was as swift as the rise of the United States at the beginning of the twentieth century. The two great wars in which Britain and America were major combatants accelerated this process of rise and decline. Britain emerged on the winning side from both wars, but it lost a sixth of its wealth in World War I and a quarter of what remained in World War II. The United States, on the other hand, emerged from the first as a creditor nation rather than a debtor and from the second as the producer of half the world's manufactured goods. By the end of World War II, the answer to the question "who shall lead the world?" had become clear: the United States had completely overtaken Great Britain as the global leader in almost every aspect.

After 1900 it became gradually apparent that the British position in the world was weakening. The most obvious signs of its decline were in the very sectors from which Britain had derived its earlier preeminence: the efficiency of its manufacturing industry and its preponderant sea power. At the dawn of the twentieth century, America's wealth, population, and industrial capacity had surpassed those of any nation in Europe. In 1860, Britain produced 19.9 percent of the world's manufactures, the United States only 7.2 percent. By 1900, Britain's share dropped to 18.5 percent and the United States' share skyrocketed to 23.6 percent. By 1928, the figures were 9.9 and 39.3 percent respectively.[2] In 1938, the total gross national product (GNP) of the United States was about four times that of the United Kingdom. By 1950, at which point the US GNP was US$434.7 billion and that of the UK US$63.4 billion, the ratio had become 6.85 to 1. In 1938 the American standard of living was about 1.8 times as good as the British. For 1960 the figure was 2.15, i.e., the American standard of living was rather more than twice as good as the British.[3]

The long march toward a "special relationship"

From the very beginning, Anglo-American ties have exhibited a two-sided, "almost schizoid" character.[4] The British could not accept the fact that those pilgrims who fled to the new world established a new country there. Embittered by the personal rejection that the American rebellion signified, King George III refused even to appoint a minister to the United States for a full decade after the establishment of the new republic. Yet in a speech to the Parliament shortly after agreeing to peace terms with the Americans, the same king approvingly predicted eventual reconciliation. He told the Parliament: "Religion – language – interest – affections may, and I hope will, yet prove a bond of permanent union between the two countries."[5]

Anglophobia, a salient feature of American political life since the founding of the republic, did not pass into the pages of history until after World War II. To the United States, Britain seemed not only arrogant in its assumption of a natural right to supremacy, but tricky and devious too. This hostility was exacerbated by the conviction of Americans that Britain's wealth was immoral, since it was based on colonialism. The British, for their part, looked upon the upstart new nation, when they deemed to consider it at all, with a mixture of distaste and disdain. America was, in the British view, a country not yet civilized, but uncouth and raw.

As America's industry started to expand and seek markets beyond its shores, it inevitably came into conflict with the British Empire. Conflict and tension led the two countries to the War of 1812. In the decades after 1812, conflicts or potential conflicts over Central America, the Canadian border, Oregon, California, Texas, fisheries, the slave trade, and British actions favoring the Confederacy during the American Civil War all threatened at one time or another to draw the two nations into renewed warfare. The presence in the United States after mid-century of several million outspokenly Anglophobic Irish-Americans gave every minor dispute the potential for erupting into a major controversy.

Yet in each case a way was discovered to calm inflamed passions, soothe wounded pride, and assuage points of contention peacefully. "As often as not, this meant a British willingness to back down before the frequently obstreperous Americans – implicit acknowledgment by London that few fundamental British and American interests clashed, that a friendly America offered advantages over one hostilely disposed."[6] Perceiving the rising American power as an unlikely threat to its interests, Great Britain had treated the United States with respect and accommodation, an attitude and policy it rarely adopted toward other powers.

When the American Civil War erupted, the official British policy was laid down in the Proclamation of Neutrality issued on 13 May 1861, recognizing the belligerency of both North and South. However, by and large the British ruling class felt a thrill of satisfaction as the ungainly republic split in two.[7] Despite the official neutrality policy, Great Britain overtly and covertly supported the South. It was assumed that without Britain's support the South could not have resisted so long, tens of thousands of soldiers would not have died, and the country would not have been burdened with colossal debts pressing down even on future generations.

When the Civil War ended in 1865, anger against Great Britain was intense throughout the victorious North. Northern anger centered upon the *Alabama* and the other Southern cruisers built in Britain. Sailing under the Confederate flag, the *Alabama* destroyed nearly 60 Northern ships before finally being sunk in 1864. By allowing these warships to be constructed the British had revealed their desire for Southern victory and the destruction of the sacred union. In 1864 the British minister in Washington, Lord Lyons, reported that "three-fourths of the American people are eagerly longing for a safe opportunity of making war with England . . ."[8] Northern resentment would take several decades to abate. Americans were also infuriated by the continued British presence in North America. Ben Tillman, leader of the Populist movement in South Carolina, spluttered, "America for Americans, and to hell with Britain and her Tories."[9]

In November 1868 Ulysses S. Grant was elected president of the United States; the next month William E. Gladstone became prime minister of Great Britain. The change of governments gave the two countries time for the dark Civil War passions to subside and for favorable influences to make themselves felt. The 1871 Treaty of Washington and the subsequent 1872 Geneva arbitration successfully ended the *Alabama* claims. Prime Minster Gladstone must be given credit for his willingness to compromise for the peaceful settlement of this dispute.[10]

After the Civil War, the United States emerged as a great power. The Union army mustered over one million men, equipped with weapons as advanced and abundant as any military power in the world. At sea, the once derisory Union navy had 671 vessels of war, mounting a total of 4,610 guns; of these 39 were ironclads and a further 29 were being built – this was at a time when

Great Britain had only 30 ironclads in the Royal Navy.[11] On the American continent the United States was clearly invincible; at sea she equally clearly enjoyed superiority in American waters. Economically, the Civil War marked a shift for the United States from colonial to metropolitan status. No longer would it simply produce raw materials and exchange them for imported manufactures, mostly from Britain. Henceforward this particular cycle of the Atlantic economy was broken, never to be reconstituted. By 1874 the United States was enjoying a favorable balance of trade. Similarly, America's heavy dependence upon the London financial market was coming to an end. The decade after the war saw the emergence of a new global money market in New York.

Mid-Victorian Britain and "manifest destiny" America were learning to live and let live. The two great Atlantic powers had found a world large enough to accommodate them both. The various disputes between the two countries seemed of relatively minor importance when set against Britain's conflicts worldwide, and the British chose to appease Washington's demands. Within a decade the United States became a major force in the Caribbean and the Pacific. When the United States took the Philippines from Spain in 1898, the London weekly the *Spectator* commented that ". . . we have more of the world's surface than we can well manage . . . It would be a relief if another English-speaking Power would take up a portion of our task."[12] America's rise was not and would not be blocked by Great Britain.

But the relative peaceful relations came to a sudden end in 1895 when the Venezuela dispute exploded. A long-time disagreement between Britain and Venezuela over the precise boundaries of British Guiana burst into flame at American insistence that Britain should submit the dispute to arbitration. In a dispatch dated 20 July 1895, Richard Olney, secretary of state in the Cleveland administration, invoked the claims of the Monroe Doctrine, accused Britain of violating it, and concluded with a reminder that "today the United States is practically sovereign on this continent." Lord Salisbury declined to accept the right of the United States to insert into the code of international law a novel principle. On both sides of the Atlantic there was talk of war. What did it all mean? "Psychologically, what was at issue was a clash between an Old World power, oversecure in its long tenure of far-flung dominion in regions intrinsically of minor importance to it, and a newly arrived actor on the international stage, confident in its capacity to dominate neighboring areas and giving to that concept of 'neighboring' an interpretation as wide as its new dynamism felt appropriate."[13] It is further evidence of America's rising strength that Britain finally agreed to a restricted arbitration of the dispute in 1896. In January 1897 the two countries signed a treaty agreeing to submit in future all major disputes to arbitration. The significance of the Venezuela crisis is that it altered the future conduct of Anglo-American relations.

The rapprochement was further enhanced by the extraordinary demonstration of pro-American feelings in Britain in 1898. In April of that year, the United States had gone to war with Spain. In the face of almost universal

European support for the Spanish cause, Britain announced her neutrality and made her pro-American sympathies clear. American Independence Day was celebrated that year throughout Britain. Washington returned the favor during the Boer War just over a year later and allowed Britain to finance 20 percent of the cost of the war on the US securities market.[14] The Spanish–American War changed America's position in world affairs. The United States became the owner and controller of territories far beyond its shores. It acquired the authority and the responsibilities of an imperialist power. The United States now saw itself as being in the same diplomatic and military league as the great powers of Europe.

As the two nations entered the twentieth century, they found themselves with complementary interests in many areas of the globe. A newly assertive Germany gave statesmen in both Washington and London a common point of concern. Britain was content to leave unchallenged American pretensions to hegemony in the western hemisphere, while the United States remained uninterested in Britain's new aspirations in Africa. In 1906, *Jane's Fighting Ships* for the first time listed the United States Navy as the world's second largest. From then on, the British government recognized the immense cost of a war with the United States, or even trying to keep too far ahead of her in naval armaments.[15]

World War I proved a pivotal point in British–American relations. The United States sent two million men to fight in Europe. Hereafter, America would be the arbiter of Europe's destiny, even when Washington actively sought to escape that role. The war years also saw the pound sterling displaced by the US dollar as the preeminent world currency. Even the Royal Navy, for centuries unchallenged on the high seas, now faced a rival mightier than any since the Spanish Armada more than 300 years earlier. Despite some British historians' claim that Britain still had a strong economy, overseas wealth, a stable currency, and the ability to sustain its status as a great power in the 1920s, while the American power was "more potential than real,"[16] a transition of global leadership was unmistakably taking place.

The long march toward the "special relationship" had never been smooth. Despite their shoulder-to-shoulder fight during the later part of World War I, Anglo-American relations after 1919 were frequently soured by differences over such issues as war debts and naval parity. American suspicions of British intentions did not fade quickly. As late as the end of 1916, President Woodrow Wilson had made few distinctions between Britain and Germany; both were considered hostile to American neutral rights. America entered the war with obvious reluctance. Wilson's performance at the Versailles conference, marked by the smug posture of disinterestedness, rankled the British further, especially in combination with the president's tendency to magnify America's role in bringing victory. America, having foisted an imperfect treaty on Europe, had then turned its back on the League of Nations and left European powers to cope at best they could with Wilson's proposals. Once again, the two Atlantic powers resorted to diplomacy to resolve their differences. The

Washington Treaties of 1921–2 successfully defused British–American naval competition, and the creation of the Irish Free State eliminated a second major irritant in Anglo-American relations. Major sources of disputes were removed during the two interwar decades.

World War II turned out to be the high-water mark of British–American collaboration. While the United States fought with Great Britain as an "associate power" during World War I, they eventually became full-scale allies during World War II. France's defeat and Britain's forced evacuation of the Continent awakened many Americans to the fact that they could no longer leave to others the responsibility for thwarting Hitler's designs. The common objective of fighting against Hitler brought Great Britain and the United States closer than ever. The Combined Chiefs of Staff (CCS) came into being in January 1942. The two sides enjoyed full and frank exchanges of information. The war further fostered habits of consultation, cooperation, and compromises between the two nations. "If World War I had been the point at which the United States matched and then surpassed Great Britain in relative economic strengths, World War II marked that point in the psychological sense."[17] No longer would Britain be anything other than the junior member in the British–American equation. A power transition was complete. Much of the world's subsequent history would be determined by how wisely the United States exercised that power, and how gracefully the British adapted to their new position of unequal and subordinate partner.

While the war had enriched America, it had impoverished Britain. Britain's growing dependence on American economic aid in the form of Lend-Lease led to a disturbing degree of American control over British gold and dollar reserves. Most ominous of all was the widening gap between the two economies. For the United States the war had been in many aspects a liberating experience. Defense spending had finally lifted the country out of its decades-long depression, invigorating not only the war industries but also the entire economy. Between 1939 and 1945 the nation's GNP soared from US$91 billion to US$212 billion. Manufacturing volume nearly tripled; raw material output increased by 60 percent. Ostensibly victorious, Great Britain in 1945 found itself nearly as exhausted as its former enemies. Having begun the war with a net creditor position of approximately £3.5 billion, Britain ended it a debtor with liabilities of roughly £2 billion. Exports from Great Britain at the end of the war were barely one-third their prewar volume.[18]

Driven by common interests and sustained by cultural sharing, personal friendships, and institutionalized exchange of information as well as sturdy networks of military and diplomatic cooperation, the collaboration between the two allies during World War II eventually developed into a special relationship. The dynamics of Anglo-American interactions (1865–1945) and power transition can be examined with the multilevel framework developed earlier in this book.

The international environment

The United States and Great Britain started the nineteenth century at war with one another. They then spent decades eyeing each other suspiciously and maintaining fortifications and garrisons along the Canadian border. By the beginning of the twentieth century, however, the two countries had not just settled their disputes but become lasting partners. After decades of mutual suspicion punctuated by overt hostility and, twice, actual war, the two Atlantic democracies in the spring of 1940 found themselves suddenly drawn together by a common repugnance against Nazism. It was this alliance that was seen on both sides of the Atlantic as being the only one able to stand up to the Soviet menace.

The full and frank exchange of information between London and Washington suggested that a special relationship existed between Great Britain and the United States before the outbreak of World War II. The British sent the Americans the same materials as were circulated to the Cabinet and the Dominions; the Americans reciprocated accordingly and even let London know of the ensuing Nazi–Soviet Pact, though the information did not get through to London in time because of a spy in the decoding department of the Foreign Office.[19] In a world where nations compete for power and influence, Great Britain and the United States increasingly saw one another as benign powers. In fact, both Britain and the United States started leaving the Canadian border undefended in the 1870s.[20] Without mutual trust, this could never have happened.

While the relationship was never bereft of conflicts, mutual trust and responsiveness led to the establishment of a security community.[21] War essentially became unthinkable between them. The best indicator of mutual attribution of benign character was that each state stopped planning for war with the other. British naval planning had long been based on the "two-power standard," which meant that the island nation's navy must be at least as large as the combined forces of the two next-largest navies. In a memorandum from early 1901, First Lord of the Admiralty Mr. Selborne adjusted the standard by explicitly excluding the United States from it. When Britain and Japan renewed their alliance in 1905, both powers agreed that their combined forces should be capable of matching any two potential rivals, but Britain had difficulty convincing Japan that the "two rivals" should exclude the United States. The clearest evidence of the United States not wishing to fight with Britain was a statement by President Theodore Roosevelt to a junior British diplomat in 1905: "you need not ever be troubled by the nightmare of a possible contest between the two great English-speaking peoples. In keeping ready for possible war I never even take into account a war with England. I treat it as out of the question."[22]

Realists argue that Britain was militarily weaker than the United States and that threats emanating from Germany and Russia persuaded its policy makers to appease the United States. Britain viewed the Americans as a less threatening power. Balancing against Germany before and during both world wars did help consolidate Anglo-American links, but it is not the only factor behind Anglo-American rapprochement. Germany's geographical proximity to Britain clearly played a role in London's decision to challenge the rise of German power while, in contrast, it sought to accommodate the rise of the United States an ocean away. In addition to a common language and history, Great Britain and the United States have "a common fate," declared US Secretary of State Dean Acheson. A common fate entails a common enemy and a common interest in defeating or containing it. The Anglo-American relationship was a combination for a purpose – "first a *pax anti-Germanica* and then a *pax anti-Sovietica.*"[23] The special relationship was not automatic. It was at its strongest, as with all alliances, in the face of powerful common enemies. Without the actions of the aggressor states, relations might well have been dominated by disputes over economic and other questions.

After the end of World War I, Britain shared American determination to revive Europe. The American policy of peaceful change and economic reconstruction of Europe was welcomed by the British government and British people. But the two powers differed over how to divide the costs of rebuilding Europe and paying for the war. In defeating Germany's challenge, Britain inadvertently cleared the way for America's rise to economic preeminence. Weighed down with huge debts and antiquated factories, the British felt outclassed by America's economic strength. The British planned postwar policy with a worried eye on American challenge. John Maynard Keynes, the influential economist, warned that squeezing Germany too hard would destroy a valuable customer. Like others, he believed that the best way to revive Germany and fill Europe's dollar gap was at the expense of the United States. The British hoped to tap American riches with the Keynes plan, which Lloyd George handed to Woodrow Wilson in April 1919. Wilson's rejection of the Keynes plan was hailed by United States Treasury officials, who resented the Allies' eagerness to milk America. Although Washington's opposition defeated the Keynes plan, the British did not abandon the hope of redressing the economic imbalance with America. From 1919 to 1933, they repeatedly tried to reduce or cancel war debts, tap the US money market, shut Americans out of the Empire, or force them into inflation.[24]

The formation of a special relationship with America was also a result of the British recognition that the United States had become the most powerful nation in the international system after WWI. By the early decades of the twentieth century, America's preeminence had become a fact that permeated Europe. This was "our century," concluded Edwin L. James after spending the 1920s as chief *New York Times* reporter in Europe. America's economic supremacy produced "enormous political influence ... There is no country where the power of the dollar has not reached. There is no capital which does not take the United States into consideration at almost every turn ... Isolation is a myth. We are not isolated and cannot be isolated. The United States is ever present."[25]

America's powerful political and economic influence in the world was recognized by the British. "No final settlement of any major international issue can be reached without the approval of the United States of America," remarked British Foreign Office experts.[26] Between 1904 and 1906 Britain withdrew its remaining garrisons from the West Indies and from Canada. This meant a British strategic abandonment of the western hemisphere . Precipitated by economic necessity, the decision also reflected a realization that in the unlikely event of an American attack on either Canada or the West Indies, Britain would not be able to defend the territories. During the inter-war years, Americans promoted the Kellogg–Briand Pact to reduce chances of military conflict, while they aggressively penetrated foreign markets. A British financier commented, "No country is independent except the United States, which secures independence through its dominion over all others."[27]

After the fall of France in June 1940, Anglo-American interests coincided again: prevent German domination of Europe, protect North Atlantic life-lines, and ensure Britain's national survival. For the British, survival was an end in itself; for Americans, these interests were the means with which any strategy of defeating Germany had to be implemented. The vast wealth and industrial capacity of the United States was quickly translated into the tan-gible expressions of power: troops, ships, airplanes, and other implements of war. The United States demanded concessions from Britain. It acquired bases essential to national security and the wider projection of her strength. Some argue that America did not enter World War II to save its British ally, it did so to preserve and extend American financial, political, and strategic interests.[28]

Two weeks after Pearl Harbor, Prime Minister Churchill was in Washing-ton to consult with President Roosevelt. Known as the Arcadia conference and lasting until January 1942, these meetings created the Anglo-American wartime alliance. Their genesis lay in August 1941, when Churchill and Roos-evelt met at Placentia Bay, Newfoundland, and issued the "Atlantic Charter." The alliance was at once the savior of Britain and the reason for the loss of British global preeminence. Churchill and his successors were compelled to follow the American diplomatic lead. Britain simply lacked the material and military resources to do otherwise.

Whether the special relationship between Britain and the United States was out of choice or necessity is open to debate. As far as Britain was con-cerned, the need for a special relationship with the United States certainly arose from an awareness of its diminished strength in the postwar world. A report dated 29 June 1945 from the Post-Hostilities Planning Staff, the body charged with assessing Britain's postwar security requirements, observed that even a united British Empire would be incapable of securing its inter-ests against the most likely potential aggressor, the Soviet Union, without the support of powerful allies. It was therefore "vital to ensure the full and early support in war of the USA."[29] America's loan to Britain at the end of 1945 was vital to the latter's economic reconstruction. Without America's economic support, Britain would face the prospect of a "financial Dunkirk" in the postwar years.

Domestic debate and foreign policy

In Anglo-American relations skepticism pre-dated specialness. This skepticism was evidenced in domestic debate on both sides of the Atlantic. In a private conversation to his sister in 1937, Neville Chamberlain remarked, "it is always best and safest to count on nothing from the Americans except words."[30] In America, congressional and public views of the transatlantic relationship were dubious. Anglophobia as a salient feature of American political life did not disappear until after World War II. Only the change of international situation and the ensuing domestic development would push the two Atlantic powers together.

From the 1890s onward both sides were pursuing policies designed to bring the United States and Great Britain closer to some sort of understanding. Britain intuitively assumed that American and British interests would in the end prove complementary in the central conflicts of international politics. Since the 1890s the dominant element in the British establishment had known in its heart that the United States would take over an increasing share of the burden and use its new strength to further Britain's original purposes. Many British public figures felt the need to believe that the displacement of power from Britain to the United States need not directly damage British interests.[31]

Britain emerged from World War I owing over US$1 billion to the United States, running a growing trade deficit with it, and having lost markets in Latin America to the new rival. By the end of the 1920s the United States had replaced Britain as the main trading partner of China and Japan and had displaced Britain as the chief foreign investor in Canada and Latin America. Britain was also in retreat in South American markets, accounting for only 16 percent of the region's imports at the end of the decade against 38 percent for the United States.[32] As British power continued to decline, a conflict with the United States was simply not an option.

US entry into World War I brought British and American societies even closer. The security community across the Atlantic was strengthened. School history textbooks deemed hostile to Great Britain were revised or removed from the curriculum; the American Revolution was to be blamed on George III, a German monarch under the sway of a "junker aristocracy." A federal judge even went so far as to jail one filmmaker producing a documentary entitled *The Spirit of '76* on the grounds that it portrayed the British in too negative a light.[33]

Both governments, but particularly the British, had worked hard to strengthen the ties. The new closeness of the two powers was marked, in April 1914, by the first official visit of a British cabinet member – Secretary for Foreign Affairs Arthur Balfour – to the United States during his term of office. Institutions such as the Rhodes Scholarships and the Pilgrims Trust were set up at the turn of the century to nurture closer relations between the two English-speaking nations.

The relationship was special, but it had to be nurtured and, above all, negotiated. At the root of the relationship lay the matter of comparative power. Because of the asymmetries of power between the two, the British were always more conscious of Anglo-American ties than were the Americans. Stated boldly, Great Britain needed the United States more than the Americans needed Britain. Bereft of many of the traditional measures of power, officials at Whitehall sought instead to exert influence. The British feared losing American support even as they resented the very dependence they feared losing. As part of this strategy they endeavored to make their ties with the United States *the* special relationship, whereas the Americans always preferred *a* special relationship, less exclusive, less confining, less overt than what the British had in mind.[34]

Britain's aim was simply to harness the much greater military, political, and economic power of the United States in support of its own objectives. As an anonymous Foreign Office official patronizingly put it in March 1944: "If we go about our business in the right way we can help to steer this great unwieldy barge, the United States of America, into the right harbour. If we don't, it is likely to continue to wallow in the ocean, an isolated menace to navigation."[35] The Anglo-American "special relationship" has been seen in British eyes as a means of influencing Britain's successor as the leading democratic nation and directing it toward policies helpful to the maintenance of Britain's world position as a maritime and imperial power.[36]

Post-WWII Great Britain, if it were to enjoy American friendship, protection, and aid, would have to defer to American wishes. Such attitudes had certainly begun to manifest themselves long before the end of the war, particularly in reference to the question of atomic bombs. Scientific exchanges of atomic research began as early as 1940, but as work moved beyond the purely theoretical stage the leaders of the American team began to doubt the wisdom of continued British involvement. Secretary of War Stimson believed that shutting out the British was perfectly acceptable given that "we were doing nine-tenths of the work."[37] By the end of 1942 British researchers found themselves virtually cut off from important atomic information. In the spring of 1943 Churchill convinced Roosevelt that the partnership had to be restored since otherwise Great Britain would be forced to divert money and manpower from the war effort in order to pursue its own atomic energy program. The revived partnership was sealed in the Quebec Agreement, a secret arrangement signed on 19 August 1943. Aside from promising that the atomic bomb would never be used by either side against the other, it established that neither would use it against a third party without the other's consent.

In August 1947, Prime Minister Clement Attlee, in an apparent attempt to break the deadlock over the exchange of atomic technology, made public the terms of the heretofore secret Quebec Agreement. Members of Congress expressed outrage that such an agreement could ever have been signed. Arthur Vandenberg, chairman of the Senate Foreign Relations Committee, called the agreement's terms "astounding" and "unthinkable." He and others demanded that the Quebec Agreement be immediately rescinded, and promised to block "any future aid to Britain" as long as the issue remained unresolved. After a few months of negotiation, the State Department assured them that "the obnoxious agreement" would be cancelled, and the crisis passed.[38]

The increasing tendency of the US government to treat the British as subordinates was also demonstrated in the American demand for overseas base rights. As the Japanese were slowly driven from their strongholds in the Pacific, the inevitable question emerged of what should be done with these newly conquered islands. The British Foreign Office suggested a mandate system, but this immediately came under fire in the American press as a scheme to expand the British Empire in the Far East. In November 1945 the State Department sent to the British Embassy a list of locations in which the United States sought long-term base rights, adding that the British were expected to support and assist the Americans in negotiations to receive them.

On 5 March 1946, Churchill made a famous speech in Fulton, Missouri, in which the former prime minister claimed that the Soviets had drawn an "iron curtain" across the heart of Europe. Only a closely knit Anglo-American partnership could resist Stalin's ambitions. Some conservative anti-communists welcomed the remarks. To most others, especially liberals, Churchill appeared to be calling for an Anglo-American alliance directed against the Soviet Union, which was not yet identified as an enemy by the United States. The editorial pages of major newspapers accused him of promoting anti-Soviet hysteria, of attempting to chain America to an "old and evil empire" that had imposed "slavery" over three-fifths of the world's surface, and called the speech "an ideological declaration of war against Russia."[39] The hostile reaction of the liberals and former non-interventionists might have been expected, but the spontaneous expressions of disdain of the British from grassroots America were not. Letters and telegrams poured into the White House from across the country. America should refuse to be held hostage by British politics, suggested many Americans.

Anglophobes in Congress also criticized British trade policies. The British were more concerned with furthering their own postwar trade than they had been with actually winning the war. Representative Daniel A. Reed (D-NY), for example, charged that by means of the "imperial preference plan," Britain monopolized world trade. Senator Edward H. Moore (D-OK) assailed what he called Britain's "international banditry," while Senator Wayne L. Morse (D-OR) referred to English policy as "international war against the United States."[40]

President Truman terminated Lend-Lease on 21 August 1945, claiming that it was meant to be nothing more than strictly a wartime measure.

Though popular at home, Truman's decision was greeted with shock and indignation in Britain. Less than one month later a delegation headed by John Maynard Keynes arrived in Washington to negotiate a loan of US$6 billion. Sympathetic to Britain's plight, yet realizing the state of congressional opinion, the administration agreed in early December to a loan of US$3.75 billion. Yet even this watered down version of the loan faced an uphill fight in Congress. Some protested that the loan might needlessly provoke the Soviet Union. Public opinion surveys taken at the end of 1945 showed only about 30 percent in favor of the loan, and only one in eight believed that it would ever be repaid. Representative Karl Mundt (R-SD), for example, labeled the measure "Russia-baiting dollar diplomacy and monetary imperialism," which would threaten the peace and undermine the newly established United Nations by "dividing the world into armed camps."[41] In mid-1945, a majority of Americans surveyed in a public opinion poll claimed to have faith that the Soviet Union would cooperate with the United States in the postwar world.

By 1948 the Soviets had consolidated their hold over nearly all of eastern Europe, were clearly supporting a left-wing guerrilla movement in Greece, were pressuring Turkey and Iran for concessions, and were channeling funds to communist parties in western Europe. In such an uncertain international climate, sniping at Britain was a luxury that few believed the United States could afford. International development changed domestic politics and public opinion on both sides. Clearly communism, not imperialism, had become the chief concern now. As the Cold War intensified, a bipartisan consensus emerged on US foreign policy, one which considered Great Britain a valuable partner. In 1947 the Senate passed the Marshall Plan, in which billions of American dollars poured into Britain and Europe to aid in postwar reconstruction. Two years later the North Atlantic Treaty Alliance (NATO) was ratified, and the United States became involved in its first entangling alliance.

Disputes and misunderstandings between the two countries would, of course, continue throughout the Cold War, but from the late 1940s onward such difficulties were increasingly matters purely to be dealt with between the State Department and the Foreign Office. Gone were the days when any difference between the two powers immediately became a subject for congressional or parliamentary debate. No longer was there a receptive public audience for anti-British or anti-American rhetoric in each society. Despite earlier suspicions and differences, a domestic consensus had been reached in both countries with regard to the importance of Anglo-American cooperation in international affairs.

Decision makers

Visionary, committed individual leaders from both sides helped foster a close bilateral relationship across the Atlantic. Accommodation was necessary to resolve conflicts between the two nations peacefully. Prime Minister

Gladstone played an instrumental role in settling the dispute over the *Alabama* claims following the American Civil War. It took some time for Britain to accept, emotionally and psychologically, the reality of American independence. For Britain the American War of Independence was an inglorious episode. Though Yorktown and the ensuing need for peace were bitter pills for Britain to swallow, the act of separation had to be forgiven and forgotten.

Peace once made, hopes revived. George III's prediction of eventual reconciliation between the mother and daughter countries also reflected the aspirations of his prime minister, Lord Shelburne, who envisioned a settlement in which everything would be staked upon a mutual recognition that, when all was said and done, Britons and Americans were economic men. The year 1776 saw the publication of the great manifesto of the economic Enlightenment by which nineteenth century Britain was to live and prosper – Adam Smith's *Wealth of Nations*. The hopes of Shelburne and his supporters rested on the belief that the future of Britain lay with Adam Smith and free trade and that the enlightened Americans would see their future in similar terms. The natural unity of the North Atlantic economy would reassert itself and would bring about a mutual rapprochement, perhaps even some degree of political reunification.

Friendly statements by politicians from both sides were helpful for the formation of a friendly relationship. Some of the firmest statements on the American side were from Theodore Roosevelt. As early as 1901 he stated that the United States had "not the least particle of danger to fear in any way or shape" from the British. By 1905 he made it clear that "I regard all danger of any trouble between the United States and Great Britain as over, I think forever," and that "England has a more sincere feeling of friendliness for us than has any other power." British leaders made similar statements. Selborne, First Lord of the Admiralty, stated, "there is no party in the United Kingdom or even in the British Empire which does not contemplate war with the United States of America as the greatest evil which could befall the British Empire in foreign relations." On the verge of taking office in 1905, Prime Minister Sir Edward Grey confirmed that he would stand by the "cardinal features" of British foreign policy, the first of which was "the growing friendship and good feeling between ourselves and the United States, a matter of common ground and common congratulation to all parties in this country."[42]

At the early twentieth century, strategists on both sides no longer considered one another as real or potential enemies. Lord Fisher, the Admiral of the Fleet from 1904 to 1910, never accepted that war with the United States was possible. On the American side the strategist Alfred Thayer Mahan, while never advocating challenging British naval mastery, only envisioned division of areas of interest.[43] Suspicions of Germany and Japan meant that an American navy, originally anti-British, became more sensitive to the need to cooperate with the Royal Navy.

The Anglo-Japanese alliance was established in 1902. In 1905 President

Roosevelt was consulted by the British government about the revision of the alliance. This showed that Britain was not prepared to commit itself to fight the United States. Under the revised alliance Japan and Britain bound themselves to maintain a force in the Far East superior to that of any "European" power, a change from the original "outside" power, and neither state was obliged to go to war with any country with which it had a general treaty of arbitration. The alliance was constructed in such a way that it would not incite Anglo-American rivalry.[44] Many British leaders, notably Joseph Chamberlain, looked longingly across the Atlantic for an ally; and though Washington did not respond immediately, there was, as Henry Cabot Lodge observed, "a very general and solid sense of the fact that . . . the downfall of the British Empire is something which no rational American could regard as anything but a misfortune to the United States."[45]

Within the British policy-making elite, there had been three broad divisions: Atlanticists who firmly believed in pan-Anglo-Saxonism and saw the United States as Britain's natural ally because of a supposed shared history and common political and cultural ties; imperial isolationists who saw the Empire as the *raison d'etre* of Britain's position as the preeminent world power and who wished to preserve the imperial edifice at all costs; and "world leaders" who strove to maintain Britain's predominant position as the only global power by cooperating with potential friends and competing with potential foes.[46] Not all members of the British foreign-policy-making elite can be identified exclusively with one trait. A large number of men held two or even all three views concurrently. Depending on the situation, one trait would dominate while the others receded into the background. When the situation changed, opinion might change. Winston Churchill, a firm advocate of Atlanticism, used to be one of the most vociferous anti-Americans and imperial isolationists in the Cabinet during the naval deadlock of the late 1920s.[47] For many years, "world leaders" dominated the British Foreign Office. For British "world leaders", the United States became an increasingly important factor in British diplomatic calculations because of the increasing power and influence of the United States. As the German threat increased and British strength declined, more and more Foreign Office officials became Atlanticists.

It is true that Woodrow Wilson and Lloyd George did not see eye to eye in making the Peace of Versailles. It is also true that the United States, after rejecting the League of Nations, retreated into its old shell of political isolation. But the numerous Britons represented by Sir Robert Cecil, and the much larger body who were long led by Ramsay MacDonald, did think and act in general harmony with the Wilsonian liberals in America and with the American exponents of democracy. Beneath occasional surface irritations, the two nations fundamentally trusted one another as lovers of peace, freedom, and orderly progress.

The effects of the Great Depression and a renewed possibility of war in Europe in the 1930s made most Americans all the more determined to isolate and insulate themselves from the quarrels in Europe. When the question of a postwar American loan to Britain arose later in 1945, members of Congress were quick to ask why the United States should subsidize "too much Socialism at home and too much damned imperialism abroad."[48] By the early 1930s the world economy had collapsed into depression, and threats to peace were already apparent. In 1931 Japan took Manchuria from China, with only ineffectual protest from the League of Nations. After Hitler came to power in January 1933, he rapidly rearmed Germany and planned a vast Aryan empire in Europe and beyond. The Italian dictator Mussolini, emboldened by Hitler's success, invaded Ethiopia virtually unchallenged in 1935, and from 1936 both dictators intervened on the side of Franco and the fascists in the Spanish Civil War. At first Britain and America watched these events from the sidelines. Gradually the two powers were forced to stand shoulder to shoulder in their external relations. These international developments certainly affected the perceptions and views of political leaders. Churchill considered an Anglo-American alliance inevitable. The British Empire and the United States "will have to be somewhat mixed up together." And "for my part . . . I do not view the process with any misgivings. I could not stop it if I wished; no one can stop it. Like the Mississippi, it just keeps rolling along. Let it roll. Let it roll on – full flood, inexorable, irresistible."[49] The British prime minister was determined to transform his personal ties with Roosevelt into a broader understanding between their two nations that would ensure a continuation of the wartime collaboration.

Winston Churchill, the son of Lord Randolph Churchill and Jennie Jerome of New York, was an ardent proponent of strong Anglo-American ties. Not even American hostility to the British Empire seriously disturbed his belief that Britain would find her main security in a transatlantic relationship. His faith in the American connection was remarkably strong and consistent. The Anglo-American cooperation centered on the remarkable relationship of Roosevelt and Churchill. They met on nine occasions; they exchanged voluminous messages constantly. Between May 1940 and April 1945, Churchill sent Roosevelt a message, on average, once every 36 hours. "No lover," he said after the war, "ever studied the whims of his mistress as I did those of President Roosevelt." [50] There was a real, if wary, friendship between the two men. Being half American, Churchill had bet his all on the prospect of an Anglo-American alliance. Throughout his dealings with Roosevelt, Churchill was on his very best behavior. He was exceedingly careful never to offend Roosevelt.[51]

After World War II, British officials saw several ways to compensate for their dearth of resources. They might look to the nearly created United Nations to ensure their security. They might make Britain's ties to the Commonwealth and Empire the center of British postwar policy. They could promote the formation of a Western European bloc led by Britain and a revitalized France. Or they might seek to carry the wartime partnership with the United States into the postwar period and rely upon the combined might of the two Atlantic democracies to defend Britain's essential interests.[52] Each of these approaches possessed liabilities, but of the four only the last, the maintenance of close ties with the United States, promised immediate help. Churchill was the leading proponent of this approach. "Our friendship is the rock on which I build for the future of the world, so long as I am one of the builders," he wrote Roosevelt shortly before the president's death.[53] A year later, and now out of office, he repeated this refrain in his much-publicized "iron curtain speech" in Fulton, Missouri: "Neither the sure prevention of war, nor the continuous rise of world organization will be gained without . . . the fraternal association of the English-speaking peoples."[54] Churchill is a representative of committed leaders on both sides who cemented the special relationship.

Societal links

In his famous Farewell Address of 1796, George Washington admonished his countrymen to avoid "excessive dislike" of any particular country. Though he mentioned no specific nation or nations, there is little doubt that Washington had Britain in mind. By this time a two-party system had begun to develop, and one of the issues that set them apart was their attitude toward Great Britain. On the one hand, the Federalists, with Alexander Hamilton as their leader and New England their main base of support, were inclined to view the British as potential allies against the radicalism of revolutionary France. Their opponents, the Democratic Republicans, led by Thomas Jefferson and strongest in the South and West, were far less willing to forgive and forget the role of Great Britain as the enemy of American liberty.[55] This battle between anglophiles and anglophobes would continue into the twentieth century.

In addition to language and history, there were cultural, sociological, and psychological forces which powerfully conditioned American relations with the British. The most powerful of these was the "Mother Country" syndrome. Even after the large-scale German and Scandinavian immigration, the overwhelming majority of white Americans continued to think of Britain as the "Mother Country," and to be proud of a heritage that they assumed was American as much as it was British.[56]

American expatriates in Europe rarely had the necessity to come to terms with European countries morally and psychologically, but Britain was from the beginning a special case. A good many Americans who visited and wrote about Britain did so in order to express their passion and anxiety about the Mother Country. Passion and admiration are accompanied by resentment and hostility at times. There is little doubt that, throughout much of its history, the most vocal attitude in the United States toward Britain was one of suspicion and hostility. This was combined with an unwilling respect for a power that was still richer and more important than the United States, and much more experienced in the business of international politics. If the United States had an enemy, it was Britain. Independence had been won in a war with Britain. The same power had been the enemy in the War of 1812, the only foreign war, apart from Mexican wars and the brief Spanish–American War, in which the country was involved between the War of Independence and World War I.

But for Britain, in each of these two wars no such concentration of hostility occurred. The war of American independence rapidly turned into a war in which Britain had to try to cope single-handedly with almost half a dozen European foes. The decisive battle, that of Yorktown, was lost because Britain's European enemies caused it temporarily to lose control of the sea. As for the War of 1812, it is notorious that this war, which bulks large in American history, is almost or totally unknown to the average Briton. To Britain it was a mere exasperating sideshow in the fight for survival with Napoleonic France.[57]

To Americans, Europe was the Old World, essentially inferior and outmoded, mired in ceaseless conflict among classes and races, its leaders bent on oppressing their subjects and making war on their neighbors. The United States was, by contrast, a land of equality and opportunity. The leitmotif in the American criticisms of Britain is that Britain represents old ways, old habits, old institutions, from which the United States has freed itself – as in fact, the thirteen colonies freed themselves from their allegiance to the Crown in 1776. All the evidences of life in America in the nineteenth and early twentieth centuries testify to the existence of strong anti-British feelings. The literature, the journalism, the reports of foreign travelers in America, all demonstrate that this was the case.[58] Americans have traditionally defined themselves by pointing toward Europe and particularly Great Britain as being what they were not.

But with the years, the tone of American comment changed. Earlier, the criticism was loud to mask an inner unease, for after all Britain was still powerful, and no doubt wicked, but significant. Later, the tone modulated. It lost its acerbity as Britain lost its power. American comment began to acquire a tone of genial condescension. Most American travelers to England discovered that, though England might have been the best of all nations, it was the United States that commanded the future. As Ralph Waldo Emerson commented, "there [America] and not here [in England] is the seat and centre of the British race; and that no skill or activity can long compete with the prodigious natural advantages of that country in the hands of the same race; and that England, an old and exhausted island, must one day be contented, like other parents, to be strong only in her children."[59]

While Americans admired and respected the British as a law-abiding, thrifty, practical, and proud people, what Americans disapproved of in the British – and more particularly the English – character and society was the class system, ubiquitous and pervasive.[60] It is not political, it is only in small part economic; it is social and psychological and philosophical. While politically they have achieved as great a degree of democracy as any other people, the English remain class-conscious and, until recently at least, it could be said that every Englishman is branded on the tongue with his class mark. The class system was what many Englishmen had immigrated to America to escape; it was by its very existence a challenge to what Tocqueville thought the most pervasive of all American traits – equality. Some Americans, like Columbia University professor Henry Steele Commager, were amazed that this class system did not poison interpersonal relationships among the British.[61]

On the British side, attitudes to America had always combined disparate and contradictory elements. It is regarded as an England that has gone off on strange courses. As America marched on its own unprecedented fashion from success to success, creating a new society unlike any that had ever been, it was a certain comfort to the older country to remember that, even if America was to be regarded as "an England gone funny," it was still England, and not some other country, that had fathered this extraordinary child. The success of the United States could, with some minimal mental dexterity, be regarded as a kind of vicarious success for England. The failures of America were naturally all its own and had nothing to do with England.

Most British assumed an unmistakable superior character and standard over Americans. Earlier British travelers were offended by the barbarous existence of slavery in America. One traveler defined the chief distinction between Britain and the United States as the latter country's "total want of refinement."[62] Later on British travelers looked at the new society with great curiosity. They admitted that American democracy was more vibrant. America was the land *par excellence* of conferences, discussion, and argument, of endless public debate about all kinds of issues. Many travelers reported that they were deeply impressed by the American spirit of being the pioneer and the lavish American hospitality. They admired American democracy, the equality of opportunity, the insistence upon educating the masses. They marveled at America's unrivaled wealth, intelligence, and general comfort and happiness.

Americans seemed to have a clearer view than any other people of the democratic fundamentals. The United States is the supreme example of a federation in being, a federation which recognizes the rights and individuality of the parts, but accepts the overriding interests of the whole. If the world is ever to have prosperity and peace, there must be some kind of federation of states which accepts the rule of law. "In such a task she (America) seems to me to be the predestined leader," remarked Lord Tweedsmuir, who was appointed Governor-General of Canada in 1935.[63]

In 1630 Governor John Winthrop predicted that America would become a model for the world – "a City Upon a Hill" with "the eyes of all people" upon it.[64] Americanism meant a pragmatic, optimistic outlook on life; a peaceful, rational compromise of political differences; an efficient, modern way of organizing work that emphasized machines and mass assembly production; rising standards of living with declining class antagonisms; scientific use of statistics and other information; and the predominance of popular culture.

Without doubt the American preeminence often generated resentment in many places. The dislike of America which grew up in Britain was due to the fact that world empire had passed from Lombard Street to Wall Street. Whether Europeans reviled America or respected it – and many did both – they saw in that secular city on the hill the image of their own societies' future.

In 1898, the United States, long the denigrator of imperialism, itself became an imperial power. It annexed the Hawaii Islands, and acquired, as the result of victory in the Spanish–American War, possession of Puerto Rico, Guam, and the Philippines, and control of Cuba. In general, the British looked at the rise of American power positively. As Britain cast about for support in the playing of its world role, it was natural to turn to where the claims of kinship might produce a response, that is, to the self-governing white parts of the Empire and to the United States. *The Times* of London reacted to America's move into the western Pacific after the Spanish–American War with "equanimity and indeed with satisfaction." "We can only say that while we would welcome the Americans in the Philippines as kinfolks and allies united with us in the Far East by the most powerful bonds of interest, we should regard very differently the acquisition of the archipelago by any other power."[65] The British broke with their European counterparts in supporting the United States in the Spanish–American War; the United States reciprocated by supporting the British in the Boer War.

The almost three years of American neutrality, 1914–17, in World War I caused a puzzled resentment in Britain. The British government refrained from openly criticizing the US position. With the end of World War I anglophobia made its return in America. Whereas this new wave of anti-British feeling appealed to many of the same themes as the old – to traditional Americanism, to the evils of monarchy and aristocracy, to the threat of the Royal Navy and the dangers of British imperialism – it sprang from different origins. It now arose from certain ethnic groups in the United States who resented the Anglo-Saxon upper classes. These Americans, especially of German and Irish decent, refused to accept the idea of Anglo-Saxon unity, and saw efforts toward this as an attempt to marginalize their role in society.[66] But this new wave of anglophobia had more to do with demographic change in American society than with any actions on Britain's part; it would subside only when these more recent immigrants felt they had reached a position of social equality with the Anglo-Saxon elite.

Though most British people had little informed knowledge of the United States, America in the 1920s seized the imagination of a new generation in Britain. For a decade, until the depression of the 1930s, everything American seemed alluring, offering the prospect of escape from life in Britain, which was drab by comparison. America was modern. America was rich. America was the future. American culture, as well as American goods, invaded Britain. Jazz began to catch on among the fashionable in the 1920s. American bands performed to wild acclaim in Britain. Gradually a market for American records developed and British dance bands began to give their music American touches, with greater syncopation and the addition of drums, banjos, and saxophones. The Prince of Wales's well-known enthusiasm, particularly for drumming, helped give jazz a seal of approval. Hollywood movies also attracted British theater-goers. The popular newspaper the *Daily Express* complained in 1927 that the bulk of moviegoers were being Americanized. "They talk America, think America, and dream America. We have several million people, mostly women, who, to all intent and purpose, are temporary American citizens."[67]

During World War I, Hollywood invaded European and other world markets. Young Men's Christian Association (YMCA) representatives entertained Allied troops with American films, and the "movie habit" caught on among civilians and soldiers. In the 1920s, American films were international box-office hits. Netting 60 percent of total world film revenue, Hollywood produced extravaganzas with which Europeans could not compete. By 1925, American films made up 95 percent of the total shown in Britain, 60 percent of the total in Germany, 70 percent in France, 65 percent in Italy, and 95 percent in Australia and New Zealand.[68] After 1925, Britain, Germany, and France tried to check the trend. Governments enacted measures to limit the number of imported Hollywood films and encouraged domestic production. This policy diminished but did not eliminate Hollywood's dominance in Europe.

Interestingly, Hollywood movies on British topics were also popular in America. The 1930s saw a rash of American movies based on books by Charles Dickens and Rudyard Kipling. Some were enormous box-office successes, such as *The Lives of a Bengal Lancer*, starring Gary Cooper. Other money-makers, such as *A Yank at Oxford* and *Goodbye, Mr. Chips*, gave stereotyped portraits of the English university and public school. But the British monarchy was the biggest hit in America. *The Private Life of Henry VIII* grossed over US$2.5 million.[69]

For many Americans, the monarchy provided the most fascinating real-life British story. King Edward VIII's affair with the American divorcee Mrs. Wallis Simpson was a matter of intense interest in the United States. In December 1936 Edward VIII was asked to choose between his throne and Mrs. Simpson. He chose the American woman he loved. The love story, which might be an embarrassment to many in Britain, was perfectly designed to satisfy America's fascination with monarchy. Likewise, a historic royal visit to the United States by King George VI in the summer of 1939, the first reigning British sovereign to set foot on the soil of the former colony, was greeted by enthusiastic crowds everywhere the royal couple went. Public mood changed with time. Gradually the British and Americans began to see each other more in a positive light. This favorable public opinion proved a critical factor as the grassroots foundation for a close relationship between the two English-speaking nations.

A union of mind and purpose

According to Aristotle, there are three kinds of friendship: friendship based on utility, friendship based on pleasure, and friendship based on goodness.[70] Of these three, only the last is perfect. Such friendship rests on the character of the partners themselves, on mutuality, and specifically on goodness. The Anglo-American relationship probably resembles this perfect friendship. The association between the two powers is deeper than formal alliances, based on affinity and tradition as much as interest, though some question the quality of Anglo-American friendship, since it was the British who took the initiative and were always conscious of the continuing anglophobia latent in American politics, and the Americans always expected and received concessions from Britain.[71]

Whereas many realists attribute the dramatic rapprochement between Great Britain and the United States to the rise of Germany and the threat it posed to the British, liberals place greater emphasis on the political and cultural affinity between Great Britain and the United States. Liberals would argue that it was the democratic affinity that persuaded Britain to choose to appease the United States instead of Germany. A list that combines the realist and liberal explanations can be made with regards to the attributes of the Anglo-American relationship that contributed to the development of a special relationship and a peaceful power transition. The following explanations also confirm the validity of the multilevel analysis framework.

1   The foundation of the special relationship between Britain and the United States is first of all demographic and ethnic, the basic fact that to a considerable extent the population of the United States derives from British sources. Estimates indicate that at the time of independence the American people were composed, as to origins, of 82.1 percent English, 7 percent Scottish, and 1.9 percent Irish, with a total from the British Isles of 92 percent. In 1930, the percentage of the American population of British origin was still as high as 61 percent.[72] In the decades between 1830 and 1880, immigrants came mostly from northwestern Europe and Germany. Beginning about 1880, there came the "new immigration" of people from Italy, Poland, Russia, and the Baltic states.

During the roughly eight decades of high-level US immigration, many other elements also contributed: for example, Chinese and Japanese immigration on the west coast and Mexican immigration across the border. None of these, however, rivaled in numbers the "new" European immigration. With the imposition of the quota system based on national origins, which prevailed from 1921 to 1967, the total flow was restricted with the objective of favoring the "old" as against the "new" sources. Throughout US history, the English-speaking contribution to the American population has been the biggest of all the national and racial groups. The number of Americans of British stock has always exceeded all other groups. Every nineteenth-century American president was of

British stock, except Martin Van Buren (1837–41), whose Dutch family emigrated in 1631.

On both sides of the Atlantic, there were proponents of the "Anglo-Saxon race" theory. "I refuse to speak or think of the United States as a foreign nation," Joseph Chamberlain told a Toronto audience in 1887. "They are our flesh and blood." He hoped that the Stars and Stripes and the Union Jack would wave together over an Anglo-Saxon alliance. Prime Minister A. J. Balfour (1902–5) was convinced that "the two great co-heirs of Anglo-Saxon freedom and civilization" had a common mission. Americans were "our kin beyond the sea." On the American side, Josiah Strong, an Ohio minister and one of the leading exponents of this thesis, said that "God is training the Anglo-Saxon race for an hour sure to come in the world's future ... Then will the world enter on a new stage in its history – *the final competition of races, for which the Anglo-Saxon is being schooled* ... And can any one doubt that the result of this competition of races will be the 'survival of the fittest' "?[73]

Between 1815 and 1860 approximately 2,877,000 immigrants entered the United States from Britain, substantially more than those entering from all other countries combined.[74] What this meant for the political, economic, cultural, and social relations between Britain and the United States could not be more obvious.

2   A common language, like the common racial origins, gives the two countries an unusually close bond and provides a basis for community building across the Atlantic. Many speak of the relationship in terms of a cultural unity shown by the English-speaking peoples, of this being the natural force for the peace and order of the world. The fact that the British and American peoples speak and write the same language probably underlines their sense of kinship tremendously, eases their cooperation, and reinforces the sense that their relationship is unique. For H. C. Allen, the cultural is probably the most important of all the ties binding the two countries since the two peoples understand one another much better than those who do not possess a common tongue.[75]

The natural concomitant of the common language is the common literature. The great literature of the British and American peoples is genuinely a common treasure, owned and created jointly. Not until the nineteenth century would American authors begin to be much read in Britain. But once the books of Washington Irving, Nathaniel Hawthorne, and James Fenimore Cooper came from the press, and were cordially read and much reprinted in Britain, the bond between British and American culture was reinforced: a common literature softened on either side the bitter memories of the War of Independence and the War of 1812. Nearly all classic books were published on both sides of the Atlantic. William Shakespeare, Charles Dickens, and Geoffrey Chaucer have been must-reads in American schools. Mark Twain's *The Adventures of Tom Sawyer* sold far more copies in Britain than in the United States.[76] All major authors are well known on both sides of the Atlantic. Americans and English knew each other from early childhood. American children read *Mother Goose* and *Alice's Adventures in Wonderland* and, a bit later, *Tom Brown's Schooldays* and *The Jungle Book* as English children read *Little Women* and *Tom Sawyer*, and when they grew up they continued to read each other's novels and poems without finding them in the least alien. Americans and English read the same Bibles – the King James Version or the Douay – and they embraced, on the whole, the same religious precepts and moral values. They even shared each other's heroes and villains.[77] A common language and, for a long time, a common history encouraged the mutual preoccupation. Jefferson wrote in 1810 that "American laws, language, religion, politics, and manners are so deeply laid in English foundations that we shall never cease to consider their history as part of ours, and to study ours in that as to its origins."[78]

3   Extensive personal ties and social links strengthened the alliance and security community. The upper classes of both countries had much in common, including marriages. Typically an earlier union was between an American heiress and a British aristocrat or high governmental official. Many British men of considerable power were married to Americans at the end of the nineteenth century.[79] After the German defeat in World War II, perhaps as many as 20,000 American GIs returned home with new British wives.[80] Such transatlantic unions doubtless had wide influence on policy. A common language and personal ties made possible a steady flow of people and ideas in both directions across the Atlantic, particularly when the steamship, introduced in the 1840s, reduced the voyage from two months to two weeks.

Britain devoted considerably more thought and energy than the United States to ensuring that business between the two nations went as smoothly as possible. British officials actively sought to mold American opinion – and through it, American policy. London continued to fund its overseas publicity and information services generously – a recognition of the heightened interconnection between opinion and diplomacy in democratic America, but also implicit acknowledgment that Britain's economic and military decline left it more dependent upon less traditional forms of diplomacy. Personal ties and the creation of contacts within the American government remained a priority for all British officials. The cultivation of friendly relations with American journalists was considered essential. Consular officials conducted extensive surveys of grassroots opinion in the various regions of the United States. American visits to Britain were promoted. The BBC beamed broadcasts from the United Kingdom specially designed for American audiences. The New York-based British Information Services (BIS) maintained a staff of over 200 in the late 1940s.[81]

Intellectually, the bonds between the two lands had been multiplied and strengthened. The free interchange of newspapers and magazines, the binational character of most great publishing houses, the mass circulation of American books in Britain and British books in America, the Rhodes scholarships, the increasing exchange of teachers and students, the movies, the radio, and the facilities for swift cheap travel had shortened the physical distance separating the two nations and made them neighbors psychologically.

4   What brings the two nations together also lies in the similarity of law and political institutions. Both were political and economic democracies. Both cherish as basic principles the rule of law, the importance of the individual, the necessity of adequate discussion, and the supreme importance of basing government on persuasion and consensus, and on some decent compromise between the rival claims of liberty and authority. Their systems of government form the two great exemplars of the two major versions – presidential government and parliamentary government – of constitutional and democratic rule that have been developed in the world. "Of this kind of governance, constitutional and democratic, they are the outstanding, and oldest, examples, with the greatest record in continuity and success of any major countries," remarked A. C. Turner.[82] Their resemblance on this point is far more significant than the differences in their versions of democracy. Personal freedom, private property, government under the law – these were liberties established long before in Britain, inherited by America, and then championed by both countries in the twentieth century against autocrats, fascists, and communists alike. Similar democratic cultures and institutions result in the expectations on both sides of mutual understanding and peaceful resolution of conflicts.

The widening of the franchise by electoral reform bills had greatly altered the British social structure. No longer in 1900 was Britain the aristocratic and somewhat arrogant nation that had so irritated republicans like Thomas Jefferson and James Madison 100 years earlier. If a more democratic Britain had greater appeal for the ordinary American, the United States no longer seemed a subversive rabble-rousing republic to upper-class Britons; on the contrary, with her written constitution and Supreme Court she seemed to many of them a welcome element of order and stability in a turbulent world. The industrialization of the United States had given its society many of the troubles, problems, and attitudes characteristic of industrial Britain. After all, America was simply taking a road that Britain had traveled a little earlier. America, too, had become crowded with great slums, restless laboring masses, and heavy tasks of relief. It was no accident that the first two Secretaries of Labor were British born. When the United States under Woodrow Wilson and Franklin D. Roosevelt wrote its first welfare and social insurance legislation, it turned to Britain for models.[83]

5   Strong economic and trade relations stabilized and promoted bilateral ties. Reference had often been made to transatlantic economic relations, and to their restraining influence whenever thoughts turned to war.

In the 1890s Great Britain was by far the principal market for American goods and the chief supplier of imports and capital. In 1890 Britain took US$448,000,000 worth of American goods, whereas the second largest market, Germany, took only US$86,000,000 worth. In 1898 the corresponding figures were US$541,000,000 and US$155,000,000. As for American imports, in 1890 Great Britain supplied US$186,000,000 worth, and Germany (the next largest supplier) US$99,000,000 worth. Eight years later the figures were US$109,000,000 and US$70,000,000. The United States was similarly important to Great Britain. For the five-year period 1890–4, an average of 11 percent of all British exports went to America; for 1895–9, 8.6 percent. For the former years no less than 23.4 percent of British imports came from America; and for the latter years 24.4 percent.[84] By the end of the nineteenth century a large community of business people and financiers moved back and forth between the two countries, at home in both. Such people and interest groups enjoyed public esteem; governments heeded their counsel. As economic ties deepened, so did the British–American friendship. It is hard to imagine that, without such deep economic interdependence and the support groups behind it, cross-Atlantic relations could have overcome difficulties and become so close.

6   The two nations removed contentious issues from their agenda through peaceful conflict resolution. The foundations for a union had always remained thanks to the two nations' determination to peacefully settle their differences.

Great Britain and the United States had a remarkable diplomatic record. A series of comprehensive treaties were negotiated and signed – the Jay–Grenville Treaty, the Webster–Ashburton Treaty, the Oregon Treaty, the Clayton–Bulwer Treaty, the Marcy–Elgin Treaty, the Treaty of Washington, the Bering Sea Treaty, the Venezuelan Treaty, and others. The United States and Great Britain also had an arbitration record that no other two countries could rival. Most extraordinary were the six full-scale arbitrations held during what may be called the heyday of arbitration, from 1872 through 1899. Five of them concerned disputes that, left unsettled, could have had grave consequences – disputes over the *Alabama* claims, the San Juan boundary, the fishery articles of the Treaty of Washington, the Bering Sea fur seals, and the Venezuelan boundary.[85] These treaties and arbitration reflected a willingness to compromise and the desire to settle disputes peacefully from both sides. Through a series of peace treaties in the nineteenth century, war had been removed from the menu of choices in transatlantic relations.

Favorable factors and conditions at all four levels, such as the common heritage, Anglo-Saxon race patriotism, the close and extensive economic and social links, the absence of clashing vital interests, the rise of British democracy and of admiration for American institutions, the emergence of a common international threat, and the willingness to compromise, are all positive forces that molded British–American relations. Each of these factors alone may not be sufficient by itself to bring about a harmonious relationship, but together they have produced solid and intimate bilateral relations with no comparison in history.

How to accept a secondary role gracefully

The United States had become indisputably the global leader in political, military, and economic affairs after WWII. "The United States is also now groping toward a new order of things in which Great Britain . . . will be expected to take her place as junior partner in an orbit of power predominantly under American aegis," a British diplomat in Washington told Foreign Secretary Bevin on 9 August 1945.[86] But how would Britain accept its secondary role gracefully? If Great Britain had refused to face the reality of its decline and accept its junior partnership to the United States, the special relationship across the Atlantic would not have been formed or lasted long and the power transition would have become violent. In fact, the concept of being the first-rank power died hard in Britain. Even during the 1950s, despite differences on such issues as trade and China, the British still considered itself an indispensable power in the world. "The close cooperation between the two great branches of the English-speaking peoples is vitally important for the peace of the world and for the defense of democracy," remarked Prime Minister Clement Attlee.[87] It was not until the 1960s that the word "decline" lodged itself firmly in the British vocabulary and consciousness.

As Britain's power declined, a British scholar warned that Britain had to change certain "habits" such as temptation to act as the world mediator and its condescending attitude toward other countries now equal in rank to Britain, especially West Germany and France. In other words, Britain had to come to terms "psychologically with what it means to be in the second rank of nations."[88]

Mutual patience, conciliation, and tact enabled the United States and Britain to settle their differences by peaceful means. Stressing the intertwining of their economies, as well as the cultural and racial ties between the two peoples, Britain and America reached an astonishing series of general treaties and arbitration agreements and established special commissions that began with Jay's Treaty in the 1790s and culminated in the Treaty of Washington and the subsequent settlement of all outstanding issues by the 1890s. By the middle of the nineteenth century, the United States, relatively content with its continental empire, ceased to threaten British interests in Canada, and Britain gave up the policy of trying to contain America's restless expansion. In the process, the British made a series of concessions to gradually defer to America's global leadership. The special relationship between the two countries is a genuine diplomatic victory – one in which there were no losers, only winners.

Britain's reaction to a new power flexing its muscles was to accommodate it as long as there was no serious conflict with British interests, particularly since it seemed a country so close in values and kinship to her own. America's growing involvement in the western hemisphere was welcomed as an extension of Anglo-Saxon influence. In Prime Minister Balfour's words, "The Monroe Doctrine has no enemies in this country that I know of. We welcome any increase of the great influence of the United States upon the great western hemisphere ."[89] After President Wilson's proposed League of Nations failed to win Senate approval, British Prime Minister Lloyd George said: "America had been offered the leadership of the world, but the Senate had tossed the sceptre into the sea."[90] For example, the United States and Britain often found themselves at odds over economic and trade practices. To counter Britain's "free trade" the United States sought to nurture its own infant industries behind protective tariffs. In the United States there was a widespread conviction that Britain's Empire gave it unfair competitive advantages such as monopolies of raw materials. A case in point was the successful American campaign to counter the burgeoning British oil monopoly in the Middle East, where it controlled production in southern Persia and threatened to do the same in Iraq. It was here that American interests, represented by Turkish Petroleum, secured a share of the concession in 1925. The supply of rubber was another source of contention. Britain already controlled three-quarters of the world output when it decided to cut production in 1922 to 60 percent of its 1920 total. The United States, consumer of two-thirds of the world's rubber, chiefly because of the automobile boom, was faced with a price of US$1.21 per pound by 1925, compared with just 16.3 cents in 1921. In the ensuing diplomatic squabble the British were forced to abandon their quotas for rubber production in 1928, by which time they controlled just half of the world supply.[91]

"Possibly the most noteworthy point about Anglo-American relations in the twentieth century is the extent to which the relationship has been a one-sided affair, in which Britain played the role of a nervous suitor, anxious by any means or any concession to court the favor of the superbly indifferent object of his affections," commented A. C. Turner, a leading expert on Anglo-American relations.[92] There were many occasions when Britain gave up a British interest, or changed a policy, in hope of pleasing the United States. Examples of a reciprocal amiability on the part of the United States are few or nonexistent. Perhaps there was no choice; perhaps a sedulously cultivated American friendship paid higher dividends than any alternative policy would have done. After all, for Britain the American alliance made possible victory in World War I; and first survival, and then victory, in WWII.

To British statesmen in the 1920s and 1930s, American goodwill was a lock-away security, not expected to produce any dividends in any immediate future, but whose purchase was worth considerable effort. To this end formidable concessions continued to be made. In the Washington conference of 1922, Britain gave up its traditional policy of maintaining the largest navy. A 5:5:3 ratio was accepted for the relative strengths of the British, American, and Japanese navies. At the same time, as a matter of simply yielding to American pressure, seconded by Canada and to some extent by other Commonwealth countries, Britain gave up the Anglo-Japanese alliance which had lasted for twenty years and had served Britain well. In 1923 Stanley Baldwin, as Chancellor of the Exchequer, went to Washington to negotiate the terms of settlement of Britain's wartime debts to the United States. He was under explicit instructions from the prime minister, Bonar Law, as to the basis of settlement and the maximum concessions to be made. In practice, he went far beyond these, and agreed to terms which were far more onerous on Britain, amounting to a substantial acceptance of the US demands. Nevertheless, on his return the British government, instead of repudiating his concessions, confirmed them.[93] On all these episodes – acceptance of US navy parity, repudiation of the Anglo-Japanese alliance, agreement of the Baldwin-conceded debt repayment terms – the British policy of seeking American goodwill as a card that trumped all other policy considerations is obvious. British officials did not think much of this appeasement of the United States.

Britain had for centuries depended upon the Royal Navy to protect herself and her empire, so it was a bitter pill to accept parity with anyone. But she had recognized over a decade earlier that she could not afford a war with America, and the formal surrender of supremacy was accepted with generally good grace. Britain never willingly relinquished power or influence, but her position was so exposed, her resources so inadequate, that she had no choice but to treat the least menacing of her foes as a potential friend. Economy and *realpolitik* ruled out a war with the United States. Britain's huge national debt, mass unemployment, and outstanding war debts to the United States were a basis for appeasement, not a state of conflict.

By 1945 it was beyond denying that the ultimate guarantee of British security lay in the hands of another nation, a galling situation for a proud people who within living memory had dominated the international scene. By the end of 1946, the British were increasingly content to cede the task of resisting provocative Soviet actions to the United States. In part this reflected Whitehall's growing appreciation of the limited resources at its disposal; in part it represented a conscious attempt to encourage Washington to accept the great responsibilities inherent in American power.[94] As one of the victorious Big Three, Britain expected a place of equality with the Soviet Union and the United States. And yet the paucity of her resources for such a role could scarcely be denied. As one scholar commented, "Britain's root problem is that she has been attempting for too long to do more than her own capabilities . . . would support or afford."[95] By 1950, the United States had accepted, even embraced, leadership of the anti-Soviet force around the globe, a role Britain had encouraged Washington to assume. Britain had clearly been relegated to the status of junior partner to the United States. Britain's dependence upon the United States had become too obvious to ignore.

Inferences and summary

From the above survey and analysis, some observations can be made about Anglo-American relations and power transition from 1865 to 1945:

The two countries ruled out war as a method of conflict resolution early in their relationship.
With the establishment of a security community across the Atlantic, all disputes were expected to be resolved peacefully. According to the historian H. G. Nicholas, the 1814 Ghent peace treaty that ended the War of 1812 ushered in "a period of Anglo-American pacification." The consequence of the peace treaty was that both sides recognized that war was "too costly a method of resolving their differences," which brought about certain lasting changes in their mutual relations.[96] With war removed from their menu of choices, transatlantic commerce flourished and political relations improved. Though talk of war emerged on both sides of the Atlantic later on, especially during the 1895 Venezuela dispute, it never materialized. Britain rejected initially but finally agreed to a restricted arbitration of the Venezuela dispute. For the peaceful settlement of this crisis – sometimes seen as the last threat of war between Britain and the United States – the British "sacrificed their prestige to their belief that war with the United States was unthinkable."[97] Through a series of peace treaties in the nineteenth century, the two countries had learned to resolve their disputes through arbitration and negotiations.

Compared with Germany, the United States had no intentions toward the Old World and kept a low profile during its rise as a great power. As a result, Great Britain felt less threatened.
Despite the Monroe Doctrine in Latin America and the proclaimed Manifest Destiny in Asia, the United States did not seem to have many political, economic, and cultural ambitions in the Old World. It was geographically far away with no immediate threat to the British isles. And its involvement in both world wars was involuntary. Great Britain had been the predominant power for over a century; its colonies were established in every corner of the earth. It increasingly felt threatened by rising powers, especially by Germany and Russia to its interests in the European continent, and by Japan to its interests in Asia. Comparatively speaking, the United States was a benign emerging power, with no aggressive ambitions toward the British.

Despite historical problems, relations were cordial at both the high level and the grassroots level between Great Britain and the United States.
The cordial relationship came a long way. During the early years of American independence, animosity could be found on both sides. While the young America looked down upon the old and rotten way of life in Britain, the British considered the new republic as a child going astray. The first steamship made her initial voyage across the Atlantic in 1819. Frequent travel across the Atlantic greatly enhanced mutual understanding and respect between the two nations. The strong and special relationship had been fostered not

only by frequent exchanges between the two peoples, but also by purposeful cultivation of leaders on both sides, especially during the interwar years. What united the two great peoples was not just common cultural and historical heritage, but also the love of peace. Favorable public opinion and committed leaders on both sides made a union possible.

British appeasement of the United States during the latter's rise was well received and reciprocated by the United States.

Facing more direct and dangerous rivals in Europe, Great Britain sought to reduce the threat posed by the United States. The British took the initiative and were always conscious of the continuing anglophobia latent in American politics. The Americans always expected and received concessions from Britain; this showed the measure of Britain's need and of her determination to achieve an Anglo-American entente. Britain acquiesced in the United States' dominant role in the Americas. The United States appreciated the gesture and supported British policies on many occasions in return. Mutual accommodation was essential in sustaining this special relationship.

The British were willing to give up their global leadership gracefully to the United States.

It was remarkable that Britain was prepared and willing to deal with and later cooperate closely with its former colony on the basis of equal status. If the British had attempted to block the rise of the United States, the power transition across the Atlantic would have been violent. Unable to sustain its global predominance, Great Britain realized that its leadership role had to be passed on to someone else. It determinedly rejected turning the leadership role to Germany, Russia, or Japan. During the interwar years, it became evident to British statesmen that an alliance with the United States, in which the United States assumed the leading role and Britain a junior supporting role, would be the only viable path toward peace. With little grudge, Great Britain gracefully passed the baton to the Americans.

A revisit of hypotheses

These observations and inferences once again confirm the validity of the hypotheses proposed for this research:

H1: The further a rising power is incorporated into the international system, the less likely it is to challenge the status quo violently.

Great Britain accepted US hegemony in the Americas first. Despite its occasional "non-entangling" rhetoric and policy, the United States had been heavily involved in European affairs, except the short period of political isolation after the League of Nations failed to pass Congress. The United States had become a full member of the international system. By the end of World War II, it became evident that it was almost impossible for the United States to adopt an isolationist policy. The United States had become the global leader in military, political, and economic affairs. It was in US interests to maintain the new international political and economic system that it helped to shape and form. And for its own interests, Great Britain stood with the United States and supported its new leadership role.

H2: The more a rising power recognizes and respects the dominant power's vital interests, the less likely it is to be perceived and treated as a threat by the dominant power.

Respect and accommodation are mutual. The United States, through its policies and actions, demonstrated that it did not pose a threat to Great Britain and its interests. Furthermore, it recognized the importance of containing German and Russian powers for the very survival of Britain and joined hands with the British, fighting shoulder to shoulder with them during two world wars. The British, in return, considered the United States a benign power posing no threat to their interests.

H3: The more the dominant power respects and accommodates a challenger's vital interests, the less likely the challenger is to become dissatisfied with the international order and its relations with the dominant power.

Britain took the initiative to accommodate the United States and strove to establish a friendly and close relationship with its former colony. The United States felt satisfied with the respect and accommodation accorded her by Britain. This research suggests that, if the British had not taken the initiative to accommodate the United States, the bilateral relationship might not have developed into a special one. And if the United States had been dissatisfied vis-à-vis Great Britain, the power transition would not have been peaceful.

H4: The more extensive and strong links the two societies have, the less likely there is to be war between them.

The British–American relationship has probably been the strongest in all bilateral relations. The extensive and firm ties cover all aspects of life across the Atlantic. Though an ocean apart, the two English-speaking nations are close neighbors psychologically. Enormous business transactions, personnel exchanges, and other activities across the Atlantic linked the two societies in a strong security community. The democratic cultures accepted by both societies made it inconceivable to resort to war as a solution of bilateral differences.

H5: The more committed national leaders are to a stable bilateral relationship, the less likely there is to be war between the two powers.

The special relationship is a result of persistent and purposeful cultivation by national leaders, especially on the British side. Without visionary and committed leaders like Winston Churchill, Joseph Chamberlain, Woodrow Wilson, and Theodore Roosevelt, a strong alliance across the Atlantic might not have been established.

General hypothesis: If the government, the public, and top leaders in both the dominant power and the challenging power have positive evaluations of the bilateral relationship in a friendly international system, power transition will end in peace.

The British–American case is a prime example of how two powers feel satisfied with an interdependent relationship in an unstable, changing world. A strong and stable alliance was essential for Britain's survival and postwar reconstruction. Despite some grudges, Great Britain gracefully handed the leadership role to the United States; and the United States, despite its occasional isolationist policy in history, happily assumed the new role as the guardian of the new international system. With the establishment and consolidation of a pluralistic security community, the two powers developed mutual understanding and mutual responsiveness. They coordinated their foreign policies and together shaped the international political and economic system. The British gracefully ceded world leadership to their closest friends across the Atlantic. A peaceful power transition was complete at the end of World War II.

It must be pointed out that the conditions surveyed at international, domestic, societal, and individual levels were mixed in this case study. Although initially some conditions were negative, especially at the societal and individual levels, toward the end of the period surveyed, all conditions turned or were becoming positive, heralding the most successful and peaceful power transition in history. This observation is significant in that it provides hope for a peaceful power transition even between two powers with diverse and conflicting interests so long as they can control the negative aspects and peacefully settle their differences while accentuating the positive aspects of their relationship.

The transatlantic special relationship may have been the defining global partnership of the last century, but the twenty-first century's international politics is most likely to be shaped by the complex relationship between the United States and China. The next chapter looks at China's rise and US–China relations between 1990 and 2005 and predicts the future course of the relationship.

5 Sino-American relations, 1990–2005

China's rise in the twenty-first century: peaceful or not?

That the mechanism for systemic change has frequently been war in history does not necessarily mean future power transitions will always end in war. The Anglo-American power transition, though unique in many aspects, provides us with some hope that, if managed well, a power transition can evolve peacefully. This chapter, through examining Sino-American relations since the early 1990s at global, domestic, societal, and individual levels, explores whether a potential power transition from the United States to China will be able to occur smoothly in the twenty-first century.[1]

Anticipating the future of world politics is risky business, but it is prudent for decision makers to prepare for all future possibilities and make choices that have long-term impact. At the turn of the twenty-first century, the United States stands in a predominant position in virtually every measure of international power: military, economic, political, technological, and cultural. Probably no other country or empire has had a comparable global reach since the Roman Empire. Lest we forget history, it is worth recalling that the rise of great powers has always been accompanied by their fall sometime later. Whether history's pattern will change in this century is impossible to know now. For the purpose of this book, I assume that the historical cycle will continue with the gradual decline of the United States and the rise of a rival power or powers in the future. US–China relations will be dealt with in the context of a potential global power transition in the future. But even if a power transfer never takes place from the United States to China, this research is still significant in that the policy analysis and recommendations are useful for managing Sino-American relations peacefully in the early decades of the twenty-first century. And the analytical framework and policy prescriptions will also be useful for analyzing and predicting a potential power transition from the United States to another power or group of powers as well as power transitions at regional levels around the world.

How to deal with a rising China is probably the most serious foreign policy challenge for the United States in the twenty-first century. Many scholars, policy analysts, and government officials in the West seem almost obsessed with China's continuing rise toward the status of a great power. Debates rage over whether there is a "China threat," how to measure China's military and economic power, and what is the best strategy to approach China. Though the course of China's development in the future is far from certain, China's economic growth itself has caused great concerns in the United States. A US National Intelligence Council report warned that, although the United States would retain its role as the world's dominant economy and military power, by the year 2020, China and possibly India would be vying with the United States for global economic supremacy.[2] An Ohio State University professor predicted that by 2025 China would overtake the United States economically.[3] Even the US military has adjusted its forward deployment arrangement to boost its rapid reaction activities in the Asia-Pacific region in anticipation of a possible war in East Asia, especially one with China over Taiwan.[4] It seems that, despite anticipated structural problems facing the Chinese economy and society after the WTO accession and intractable resistance to further economic and political reform, some people in the United States and elsewhere are fixated on China's bullish future, and therefore worried about losing America's sole superpower status, at least in Asia.

Interestingly, economists disagree on the exact size and potential of China's economy. Some suggest that the official annual growth rate of nearly 10 percent in the 1980s and 1990s may have been exaggerated. Some suggest that, already larger than Italy's and France's by 2003, China's economy was moving up fast soon afterwards on Britain, the world's fourth largest economy. Taking into account the different purchasing power of currencies, some analysts believe that China will leapfrog into the second place, with an economy already about half the size of America's.[5] The potential of China's economic power is not to be overlooked. At least in Asia, "an inescapable process of China replacing the United States as the dominant power" has already begun, declared a *New York Times* correspondent.[6]

China's own evaluation of its economic strength is probably closer to reality. In a 2002 report released by the China Institute of Contemporary International Relations in Beijing, China's "comprehensive national strength" was considered a quarter that of the United States.[7] In his political report to the sixteenth National Congress of the Chinese Communist Party in November 2002, outgoing President Jiang Zemin also laid down a roadmap for China in the next two decades: to build China into a "comprehensively well-off society" by the year 2020. According to him, China's per capita share of GDP should jump from the current US$800 to around US$3,000 in 2020.[8] President Hu Jintao reaffirmed this national objective and told the 2005 Fortune Global Forum in Beijing that China would quadruple its GDP to approximately US$4 trillion by 2020.[9]

Realistically speaking, in the first two decades of the twenty-first century the United States will probably remain a hyperpower unmatched in every dimension of national capabilities. China will not be in a position to challenge the American military, technological, and economic supremacy any time soon. There are daunting economic, political, and social challenges that China has to deal with now and in the near future. So conflict between China and the United States derived from power rivalry is not very likely in the next two to three decades. But exactly because of this, the next two or three decades are particularly crucial in determining the nature and the future trend of the fluid relationship between China and the United States. If they can handle this complex relationship constructively, a potential power transition in the future is more likely to be peaceful.

Regardless of the ideological mismatch between communism and liberal democracy and the difficult issue of Taiwan, China's rise is bound to raise concern, discomfort, and even hostility from some quarters in the United States. With a size slightly larger than that of the United States and a population one-fifth of the world's total, China can be a real source of regional and global stability or instability. Will China follow the path of pre-WWI Germany and violently disrupt the international system? What can the United States and China do to ensure a smooth rise of China and a peaceful coexistence? As the global and Asia-Pacific regional leader, the United States probably faces no greater challenger than to ensure China's peaceful surge. Only wise policy choices from both sides can help manage the interactions between the two giants peacefully. What policy each takes and how each action is perceived will greatly affect the future course of the relationship. In this sense, great efforts are needed to understand the complexity of US–China relations in all aspects and to find out ways to manage this relationship in the early decades of the twenty-first century.

The international environment: US–China relations in a globalization era

The post-Cold War US–China relationship has been a complex mix of contention and cooperation. Since 1989, the Sino-US relationship has been driven by both domestic and international considerations. The key factors precipitating this change were the Tiananmen incident and the collapse of the Soviet Union. To a great extent, the Tiananmen incident fundamentally changed Americans' view of China. The image of an opening China of the 1980s was replaced overnight by an image of a defiant China ruled by dictators. The end of US–Soviet rivalry removed the most obvious rationale for Sino-US cooperation in international affairs. All the major differences between the two countries suddenly resurfaced. Leaders on both sides have yet to identify a new foundation upon which the bilateral strategic relationship will be built.

At the turn of the century, especially after the 11 September 2001 terrorist attacks on American soil, a new consensus seemed to be emerging in the United States with regard to the greatest threat to national security. Asymmetric warfare, including terrorism, is a greater danger to US interests and a subsequently higher strategic priority than any traditional military threat.[10]

According to the US ambassador to China, Clark Randt, the 11 September attacks demonstrated to Americans that they have real enemies, and China is not among them.[11] For the United States and China, the 2001 terrorist attacks provided some breathing space for the tense relationship jeopardized by the spy plane incident and President Bush's statement of defending Taiwan at all costs earlier that year. The two countries have cooperated well on the war against terrorism though they had differences over the US war in Iraq.

Yet the "China threat" argument within the US government and society was on the decline only for a while. It seems that the rise of China as a great power is never comforting to some in the United States. Even during the height of war against terrorism, some forces in the United States did not let down their guard against a powerful China. In July 2002 for example, two official reports submitted to the US Congress – one by the US–China Security Review Commission on bilateral relations and the other by the Department of Defense on China's military power – both portrayed China's surge as a threat to American interests.[12] The "China threat" view is nothing new. Since 1990 China has frequently been singled out as the most dangerous potential threat to US national interests. The China threat debate has been intense, especially in election years. Without seeing a real peer competitor in the international system, some people in the United States turn to China as an easy target.

China, on the other hand, has come to see its interests inseparably aligned with those of the international community. China's priority since the late 1970s has been to take advantage of the relative peaceful international environment for its modernization programs. If anything, China probably wants to maintain a good relationship with the United States and the international community for its internal development. In 1982, the PRC adopted a new constitution which for the first time contained an international interdependence theme: "The future of China is closely linked with that of the world."[13] With some twists and turns, China's door to the world and the West in particular has opened to a point that it is almost impossible to close again.

Whereas the United States considers the enlargement of areas of democracy a core element of its grand strategy, China has made no such effort, nor does it seem to have any intention, to export its ideas about market socialism. China has not replaced the former Soviet Union as a global threat to US interests and to the security of regions all over the world. China is not seeking to construct a network of client states over the world through which to challenge US and Western interests. The Chinese may work with coalitions of other countries on certain issues – such as human rights – to oppose US imposition of its interests and advance China's own programs and interests. However, China is not leading any coalition seeking to oppose the United States on a broad agenda of issues. Nor is China seeking to spread a specific ideological vision of the world and to gather other countries under its ideological leadership.

In China, some analysts see the events of 11 September 2001, while tragic, as heralding a brighter future for US–China relations. These analysts see significant potential for US–China cooperation on counterterrorism efforts, which may contribute to an improvement in overall bilateral relations. Indeed, American and Chinese officials have held regular talks on terrorism in Asia and agreed that "very encouraging progress has been made in the fight against terrorism and recognized that much remains to be done."[14] The United States has offered, for example, to provide China with security experts and other assistance in preparation for the 2008 Olympics in Beijing. Nevertheless, although the terrorist attacks and the ensuing American fight against terrorism brought the two countries a bit closer, they have not generated any new consensus in either country for closer bilateral cooperation.

Frankly speaking, the America-led war against terrorism is not China's top national security priority. Sino-US cooperation based on the war against terror is rather limited. Some Chinese analysts have already noted that the George W. Bush administration will single-mindedly and unilaterally pursue its war on terrorism if it cannot overcome its differences with friends and allies, which may result in deterioration of US–China relations. In fact, the United States probably does not expect much actual support from China. The United States should probably be satisfied with no vocal opposition from China. If the United States does seek substantial help from China in the war, it is likely that China will insist on a significant quid pro quo (especially regarding Taiwan, which is China's top security concern, and perhaps also the North Korea nuclear crisis). The United States is apparently not ready to and probably will not expend this valuable political capital in pursuit of close Chinese cooperation in the war.

In the long term, globalization, particularly in the economic and political dimensions, provides the best hope for extensive cooperation between the two countries. Economic globalization and deep interdependence of the two societies are most likely to become the foundations for a peaceful, though not very intimate, relationship between the two countries. How globalization and interdependence affect domestic policy and how domestic politics responds to multilateral cooperation will determine the course of great power interactions in the future.

It has been argued throughout the book that, if the hegemonic power can incorporate the challenging power, through multilateral approaches, into the international community where they share vital interests, wars will be less likely between them during the power transition. Weaving a rising power into an interdependent world also exposes it to international norms and practices. If the challenging power can benefit from these norms and practices, it may well accept the existing rules and is less likely to challenge the status quo violently. The mutual predictability of behavior as part of the extensive link between the two powers may substantially decrease the likelihood of armed conflict between them. Multilateral actions initiated by the dominant power and supported by other powers are more likely to be perceived as legitimate by the international community including the challenging power. In a multi-lateral and interdependent environment, contentious issues are more likely to be addressed after reaching consensus with other powers.

To a great extent, the United States has helped to bring China back to the international stage after the end of the Cultural Revolution. President Richard Nixon's groundbreaking visit to China in 1972 essentially recon-nected the People's Republic of China with the developed world. Since the early 1980s, through trade and investment, the United States has facilitated China's modernization. Through interactions with the United States and other countries in the fast changing globalized world, China has become an important regional and global player. China's growing involvement with and acceptance by the international community was highlighted by its admission into the WTO at the end of 2001 and its successful dual bid to hold the 2008 Olympics in Beijing and the 2010 World Exposition in Shanghai – the first time a World Expo is to be held in a developing country in its 150-year his-tory.

Is China a satisfied power in the lexicon of power transition? By most stan-dards, it probably is. Being an active member of such international and mul-tilateral organizations as the United Nations and the WTO, China is helping to rewrite the global rules of the game. The rules that are established with China's participation are more likely to be observed by China. Globalization, interdependence, and multilateralism have clearly all contributed to turn-ing China into a law-abiding state in the international system, which has far-reaching significance for a potential power transition in the twenty-first century.

Globalization and deep interdependence provide both the rising power and the dominant power a rare opportunity to focus on the large picture of the relationship while accommodating on specific contentious issues. With political vision, wisdom, and will from both national leaders and the public, there is no reason to think that the next power transition cannot be managed peacefully. For the past 100 years, Chinese foreign policy had been predicated on the belief, first, that China was a victim and, later, that it was a Third World leader. However, in recent years China is adjusting its worldview. An influential Beijing University scholar argued that China should walk out of the shadow of the past 100 years of the diplomacy of humiliation and begin to act like a big power in East Asia.[15] Indeed, a significant portion of China's foreign policy establishment is beginning to view today's China as a rising power, closer to the United States and Europe than to the world's poor.

In each of the historic transitions China has undergone since the end of World War II – communist revolution under Mao Zedong, reform and open-ness under Deng Xiaoping, and integration with the global political economy under Jiang Zemin and Hu Jintao – China could not afford to ignore America's role. The "American factor" is likely to carry still greater weight in China's future development. The US government has great expectations of China's younger leadership. Hu Jintao was invited to visit Washington and received as a head of state in April 2002 before the official leadership transfer in Beijing. As a historical coincidence, the late Deng Xiaoping was also invited to visit the United States before becoming the supreme leader in 1979. Deng engineered a rather constructive relationship with the United States throughout the 1980s, even in the aftermath of the Tiananmen incident. How Hu can help raise the relationship to a higher stage is worth watching.

While opposing America's frequent unilateral approach in international affairs and its high-handedness toward China on certain issues, the Chinese government has a basically positive view of the US-dominated international system. In the early 1990s China was still talking about *fandui baquan zhuyi* (fighting against hegemonism), the Communist Party's code word for US dominance in world affairs. However, starting from the mid-1990s, the Chinese Communist Party has held a more benign view of the international environment. From Deng Xiaoping to Hu Jintao, senior leaders have emphasized the importance of taking advantage of the relative peaceful international environment after the Cold War for China's economic modernization. China should keep a low profile in international affairs and concentrate on economic development, the late Deng admonished. What is necessary now is to work more for *heping yu fazhan* (peace and development) – more code words, which mean cooperation with the United States. At the beginning of the twenty-first century, Chinese leaders are continuing this development strategy and are trying to do their best to present a new image of a peacefully rising China in the region.[16]

China's role in international organizations is "distinctively system-maintaining," observed Columbia political scientist Samuel Kim, and China is "a satisfied conservative system maintainer, not a liberal system reformer nor a revolutionary system transformer."[17] Since the PRC was admitted to the United Nations in 1971, Beijing has been more interested in what the UN system can do for China's development and less interested in what China can do to reform the United Nations. The early fear that China might use its veto power to paralyze the UN Security Council turned out to be unfounded. China has very rarely used its veto power and has more often than not cooperated with other Security Council permanent members. Like most nations, China tries to use the international institutions to advance its own interests.

China's modernization requires a peaceful international environment. This means it shares a common interest with the United States in maintaining peace and stability in the Middle East, Asia, and elsewhere; preserving stable oil and commodity markets; and restricting the proliferation of missiles and weapons of mass destruction. China's efforts to shore up regional currencies during the East Asian financial crisis in the late 1990s, its willingness to agree to a code of conduct in the South China Sea, its work in the United Nations on peacekeeping, and its cooperation with the United States in the area of arms control and the Korean peninsula indicate that China has just as much interest as the United States in maintaining a predictable, rule-based international order.

The basic objectives of China's *duli zizhu de heping waijiao zhengce* (independent foreign policy of peace) since the early 1990s have centered on safeguarding national independence and state sovereignty, creating an international environment favorable to its reform, opening, and modernization efforts, and maintaining world peace and promoting common development.[18] China considers peace and development as the main themes of the times, and the international environment as presenting more opportunities than challenges to China in an era of globalization.[19] China's foreign policy has been consistent over the years. China has improved relations both with the big powers and with its Asian neighbors. Maintaining a constructive and beneficial relationship with the United States is clearly one of the top tasks on China's foreign policy agenda. China has also normalized and improved relations with former enemies on its borders: Russia, Japan, India, and Vietnam. Without a peaceful international and regional environment, China's expanded growth will be impossible.

China has professed its intention of "not seeking hegemony" (*bu cheng ba*) even after it becomes powerful. China is probably less concerned with replacing the United States in its hegemonic position than with preventing its hegemony from becoming overwhelming and final. The Chinese know that access to the American market as well as American capital and technology play a key role in their desire to become a powerful and modern country. The emerging competition is about the search for reciprocity, mutuality, and respect. It is about diversity and reciprocity. It is about multilateralism, not unilateralism. At the moment, China has neither the capability nor the intention to pose a threat to US leadership in the world. In general China benefits from the international environment dominated by the United States. China has already become part of the international establishment. If China continues to benefit from the US-dominated international system, it is not likely to challenge it or the US leadership. For the foreseeable future, China will most likely continue on the road it has been traveling for the past two decades and more, laboriously building up its economy, gradually modernizing its society and upgrading its military, and hoping that in the long term Taiwan will want to reunify with a more prosperous Chinese mainland.

The 1991 Gulf War was the first time the United States displayed its military supremacy as the only superpower. To a great extent, the 11 September attacks consolidated America's superpower status and hardened its will to go unilateral when necessary in protecting its national interests. In the security arena, China and the United States have clear common interests in North Korea, South Asia, and terrorism in the Middle East, not to mention border control, the environment, and infectious diseases such as AIDS and SARS. But US and Chinese positions diverge on Taiwan, human rights, and nonproliferation. More significantly, disputes with China over Taiwan and human rights are construed by some in China as the American design to block China's rise as a great power in Asia. If the United States continues its unilateral approach in international affairs and its high-handedness toward

China on the vital issue of Taiwan, relations between the two powers may be in danger of slipping downward.

Nevertheless, US–China relations remain dynamic and resilient. Despite differences over a wide range of issues, bilateral relations have withstood strains from several crises since the mid-1990s. During Clinton's presidency, the relationship survived the Taiwan Strait crisis in 1995–6 and the Chinese embassy bombing in 1999. The two countries succeeded in reaching agreement on China's WTO admission toward the end of the Clinton administration. The George W. Bush administration is widely believed to be more hawkish and unilateral in international affairs. US–China relations were rocky during the first few months of the Bush presidency. In April 2001, a US EP-3 reconnaissance plane was forced down on China's Hainan Island. Some wondered if the crisis had brought down not just the plane, but also the hope of a productive relationship. Toward the end of 2001, rather than the relationship being sunk by that incident, the two countries were exploring new areas of cooperation, from counterterrorism to trade liberalization and stability in South Asia. By the end of 2003, a satisfied President Bush told visiting Chinese prime minister, Wen Jiabao, that the United States and China have become "partners" in diplomacy.[20] Two major players in regional and global affairs, the United States and China have learned the importance of cooperation and realized the danger of contention in an era of globalization.

Domestic politics

The United States

Foreign policy has always been fundamentally affected by domestic politics, as illustrated by the two-level games logic.[21] This is especially true for the United States, where the tradition of open debate over public policy has been one of its founding principles. Yet the United States, like many other nations, is essentially ideological in its policy deliberation, fixated on political slogans such as defending national security and democracy, rule of law, free markets, and individual freedom. In dealing with China, the United States has often been flexible and pragmatic while upholding these ideals.

The checks and balances mechanism is a trademark of American style democracy. It ensures intense domestic debate on major issues. Congress and the White House may agree upon US objectives toward China, but they often diverge on concrete policies. Traditionally, Congress has been more outspoken and critical of the negative sides of Chinese society and has advocated tougher policies accordingly. The White House, Republican or Democratic, has tended to take a more balanced approach toward China. Though both Republicans and Democrats have held office in the White House since the end of the Cold War, the China policy objectives and practices of various administrations have remained similar; a balanced centrist road often wins at the end of the day. As America's debate over China's WTO membership in the late 1990s indicated, America's China policy is often pulled in different directions by a variety of competing interests and concerns.[22] US foreign policy toward China often swings between the extremes as a result of domestic development. American leaders from both parties have helped produce a China policy adrift, with their different rhetoric and policy orientations, which has contributed to tensions on the most sensitive issue in the bilateral relationship: Taiwan. A change of power in the White House can often drastically lead the bilateral relationship to a new uncertainty. Though both Democratic and Republican administrations still nominally stick to the "one China" policy, their approaches to the Taiwan issue and their tactics toward China may vary, creating confusion and inconsistency in a core issue between the two countries.

Like a pendulum, US foreign policy has swung between idealism and realism. With regard to China, the policy has been characterized by a combination of engagement and containment (Figure 5.1). China policies of all US administrations since the end of the Cold War could be seen as engagement to the extent that they have promoted robust economic and trade ties with China; and containment to the extent that they have firmed up security relations with allies in Asia and continued US military support for Taiwan. The combination strategy of engagement and deterrence has remained unchanged in dealing with China; what is different is the tactics. All US administrations have sought to keep China's emergence as a major power from undermining key US interests, without creating a counterproductive spiral of growing hostility.

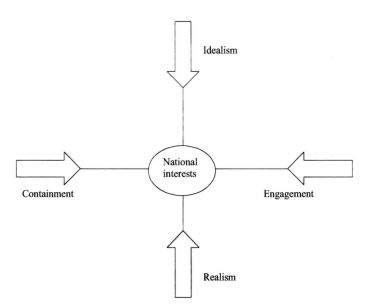

Figure 5.1 Different positions, same objectives.

US Congress

Congress has been a major player in US policy toward China. The history of American foreign policy making reveals a tug-of-war between Congress and the executive branch. America's China policy has not been determined by any single president or by Congress. Rather, it has resulted from a complex interaction between the two branches of government. Criticisms of China from members of Congress are often harsh. From human rights and rule of law to Taiwan and Tibet, many members of Congress rarely have anything positive to say about China. Several members of Congress have taken a strong personal interest in aspects of US China policy. Nancy Pelosi (D-CA) and Frank Wolf (R-VA), for example, are personally identified with concerns over China's human rights issues. Congressman Dana Rohrabacher (R-CA) and former Senators Frank Murkowski (R-AK) and Jesse Helms (R-NC) are closely identified with strong US support for Taiwan. Members of Congress who are critical of China represent interests of human rights groups, labor groups, religious groups, and arms control advocates. Congress is also a venue where partisan politics is most evident. Scholars have seen this motive behind some of the Democratic-led criticism of President George H. W. Bush's China policy, especially in the period leading up to the 1992 elections. President Bush was able to sustain enough support in the Senate to preserve the most-favored-nation status for China, in part by appealing to the party loyalties of Republican senators. Scholars and other observers also saw partisanship behind congressional Republican-led attacks against the Clinton administration's China policy, especially during his second term.[23]

Interestingly, despite its harsh criticism of China's poor human rights record and its lack of law, US Congress has never funded the rule of law program for China that was announced by President Bill Clinton in 1997 during his summit meeting in Washington with Chinese President Jiang Zemin. The tough but unconstructive rhetoric from Congress feeds the impression in China that the United States is more interested in openly humiliating China than in assisting China during its historic transformation. Even though there is strong congressional support for normal US trade and diplomatic relations with China, Congress as a whole is often perceived as an anti-China force in American politics by many people in China. For personal, interest group, partisan, and other reasons, critics of China in Congress are likely to remain active for the foreseeable future.

The partisan views of China are best summarized by Henry Kissinger in a comment in 1998: "Republicans see China as a threat; Democrats view it as a laboratory for the spread of American values. Both view China through the prism of their party's experience over the last 30 years. Unfortunately, too many Republicans have substituted China for the collapsed Soviet Union and seek to deal with it by the methods that accelerated the collapse of the Soviet empire: diplomatic confrontation, economic ostracism, and ideological warfare. Too many Democrats act as if the principal goal of American policy should be to replicate our institutions and principles in China, even at the cost of our many other interests at stake in Asia and without regard for the complexities of Chinese history."[24]

Ever since the 1989 Tiananmen incident, US media has devoted heavy attention to policies and practices of the Chinese government that are often seen in a negative light in the United States. Such coverage is viewed as always true by a not-so-well-informed American public that holds ambivalent views about the Chinese authorities. For congressional critics of China, this situation means that their criticism would very likely be publicized by US media and would receive due consideration from the American public. As members of Congress often seek to take a public stance on an important issue that will receive recognition in the media and the public, some in Congress are aware that their criticisms of China would almost certainly boost their public reputation and political benefit.[25] In other words, you can make political gains by bashing China.

Doves and hawks

In the United States foreign policy establishment, there are frequent debates between the so-called doves and hawks. For example, within the George W. Bush administration, there has been fierce debate over how the United States should deal with China. Some administration officials, particularly in the State Department, see China as a potentially valuable ally against terrorism, whereas others, particularly in the Department of Defense, tend to consider China as a potential threat to US interests. Whenever US–China relations have improved, some right-wingers would come out and complain that the administration has become too complacent about what they call a growing China threat.

Since 1990 there has been a hot debate in Washington between China hawks and China doves. Some officials see China as a strategic competitor and a potential adversary. Some would like to engage China so that China will turn out to be a benign power. Yet from a broader and longer perspective, there is no real domestic division in US policy toward China. Both the so-called doves and the hawks aim at neutralizing China as a potential threat to US interests in Asia. Their difference is only one of tactics and timing. The doves promote "peaceful evolution" through trade and engagement, while the hawks promote preemptive confrontation through military conflict. Neither advocates all-out war with China. The hawks, even at their most extreme, advocate only a proxy war through Taiwan.

President George W. Bush's first Secretary of State Colin Powell is widely believed to be a moderate whereas Defense Secretary Donald Rumsfeld and Vice President Dick Cheney are generally considered hardliners. In terms of China policy, the views and policies from the State and Defense departments often diverge. For example, on 12 July 2002, the Pentagon released its first "Annual Report on the Military Power of the People's Republic of China" under the Bush administration. Citing Beijing's deployment of missiles oppo-site Taiwan and its recent purchase of Russian weapons, the Pentagon report claimed that Beijing was pursuing "a coercive strategy" to force Taiwan to negotiate on Beijing's terms and that China's military modernization could pose a threat to Japan and the Philippines as well as Taiwan. The report concluded that China was rapidly modernizing its military with the goal of countering American power in the Pacific and pressing Taiwan to accept uni-fication.[26] The Pentagon reports in subsequent years continue to alarm policy makers of the potential threat to Taiwan and US interests in East Asia posed by the People's Liberation Army.

These Pentagon views were apparently not in line with what Secretary of State Powell said the day before the first Pentagon annual report was released. In a joint press conference with the visiting Australian foreign minister Alexander Downer on 11 July 2002, Powell remarked that China and the United States have "good bilateral relations" and "we're anxious to have more military to military exchanges with the Chinese." He said that as China develops, some of its wealth would be used to modernize Chinese mili-tary forces. That itself was not "frightening" and the United States would monitor it carefully. To which point, the Australian foreign minister added that Australia "does not have any great concerns" about modernization of the Chinese armed forces since "we haven't seen any change in China's stra-tegic posture that would cause us any concern."[27]

Citing what they perceive as a major military buildup by China, the right-wingers in the United States want the administration to provide more sophisticated weapons to Taiwan, bolster the US military presence in East Asia, and deploy a theater missile defense program that includes Taiwan. These proposals can often be heard and read from conservative politicians and publications. For example, in a July 2002 issue of *Weekly Standard* maga-zine, an influential right-wing publication, Gary Schmitt, the executive direc-tor for the Project for a New American Century (PNAC), an organization whose founding members include Vice President Dick Cheney and Defense Secretary Donald Rumsfeld, called on the United States to take advantage of China's current preoccupation with its internal problems to strengthen America's position in Asia.[28] There is very little doubt these people view China through very dark lenses. If such policy proposals were adopted by the US government, a more rocky road ahead for US–China relations could be expected.

Since 1989 the United States has been the only country in the world still imposing economic and military sanctions against China, though the busi-ness community has been eager to enter the Chinese market. These sanc-tions include the practice of US representative voting against or abstaining on many World Bank loans to China and the withholding of some US Ex-port–Import Bank China-related loans and credit guarantees. US abstention on China loans at the World Bank does not block loans to China, and under a waiver program some loans from the US Export–Import Bank to China have gone forward. As of 2005, the United States not only maintains its high-tech export ban on China sixteen years after the Tiananmen incident, but also opposes the European Union's decision to lift the arms embargo against China as well as Israel's weapons sales to China. But China's military is going to be modernized anyway. Thus these sanctions are largely symbolic. They send an unmistakable message, however, that the United States seeks to block the emergence of China as an economic and military power. The United States probably needs to move on and develop a more normal relationship with China. Invoking US domestic laws such as the Taiwan Relations Act to justify its weapons sales to Taiwan and quoting the Special 301 Item to impose trade sanctions against China is not only unacceptable to the PRC but also unjustifiable in international law. Partially in response to America's citation of the Taiwan Relations Act in defending its weapons sales to Taiwan, the PRC's National People's Congress passed an anti-session law to deter the Taiwanese independence movement in March 2005.

The Cold War united front between the United States and China against the Soviet Union disappeared with the disintegration of the Soviet Empire. Despite political and intelligence cooperation with China following the 11 September 2001 terrorist attacks, the United States has been unable to clearly articulate its future relations with China. It has yet to reach some sort of a domestic consensus and design a well-coordinated, consistent policy toward China at the beginning of the twenty-first century.

China

Though the non-transparent character of Chinese politics makes its intentions less predictable, China's policy toward the United States has been rather consistent since the end of the Cold War. To quote former President Jiang Zemin, "reducing trouble and promoting cooperation" has been a major feature of Chinese policy toward the United States. Chinese leaders have adopted a policy of keeping a low profile in international affairs while focusing on domestic development. As in the United States, there are both moderates and hardliners in China with regards to policy toward the United States. The Chinese "hawks" include the People's Liberation Army and some conservative scholars in government-funded think tanks. For example, hardline Chinese officials, angry at Washington's invitation to Taiwan's defense chief to attend a March 2002 military conference in Florida, where he met with senior US officials, demanded that Chinese Vice President Hu Jintao's planned trip to the United States be cancelled. Hu eventually made the trip with the support of President Jiang, who stressed the long-term need to develop bilateral relations.

As a developing country, China faces enormous challenges at home.[29] These challenges include, but are not limited to, chronic poverty, population growth, environmental deterioration, ethnic separatism, increasing unemployment, and the rule of law. Despite rapid growth between 1978 and 2004 that had lifted millions of people out of abject poverty, there were still 26 million people living in poverty in the countryside in 2005.[30] China's demographic transformation brings three sets of serious social problems: rapid aging, declining manpower, and an imbalance in the sex ratio. China's "graying" will be as swift as any in history. In 1995, the average age in China was just over 27 years. By 2025 it will be about 40.[31] The "one child" policy has been largely successful in the cities. But in the countryside where malpractice such as sex-selective abortion and female infanticide has been reported, the imbalance between boys and girls will mean a corresponding mismatch of prospective husbands and brides. Bride shortage will cause serious social problems in the decades ahead. Over the past generation, China's brisk economic growth has been partly due to an extraordinary increase in the work force. From 1975 to 1995, China's working age population grew by over 50 percent (or nearly 300 million persons).[32] With an aging population and family planning policy, China will have declining manpower in the years ahead.

As it moves from an agricultural-based economy to an industrial one, China has encountered serious environmental problems. Air and water quality have worsened. Sandstorms continue to hit northern China including Beijing. A 1999 study by the World Health Organization reports that seven of the world's ten most polluted cities are in China. Air pollution is so serious that, according to one report, traffic police in Beijing, breathing foul air, live 40 years on average.[33] Environmental challenges for China are no less significant than political and economic ones.

Furthermore, admission into the WTO offers China both opportunities and challenges. It is "a gamble of historic proportions."[34] State-owned enterprises have become less competitive. Tens of millions of workers are unemployed in the cities, while from 60 to 100 million surplus rural workers are adrift between the villages and cities, subsisting on part-time low-paying jobs. WTO participation also requires banking and financial systems reform and the establishment of the rule of law. All these challenges, together with the Communist Party's task to sustain rapid economic growth to maintain its legitimacy in power, will keep China busy for quite some time. While some political scientists argue that countries may take a provocative and aggressive approach in their foreign policy as a way of diverting domestic tensions, this has not been evidenced in post-Cold War China. It is very unlikely that the PRC is going to take an aggressive approach toward the United States, or Taiwan for that matter.

Interestingly, a concept called "the law of avoidance" emerged during the debate in China in the mid-1990s as US–PRC tensions over Taiwan worsened. According to the law of avoidance, a rising power that comes into direct military collision with the incumbent dominant power invariably fails in its quest for preeminence, whereas those rising powers that successfully avoid confrontation by cooperating with the reigning hegemon over a fairly long period are eventually successful. The conclusion, according to the advocates of this principle, is that China should at all costs avoid a war with the United

States. Failure to do so could result in ultimate failure of China's quest for international preeminence.[35] This principle seems compatible with the late Chinese leader Deng Xiaoping's teaching that China should keep a low profile and bide its time during economic modernization – a policy that has been followed by current Chinese leaders.

China's modernization has changed the country enormously but has also brought about severe social and political dislocations. Discontent by millions of workers and peasants as a result of growing income disparity and unemployment constantly threatens social and political stability. After two decades of economic and social transformations, today's China is freer and more prosperous than at any time in its history. Yet politically it remains a centrally controlled party-state. Sooner or later, political reform will be pushed onto the national agenda. It is perhaps a welcome sign that, at a Chinese Communist Party central committee session in September 2004, Hu Jintao and his team listed curbing corruption as a priority of government reform. The Chinese leadership will be preoccupied with complex domestic issues in the near future. Foreign relations are not likely to rate very high on the policy agenda; when they do, they will tend to be viewed in the context of linkages to the domestic economy, society, and polity.

More than 30 years after the Nixon opening, debate over China policy still rages in the United States. The debate has polarized into the competing schools of engagement versus containment. Often missing in the debate, however, are considerations of China's potential responses to these polarized policies and considerations of the domestic variables in China that will condition its external orientations. The argument that China is threatening US national interests sounds far-fetched and irrelevant in a China that is busy improving its living standards while overcoming tremendous domestic problems. For its ambitious modernization program, China wants US trade and investment, but it also wants a non-hierarchic relationship with the United States. It is fair to say that much of the tension in US–China relations is due not to China's actions but rather to American's unease with China's reemergence as a great power. A cursory survey of the relationship between China and the United States since the early 1990s indicates that problems have often been caused by drastic measures taken by the US side. And many US criticisms of China – on issues such as human rights or nuclear nonproliferation – are probably either politically motivated or intentionally exaggerated.

China is the weaker partner in this relationship and often becomes the victim of America's insensitive rhetoric and actions toward China. But China does need and want good US relations. About all China can do is protest whenever the US side creates some trouble for the bilateral relationship. For example, after Taiwan defense minister Tang Yiau-ming's participation in a Florida conference and his meeting with US Deputy Secretary of Defense Paul Wolfowitz – the first such high-level official meeting since 1979 – in March 2002, and the release the same month of the Pentagon's secret

Nuclear Posture Review which listed China – along with Russia, Iraq, Libya, North Korea, Iran, and Syria – as target nations of US nuclear weapons, China's reactions were simply to summon US ambassador Clark Randt for "solemn representations" and issue a complaint from then Vice Foreign Minister Li Zhaoxing: "Where does the US want to lead China–US relations?"[36] China initially prevented the calling of a US warship on Hong Kong, but shortly afterward agreed to allow another ship to call on Hong Kong. Most significantly, China did not cancel Vice President Hu Jintao's planned visit to the United States in late April 2002.

The imperatives of China's economic modernization require cooperation with the United States. Yet China's domestic politics dictate that cooperation should not be at the expense of core Chinese interests. China has no intentions or capabilities to challenge the US leadership in world affairs. The only likely scenario of an American–Chinese military conflict is over Taiwan. But if the conflict were to occur, it would be one most likely provoked by Taiwan or the United States, not by a defensive PRC. Compared with the United States, the Chinese government and society at large seem to have reached a consensus regarding the United States. This consensus can be summarized as seeking cooperation and avoiding confrontation with the United States while concentrating on domestic modernization.

The public mood

Generally speaking, public opinion can influence government policy. In the history of Sino-American relations, however, this has not always been the case. With their low participation in politics, the Chinese public had minimal impact on the Sino-American détente in the 1970s. Chinese foreign policy was tightly handled by the central government in the past. For example, the decision to end hostility with the United States through "ping pong diplomacy" was made exclusively by the top leadership and the public only passively reacted to it.

Now with a more relaxed political atmosphere and a growing, better-educated middle class in China, it is likely that future US–China relations will be influenced not only by the US domestic audience but also by the Chinese public. One political outcome of China's reforms and opening up is that an independent and individualistic civil society is gradually taking shape. On the issue of understanding America, public independent judgment has been strengthened, and public opinions have become more sophisticated, with maturity and sober-mindedness. A notable development, given the frequent controversies between the two governments in recent years, is that bilateral commercial relations and social and cultural exchanges reached a new peak. The Chinese public has more diverse sources from which to learn about America. Earlier simplistic and naïve Chinese views of the United States have been replaced by a more complex and diverse image with a recognition that disagreements will persist although cooperation between the two countries is necessary and possible. The Chinese public's independent thinking and observation of international affairs, especially of America, is gradually forming a public opinion not to be ignored by decision makers and, therefore, this affects the development of Sino-American relations.

The Chinese public has demonstrated a feeling of hope and disillusionment toward the United States. This is best illustrated by the phenomenon that some of the very students who protested and threw rocks at the US embassy in Beijing after the US military bombed the Chinese embassy in Yugoslavia in 1999 appeared at the US embassy the next day to apply for visas to study in the United States. In general, the Chinese public is not anti-America. The so-called anti-American nationalist feelings only surge when the Chinese public perceives that China has been bullied by the United States as in the embassy bombing case.

In 1784, the American commercial ship *Empress of China* arrived in Canton, thus initiating the encounter between the two nations. In the next 200-plus years, with the exception of the Boxer Rebellion and the Korean War, the two countries had no direct military confrontation. Some older Chinese still remember that at the turn of the twentieth century the United States used the Boxer Indemnity Fund to support Chinese students for study in the United States. And some American missionaries contributed to China's education, medicine, scientific research, and charity. Most Chinese have positive opinions of American domestic political, economic, and social developments, but negative ones of its international behavior.

Chinese views of the United States are mixed. On one hand, the United States is seen as a democratically governed, economically prosperous, technologically advanced country – a trading partner important to China's economic growth and a mecca for tens of thousands of Chinese students. On the other hand, the American government is seen as arrogant and overbearing with hegemonic ambitions. The Chinese public's favorable images of America's domestic achievements have not changed much despite the ups and downs in the bilateral relationship. According to Wang Jisi of the Chinese Academy of Social Sciences, most average Chinese have two different perceptions of America. Domestic issues received positive responses. Chinese envy America's wealth, stable political system, and advanced technology; but there are also mixed feelings on America's crime rate. Chinese views of American foreign policy, especially in Asia, are negative and often marked by perceptions of American hegemony.[37] "Democratic inward, hegemonic outward," summarizes Zi Zhongyun, a leading America scholar at the Chinese Academy of Social Sciences.[38]

Many Chinese point out America's hypocrisy and double standards on issues such as human rights and proliferation of weapons of mass destruction. For example, the US Department of State publishes country reports on human rights annually, routinely castigating human rights records of China and a dozen other countries, but never talking about America's own human rights record. When the abuse and mistreatment of Iraqi prisoners by US soldiers were reported in May 2004, one Chinese internet user commented that the United States should be ashamed of itself and is not entitled to criticize other countries at all.[39] Some Chinese are pessimistic about the long term prospects of the bilateral relationship. For some the future is uncertain at best. "China and the United States will always confront each other," according to Shen Dingli of the Center for American Studies at Shanghai's Fudan University. "They are fundamentally different, and they should collide" because "they look to their own interests."[40] Yet in one survey conducted in 2001, though 70 percent of Chinese participants believed that Americans see China as the greatest threat to US security, the majority of Chinese surveyed (70 to 80 percent) also felt increasingly optimistic about the future of US–China relations. At the Central Party School, a training center for senior Chinese leaders, 85 percent felt optimistic about a peaceful resolution of the Taiwan issue, despite widespread resentment of what they see as US interference. When asked "Why is the US rich?" most respondents pointed to America's tradition of welcoming immigrants, its abundance of natural resources, and its open market economy. This conflicts with some official explanations that cite imperialism and working class exploitation as the basis for American prosperity.[41]

In a strikingly similar scenario to the public sentiment in England and Germany before World War I, some authors and novelists in both the United States and China are now obsessed with the prospect of a future conflict between the two countries. *The Coming Conflict with China* and *Dragon Strike* are just some of the recent titles by American authors who believe an American conflict with China is inevitable and advocate forceful containment of China.[42] Robert Kaplan's article "How We Would Fight China" is a more recent addition to this camp.[43] How these semi-fictions impact public opinions and policy making in the United States is an interesting topic for further research.

One of the key intellectual developments in China in the 1990s was the emergence of a militant nationalist train of thought among a significant portion of China's intelligentsia and urban populace. The crux of this new nationalist sentiment was the vision of an aggrieved China standing up to hostile foreign powers, especially the United States. *Zhongguo keyi shuo bu* (China Can Say No) was the most famous book of this genre.[44] Published in August 1996, just after the military confrontation between China and the United States near the Taiwan Straits, this quickly written but deeply emotional book set sales records. Another book from the so-called "Say No Club" is *Quanqiuhua yinmou xia de zhonguo zhi lu* (China's Road: Under the Conspiracy of Globalization).[45] Published in Beijing in 1999 in the aftermath of the May 1999 US bombing of the Chinese embassy in Belgrade, this book claims that the existing global order was set up primarily to benefit the Western nations, who view China as a challenge to that order. China has no choice but to prepare for the conflict and difficulties of facing hostile Western powers, especially the United States. Confronted by inveterate Western hostility, China should arm itself militarily, economically, and psychologically.

Perhaps fortunately, these are not the mainstream views of China's intellectuals and populace. In fact, one of the authors of *Quanqiuhua yinmou xia de zhonguo zhi lu* (China's Road: Under the Conspiracy of Globalization) is full of disdain for the mainstream Chinese scholars with their PhDs, Western education, and affections. He holds such "mainstream," "establishment," "liberal," "pro-American" intellectuals responsible for misleading and ideologically disarming the Chinese people. "The animus he directs against them is almost as great as that directed against the West," commented a US-based China scholar.[46] In fact, books eulogizing America's success can easily be found in China. A typical example is the book *Meiguo, ni wei he qiangda?* (America, Why Are You Powerful?) written by Zhang Zeqing. A mechanical engineer, Zhang visited the United States, where his daughter was studying, several times in the 1990s. After his visits, he wrote down his true feelings about America, claiming his US trips changed many views of America he used to have. He said: "it's unsuitable to judge America with Chinese standards." Americans have, he observed, ten guiding principles: paying taxes, abiding by the law, honesty, freedom, competition, democracy, human rights, taking risks, hedonism, and self-perfection.[47]

In general, most Chinese people greatly admire America's inroads in technology, science, computers, finance, and management. American products are immensely popular. Young Chinese seem to have been seduced by American culture and ideology. Coca-Cola and McDonald's were hailed in China as symbols of modernity. In a survey, an overwhelming majority do not think America is in decline. On the contrary, it is perceived as becoming more powerful.[48] Yet nationalism is also strong in China, especially when the Chinese feel they are wronged (again) by the United States. From the Chinese perspective, crises between the two countries in recent years such as the 1995–6 Taiwan Strait standoff, 1999 embassy bombing, and 2001 spy plane collision were all caused by the United States. But on each occasion, the United States blamed China for the worsening of bilateral ties. While admiring American technology, management, and way of life, many Chinese do not feel comfortable when the United States accuses China of violating human rights and religious freedom. Many feel that China is a great nation with a 5,000-year history and the United States is a great country too but with only a 200-plus year history. They believe that China has staggered through some 4,800 of their 5,000 years without significant advice from the United States, so it is not self-evident why they must follow all the prescriptions of the United States.

When there have been problems between the two countries, the Chinese government often claims "the US action on this issue seriously hurt the Chinese people's feelings," a statement frequently taken as childish by the West. Few in the West understand that the wounded history and a sense of humiliation since the Opium Wars have shaped a distinct worldview of many Chinese. The Chinese mindset is a "prisoner of its past."[49] Chinese are much more sensitive than Americans to foreign "interference" into China's internal affairs. According to surveys done in March and April 2000, the embassy bombing, the US arms sales to Taiwan, the condemnation of China's human rights policies, and support for the Tibetan separatist movement are what hurt the Chinese people most.[50] Many Chinese do not understand why the current PRC government, the most liberalizing regime in Chinese history, is the one most attacked by the US media, politicians, and intellectuals – the same groups that in many cases tolerated both Mao Zedong's and Chiang Kai-shek's dictatorships.

The US government does not always speak or act with appropriate sensitivity to the feelings of others. Sometimes the United States does not seem to care about China's legitimate and serious concerns. For example, after China complained about the apparent upgrade of US–Taiwan military ties since President George W. Bush came to office, a senior Bush administration official shrugged off the Chinese concern by saying "we have done nothing wrong, and Beijing is going to have to learn to live with it."[51] The so-called "China threat" assumption in certain circles in the United States and US actions on Taiwan are often interpreted as America's desire to keep China weak and separate.

Comparatively speaking, ordinary Americans know far less about China than ordinary Chinese know about America. Public views of one another are not monolithic in both countries and vary from issue to issue. Most often, the first impressions of China held by Americans are hazy and based on bits of information gleaned from various sources: newspapers, movies, books, Chinese restaurants, etc. These initial impressions were generally similar among participants in a research based on forums and focus groups in communities across America. They resembled stereotypes rather than well formed opinions. When asked to examine specific issues in more detail, answers became more complex and diverse. Individual experiences, history, and biases came through to color the responses. Views on issues such as human rights also expose conflicting feelings that Americans often have.[52] A telephone survey of 1,468 adults, conducted between 15 May and 28 May 2001 by the Pew Research Center, found generally moderate views about China. Public alarm about China has not increased in spite of the rise in bilateral tensions over the April 2001 spy plane incident. As in previous surveys, most see China as at least a serious problem, but only one in five calls it an adversary. Similarly, even though as many as 40 percent recognize that relations between the two countries have worsened, the proportion who see China's emergence as a world power as a threat to the United States has not increased since 1999 (Table 5.1).

In fact, since the 11 September 2001 terrorist attacks and the general warming up of Sino-American relations, fewer Americans consider the development of China toward great power status as a threat to the United States. Based on a survey of 1,195 American adults conducted between 6 July and 12 July 2004 by the Chicago Council on Foreign Relations, those who consider China's growth as a threat to America have dropped to 33 percent from 49

Table 5.1 American views of China: still not an adversary

View of China	September 1997	March 1999	June 1999	March 2000	May 2001
Adversary	14	20	18	17	19
Serious problem	46	48	53	44	51
Not a problem	32	25	22	26	22
Do not know	8	7	7	13	8

Source: "Modest Support for Missile Defense, No Panic on China," Survey Report, 11 June 2001, the Pew Research Center for the People and the Press. Accessed from the Pew Research Center's website at http://www.people-press.org/reports.

percent two years before.[53] In January 2005, the Committee of 100, a national, non-partisan organization composed of prominent American citizens of Chinese descent, announced the results of a new study conducted by Zogby International, a national polling organization. Based on the study, 59 percent of Americans viewed China favorably in 2004, compared with 46 percent in a 1994 survey.[54]

According to research done by the Kettering Foundation based on community forums on US–China relations across the United States in 2000, ordinary Americans' views of China are ambivalent and their image of China is a work in progress. In every forum, participants called for a more accurate picture of China and of the Chinese people.[55] The participants in these forums ranged from youth to elders from all major racial groups, college and high school students, university faculty, veterans of the Korean and Vietnam Wars, and business people. On the issue of China's rise, although some participants saw China as a threat, many of these citizens saw opportunities in the possibilities for a strong China–US relationship. Many participants wanted constructive engagement with China and a deep interdependent relationship with China to create a secure world. Though they admitted they did not know much about China, they had strong opinions. While the participants did not envision military conflict with China, they strongly believe that human rights and individual freedoms are the ideals to which China should conform. In general, they are more concerned about China's domestic development than its foreign policy posture. Significantly, these Americans do not relish the thought of getting involved in a dispute with mainland China over Taiwan, but they believe in living up to any obligation that America has made on this issue. Most Americans do not seem to believe that China is a threat to America, but they want to see more improvements in China's domestic institutions and policies.

It is safe to say that while some people in both countries consider one another as the greatest potential threat, the majority in both countries seem to disagree. China and the United States may not be natural allies or even close friends, but the two countries can establish a mature relationship and become normal partners in the international community. As the participants in the China–US dialog sponsored by the Kettering Foundation suggested, more exchanges between the two peoples are needed to facilitate better understanding of one another's history, culture, domestic and foreign policies. This is important since a favorable public view of each other provides a solid social foundation for a peaceful relationship between the two countries, as demonstrated in the Anglo-American relationship.

Commitment of top leaders

In dealing with China, American presidents may use different rhetoric and adopt different policies, but the same "tough and soft" pattern can be discerned from their handling of China. A president may be tough toward China on certain issues, but soft on some other issues. Or he may be tough sometimes but soft at other times. Domestic politics, elections, and personal preferences all affect a president's foreign policy orientation. No top American officials have openly advocated containment of China, but US policy toward China has basically swung between containment and engagement. That is, the policy is openly called "engagement" through extensive trade and exchanges with the proclaimed purpose of bringing about a prosperous and peaceful China in the international community. But the engagement policy is supplemented with a strong US–Japan alliance, powerful forward deployment of forces in Japan and South Korea, and especially robust arms sales to Taiwan – all these measures are exactly some of the "containment" policies suggested by the hawks. The United States seeks cooperation with China on a wide range of global and regional issues even while it often seeks to contain rising Chinese power and influence.

Usually China is not a top policy priority for most American presidents. Because of the inconsistency in America's China policy, the policy may appear contradictory and confusing from the same president. For example, President George H. W. Bush had a deep, lifelong interest in foreign affairs and devoted much attention to Sino-American relations following the 1989 Tiananmen incident. He considers himself as a China hand and is called "an old friend of the Chinese people" by the Chinese government, yet in fact he was not so "friendly" to China during the later days of his presidency. In an effort to garner more votes for his re-election, he approved the sale of 150 F-16 fighter jets to Taiwan in August 1992, then the largest sale of the most advanced weapons to Taiwan since 1979. This move appears rather contradictory to his other conciliatory policies toward China, including his dispatch of secret envoys to Beijing following the bloody incident at Tiananmen Square. National security and personal interests always outweigh other considerations in dealing with the China.

Nevertheless, President Bush's efforts to prevent Sino-American relations from further deteriorating are to be commended. Immediately following the Tiananmen incident, the president tried to speak with Chinese leader Deng

Xiaoping by telephone. When he could not get through, he sent a personal note to Deng through the US ambassador, James Lilley. Then, on 20 June 1989, Bush wrote a long letter to Deng Xiaoping, reporting that he wrote in "a spirit of genuine friendship" and that he had "great respect" for what Deng had done for the Chinese people. He assured Deng that he felt "more strongly" than ever before that "good relations . . . are in the fundamental interests of both countries."[56] He wrote a second letter to Deng in July. Having expressed his personal commitment to the US–China relationship, he argued that both China and the United States needed to work hard to restore US–China relations. Risking domestic criticism by seemingly violating his sanctions on exchanges between US and Chinese officials, Bush sent National Security Advisor Brent Scowcroft and Deputy Secretary of State Lawrence Eagleburger on a secret visit to China in early July 1989.

President Bush was committed to the relationship and believed he understood both Chinese and American interests. In 1990 and 1991, he relied on his authority in foreign policy and his domestic popularity to wage an uncompromising battle against his congressional critics for the extension of China's most-favored-nation status. By 1992 the administration's China policy had become a favorite campaign issue for all of the Democratic Party contenders for presidency, the Democratic Party leadership, and Democratic leadership in Congress. On 1 April, presidential candidate Bill Clinton criticized President Bush for failing to use trade as a leverage against China's human rights abuses. The combination of declining popularity and campaign vulnerability weakened the efficacy of the president's China policy. He was compelled to reevaluate his strategy and pursue a more demanding China policy. In retrospect, without Bush's personal attention and efforts, US–China relations could have been much more problematic in the early 1990s given the strong international and US domestic outcry against the Chinese government's handling of the Tiananmen student demonstrations.

As power passed from George H. W. Bush to William Jefferson Clinton, US national leadership shifted from a president who paid considerable attention to foreign policy to one who did not. It moved from a man who personally cared about American relations with China to one who saw China through the eyes of advisers with competing agendas. As the new administration set about examining its worldwide responsibilities, China did not command a high priority. But, as culpable as Clinton might have been for not vigorously attacking the difficulties in the US–China relationship, it is not true that he sought to isolate China or to punish it for the human rights violations that he deplored. During his second term, President Clinton devoted more efforts to developing US–China relations. He and Chinese President Jiang Zemin exchanged state visits in 1997 and 1998. And he pushed hard for completing negotiations on China's admission into the World Trade Organization.

President Clinton called Beijing leaders "butchers" during his presidential campaign. Many people still remember his catchy campaign line about "an America that will not coddle tyrants, from Baghdad to Beijing." Previous efforts to curtail China's access to the American market had been repeatedly thwarted by presidential vetoes in the Bush years; now President Clinton planned to hold China accountable for its human rights record. He tied "overall significant progress" in China's human rights behavior to renewal of the most favored nation status. Under tremendous pressure from business groups, however, this policy failed and he had to de-link trade and human rights in 1994.

That China received scant attention from President Clinton during his first term does not mean he had no intention or did nothing to improve the relationship. In September 1993 President Clinton signed an action memorandum approving an interagency review of China policy. Henceforth there would be "comprehensive engagement" with frequent visits and regular exchanges between high-level civilian officials, renewal of military-to-military contacts suspended since June 1989, and a Clinton–Jiang summit during the approaching Asian Pacific Economic Cooperation (APEC) meeting in Seattle. Before the summit President Clinton wrote to President Jiang reaffirming Washington's interest in a strong, stable, and prosperous China. An accompanying document allegedly carried a pledge to support Chinese unity.[57] The crisis in US–China relations over Taiwan in 1995 and 1996 also prompted the Clinton administration to pay more attention to China policy.

But it was during his second term that Clinton's China policy gathered momentum. He and Chinese president Jiang Zemin announced the formation of "strategic partnership" between the two countries. He exchanged state visits with President Jiang and announced his "three nos" policy toward Taiwan in Shanghai, a statement perceived as tilting toward the PRC.[58] During the last two years of his presidency, though troubled by his personal scandals, President Clinton managed to score foreign policy points by striking a deal with China about China's WTO admission.

George W. Bush was inaugurated as the first US president of the twenty-first century on 20 January 2001, but he began the year as a question mark in the eyes of many Americans as well as the international community. To a great extent, he really became president in the days following 11 September 2001. The tragedy changed America's policy agendas and turned George W. Bush into a foreign policy president he did not intend to become. A lot of other foreign policy issues were forced into the background, and China has received a low priority in Bush's foreign policy since then.

What decision makers say and do make a great difference in foreign relations. During his presidential campaign, George W. Bush opposed Bill Clinton's concept of "strategic partnership" with China, and he began his term as president with forceful rejections of that policy. President Bush and his hawkish foreign policy team have repeatedly provoked China on the sensitive Taiwan issue since they assumed power in January 2001. In addition to selling or proposing to sell large amount of advanced weapons to Taiwan and perceptibly upgrading US–Taiwan relations, President Bush openly declared in April 2001 that the United States would do whatever it takes to defend Taiwan. At the time, neither he nor his cabinet members and advisors explained clearly whether this applied to the situation in which Taiwan's open declaration of independence provokes a guaranteed PRC military attack. Departing from the previous policy of "strategic ambiguity" – which caused both Beijing and Taipei to guess whether the United States would help Taiwan if it were attacked by the PRC – the Bush administration has made repeated categorical pledges to do "whatever it takes" to protect the island. This new rhetoric, as the Chinese government complains, will probably only embolden and encourage separatist forces in Taiwan. It may only harden the PRC's resolve and cause the PLA to make further preparation for US involvement in a potential PRC–Taiwan conflict. No wonder many people including Richard C. Bush, former Chairman and Managing Director of the American Institute in Taiwan, believe that on balance there is no compelling reason for the United States to state in advance the details of its response to the use of force against Taiwan. Spelling out exactly what the United States would do is not a good idea.[59] Others warn that writing a blank security check to Taiwan could drag the United States into a deadly conflict with China.[60]

Apparently top Pentagon officials consider Taiwan a strategic platform that must be denied to China. Some coolheaded US observers worry that hardline US "China threat" security thinkers may not know where to draw the line, even while seeming to expand it.[61] Whereas the Bush administration still accepts the "one China" principle, it asserts that Taipei is free to reject the principle, as it has done since 1999.[62] But the hawkish approach has often been counterbalanced by moderate forces within the Republican Party. Former President Bush and veteran diplomat Henry Kissinger are reported to have exerted influence on Bush Jr.'s more balanced policy toward China later.[63]

President George W. Bush, despite his straightforward talk about China and his apparent leaning toward Taiwan, especially on weapons sales, in the early months of his first presidency, attended the Asia Pacific Economic Co-operation (APEC) conference in Shanghai in November 2001, his first foreign travel after the 11 September attacks. President Bush reportedly said that if the conference had not been held in China, he probably would not have attended it.[64] He paid an official working visit to Beijing in February 2002 during his three-nation Asia tour. While in China, President Bush praised China for its efforts in the war against terror and encouraged further cooperation in economic and security areas. It is unusual and significant for a US president to visit a foreign country twice within a few months.

The Bush administration has also apparently backed down from its overtly pro-Taiwan rhetoric earlier. In August 2002, in response to Taiwan President Chen Shui-bian's "one country on each side of the Taiwan Strait" statement, the White House national security council spokesman remarked that the United States adheres to the "one China" policy and does not support

Taiwanese independence.[65] In May 2002, Deputy Secretary of Defense Paul Wolfowitz, considered a hardliner in the Bush administration, also mentioned that the United States would not support Taiwan's independence.[66] Even President Bush himself, sensing the danger of Taiwan's lurch toward independence, had to make a public statement in December 2003 warning Chen Shui-bian against changing the status quo across the Taiwan Strait.[67] In subsequent meetings and telephone conversations with Chinese leaders, President Bush has always reaffirmed America's "One China" policy and his opposition to Taiwanese independence. As Robert Hathaway of the Woodrow Wilson International Center for Scholars commented, "One has only to compare Bush's public statement in early 2001 that the United States would do whatever it takes to ensure Taiwan's security with his unusually pointed warnings to Taipei more recently about not upsetting the status quo to see how far Bush – and the US–China relationship – has traveled over the past four years."[68]

Vice President Dick Cheney, widely considered a leader of hawkish forces within the Republican Party, paid an official visit to China in April 2004, and pronounced US–China relations to be "in good shape" during his visit.[69] It is equally encouraging that Defense Secretary Donald Rumsfeld has also toned down his hawkish rhetoric regarding China. While addressing the third Asian Security Conference in Singapore in June 2004, Rumsfeld declared that the United States "seeks to cooperate with (an emerging China) in many fields – diplomacy, economics, and global security." He praised China for its efforts and leading role in helping resolve the nuclear problem on the Korean Peninsula and stated that the world welcomes "a China that is committed to peaceful solutions and whose talented people contribute to international peace and prosperity."[70]

George W. Bush is merely the most recent in a series of US presidents who took office pledging more forceful policies toward the PRC only to be reconciled eventually with the need for continued cooperation with China. Jimmy Carter in 1976, Ronald Reagan in 1980, and Bill Clinton in 1992 all acted in much the same fashion. This process of socialization of American presidents to the imperatives of cooperation with China is "largely a function of the reality of the PRC's great national capabilities and, consequently, of the very high costs the US risks if it fails to reach an accommodation with China," commented China scholar John W. Garver.[71]

Not only in the United States have top leaders attempted to maintain a strong US–China relationship in the past decade or so; Chinese leaders are equally if not more committed to a smooth and constructive relationship with the United States despite vast differences on certain issues between the two countries. Since the early 1990s, Chinese President Jiang Zemin has launched the so-called big-power diplomacy, a codename referring to promoting cooperative relations between China and the United States, Russia, the EU, and Japan. His policy has been criticized by some in China as too weak and too accommodating to the United States, especially on the Taiwan issue, during the 1999 Chinese embassy bombing incident, and over the 2001 clash of an American spy plane and a Chinese fighter jet. President Jiang's own evaluation of US–China relations is a mixed one. During a CBS *60 Minutes* interview with Mike Wallace on 15 August 2000, Jiang expressed his views on the state of the bilateral relationship: "Sometimes China–US relations are good and sometimes in a storm. There are certain people in America who do not want to see China and the US having good relations. They always make some problems."[72]

"Increasing trust, reducing trouble, expanding cooperation, and avoiding confrontation" have been President Jiang's US policy guidelines.[73] Even during rough times in the bilateral relations, President Jiang still tries hard to avoid direct confrontation with the United States. For example, he backed continued US–China negotiations on China's WTO admission in the second half of 1999 following the US bombing of the Chinese embassy in Yugoslavia and the publication of the sensational, later discredited, Cox Report, which accused China of posing a serious threat to US national interests by stealing nuclear technology from the United States. Also, he supported Vice President Hu Jintao's April 2002 maiden visit to the United States following the Taiwanese defense minister's US visit and his meeting with senior US officials at a Florida conference earlier that year. Hardline Chinese officials, angry at Washington's invitation to Taiwan's defense chief, demanded that Mr. Hu's planned trip be canceled. But President Jiang saved the situation, stressing the long-term need to develop relations.

If what was said in the United States is any indication, the new leadership of China seems equally enthusiastic about developing and expanding US–China relations. In his only public speech during his May 2002 US visit, Vice President Hu Jintao called on the two nations to step up dialog at all levels, intensify exchanges and cooperation in all fields, and seek common ground while shelving differences. He concluded by saying that the two nations will overcome interruptions and difficulties and "write a new chapter in the development of bilateral relations."[74] Since assuming the positions as Communist Party general secretary and the state president in October 2002 and March 2003 respectively, Hu has reiterated his intentions and determinations to maintain a good relationship with the United States each time he meets with American visitors. President Hu has also maintained regular telephone conversations with President Bush to exchange their views on regional and global issues.[75] It is significant to note that shortly after President Bush's re-election in November 2004 he held a meeting with President Hu Jintao when both attended the APEC conference in Santiago, Chile. At the joint conference after the meeting, both leaders reiterated their commitment to build a healthy and strong relationship, and both leaders issued invitations to visit each other's capital as soon as possible.[76] States visits to each other's capital were planned for late 2005.

Strong and extensive ties

The United States and China have closely cooperated on a wide range of issues at international and regional levels, though their national security and economic interests may not always be compatible. How can this happen? To put it simply, in an era of globalization, extensive economic and trade relations help soothe difficulties in the security area. Some studies suggest that the tendency for governments to decide for war significantly decreases if their economies have large foreign trade sectors.[77] Countries whose economic and political interests are deeply entangled with one another's are less likely to use force to solve their disputes. Great powers are also large trading nations. The flow of goods and services brings people together and has been an important initial step in the formation of the EU.

Of course, the growth of economic interdependence alone will not stop a conflict, especially where sovereignty claims are concerned. Nevertheless, growing economic interdependence between the United States and China increases the costs and therefore the disincentives for war as an option for settling the Taiwan Strait dispute. US–China relations have experienced ups and downs since the establishment of diplomatic ties in 1979. Despite such episodes as the Tiananmen Square tragedy, Taiwan Strait missile crisis, embassy bombing, and EP-3 spy plane incident, the two countries have maintained a dynamic working relationship. Bilateral trade probably has the strongest support in both societies. Economic and political interdependence and deep ties between the two societies undoubtedly have played a significant role in reducing tensions and building trust between the two countries. By the end of 2004, the United States had become China's number two trading partner while China ranks number four in America's foreign trade. The bilateral trade volume exceeded US$100 billion in 2003. US investment has been the largest source of foreign investment in the Chinese mainland after Hong Kong. According to China's Ministry of Foreign Trade and Economic Cooperation, the United States can overtake Japan as China's largest trading partner at the end of 2005.[78] Extensive economic and trade relations have become the most fundamental link between the two countries.

The 1999 US–China trade agreement that allowed China to enter the WTO is interpreted by some analysts as a calculated effort by both countries to fashion the world order of the twenty-first century.[79] The trade agreement exemplifies post-Cold War geopolitics and indicates that both sides are satisfied with the economic and trade order of the twenty-first century. This convergence of interests is very helpful for maintaining a stable relationship. The potential for economic cooperation and trade is vast. If China honors all its commitments in real earnest as a member of the WTO, China will import US$1.5 trillion worth of goods in the coming five years, a huge opportunity for US businesses. Both countries reap benefits from close economic and trade cooperation. American investment and technology play a positive role in China's modernization. Since the early 1980s, American businesses have rushed to provide China with everything from financial services to convenience stores. In return, China's growing economy benefits American consumers.

Trade relations are just part of the extensive linkage between the two countries. The strong ties are also reflected by other exchanges between the two societies. The two governments have reached more than 30 official agreements on cooperation in the political, economic, cultural, educational, and other fields. China remains one of the top Asian destinations for American tourists, with over one million Americans tourists now traveling to China yearly. In 1979–80, only about 1,000 Chinese students were studying in the United States and almost no American students were studying in China. Today there are over 60,000 Chinese students studying in the United States and more than 5,000 American students studying in China.[80] Since 1999, the PRC has replaced Japan as the leading place of origin for international students in the United States, and in the 2000–1 school year alone, PRC students comprised 10.9 percent of all international students studying in the United States (Table 5.2). According to a study by the Institute of International Education, the number of American students studying in China has increased dramatically over the past five years. While the majority of American students continue to favor Europe, Australia, New Zealand, and Latin America, in 2001 about 10 percent of American students who studied abroad chose Asia as their destination. In 2001, of the total 8,834 American students enrolled in Asia, 2,949 (over one-third) were studying in the PRC.[81]

In another example of close social connections, since 1990 tens of thou-

Table 5.2 Chinese students studying in the US, selected years between 1979 and 2004

Year	Total number
1979–80	1,000
1982–3	6,230
1984–5	10,100
1986–7	20,030
1988–9	29,040
1990–1	39,600
1993–4	44,381
1997–8	46,958
1998–9	51,001
1999–2000	54,466
2000–1	59,939
2003–4	61,765

Sources: Institute of International Education data. The pre-2000 numbers are from *50 Years of Open Doors*, CD-ROM (New York: IIE, 2000); the 2000–4 numbers are from IIE's webpage (http: opendoors.iienetwork.org).

Note
According to the *Chronicle of Higher Education*, the number of Chinese students in the United States was surpassed by that of Indian students in the academic years 2002–3 and 2003–4 (Burton Bollag, "Wanted: Foreign Students," *Chronicale of Higher Education*, 8 October 2004, accessed online at http://chronicle.com/weekly/v51/i07/07a03701.htm).

sands of American families have adopted children from China. More than 5,000 Chinese children were adopted by American families in 2000 alone.[82] According to the Alliance for Children, Inc., based in Gardner, MA, which has helped many American families to adopt children overseas, in 1991 only 61 children were adopted from China, by 2003 the number had reached 6,875, and it was expected to surpass 7,000 in 2004.[83] These families have already demonstrated their interest in China through their adoptions, and their adopted children are expected to travel back to China as they grow up. The effect that these families and children can have in helping bridge the two societies should not be underestimated.

Also, as an indication of expanding trade and personnel contact between China and the United States, transportation authorities of the two countries reached agreement in 2004 to dramatically increase commercial flights before 2010. Under the agreement, the number of weekly commercial flights between the two nations aboard US-based airlines will rise from 54 to 249. Of those additional 195 flights a week, 111 will be by cargo carriers and 84 by passenger airlines.[84] In addition to the extensive bilateral relations, the United States and China have wide-ranging common interests in regional and international issues, such as promoting peace on the Korean peninsula, maintaining Asia-Pacific economic prosperity, curbing proliferation of deadly weapons, wiping out drug trafficking, and protecting the global environment. Extensive ties and common economic and security interests in the Asia-Pacific region argue against a new Cold War. A deep interdependent and mutually beneficial relationship helps the two countries to deal with problems from a larger perspective.

The amount and type of trade may reflect the quality of the relationship. In this regard, the United States and China have not become trustworthy friends. Bilateral trade volume is huge, but the United States is determined not to provide military hardware and software to China. The United States, while actively promoting trade with China, has maintained an embargo of dual-use strategic and military sales to China since 1989. To upgrade bilateral trade and political relations, the United States probably should change this policy as a gesture to treat China not as a foe, but as a normal trading partner.

Strong economic, social, cultural, and other interactions between the two countries serve as a stabilizer and balancer against the ups and downs in political and security relations. However, deep ties and common interests alone may not be enough to deflect conflicts. Historical studies suggest that to ensure a smooth power transfer, a rising power's vital interests have to be recognized. Specifically, this research argues that the failure to accommodate a rising power's vital and legitimate interests is a major reason for bloody power transitions in history. For decades, China has repeatedly warned the United States that Taiwan is the single most important issue in US–China relations. No other issue has made US–China relations so tumultuous. But the United States has either chosen to ignore this Chinese concern or simply does not want to accommodate China on it. Though the PRC is partially to blame for the inflexibility in its Taiwan policy, nevertheless, according to power transition theory, if the vital issue of Taiwan is not handled properly by the United States, China can be expected to act violently under certain circumstances.

The Taiwan issue

As a political joke goes, the good news about relations between China and the United States is that there is only one contentious issue between them; the bad news is there is no solution to the problem. The Taiwan issue remains the most long-standing and difficult dispute between the PRC and the United States. For the PRC, the Taiwan issue concerns such vital Chinese interests as national independence, state sovereignty, and territorial integrity, which brook no foreign interference. Though Taiwan remains important for the United States for historical, economic, strategic, and other reasons, it is not vital to America's economic and security interests. For China, the Taiwan issue boils down to nation-building and national rejuvenation. If Taiwan's separation from China becomes permanent and legal, China will never be a great nation. The importance of the Taiwan issue is explained by the following official PRC statement:

> The modern history of China was a record of subjection to aggression, dismemberment and humiliation by foreign powers. It was also a chronicle of the Chinese people's valiant struggles for national independence and in defense of their state sovereignty, territorial integrity and national dignity. The origin and evolution of the Taiwan question are closely linked with that period of history. For various reasons Taiwan is still separated from the mainland. Unless and until this state of affairs is brought to an end, the trauma on the Chinese nation will not be healed and the Chinese people's struggle for national reunification and territorial integrity will continue.[85]

Though both countries wish to maintain peace and prosperity across the Taiwan Strait, the United States and China have divergent interests in this issue. Whereas the United States is interested in peaceful resolution of the dispute, the PRC government's objective is peaceful unification with Taiwan, by force if necessary. The "one country, two systems" formula, though generous from the PRC perspective, lacks creativity and does not address the core issue of Taiwan's separate identity. The PRC government believes that Taiwan's prosperity and security can best and only be achieved through Taiwan's reunification with the motherland so that Taiwan can enjoy more international space and live with the Chinese mainland free from constant military threat. The United States, on the other hand, believes the best strategy is to maintain Taiwan's autonomy, keep Taiwan from joining the communist mainland,

and provide Taiwan with sufficient military and moral support. For its own interests, the United States does not support Taiwan's official independence, neither has it expressed open support for China's unification.

Political, economic, social, and cultural developments in Taiwan in the past few decades have fostered a distinct Taiwanese identity. The PRC government feels that Taiwan is moving toward creeping independence; and worse yet, the PRC believes the United States may be tacitly approving this trend while paying lip service to the "one China" policy. No sensible and rational PRC leader or citizen would strive for the destruction of Taiwan's prosperity and freedom. The PRC's consistent, two-decades old policy of "one country, two systems," though rejected by Taiwan, clearly indicates the PRC's intention of achieving the unification peacefully and keeping Taiwan's way of life intact. It is not hard to understand why the PRC is vociferously opposed to US arms sales to Taiwan, a policy the PRC believes has emboldened pro-independence forces on Taiwan and makes peaceful reunification increasingly impossible.

The United States officially sticks to the "one China" policy and acknowledges that Taiwan is part of China. This "one China" policy is the basis of the three communiques (1972, 1979, 1982) between the United States and the PRC. But Taiwan is to be defended by the United States against potential PLA use of force, based on the 1979 Taiwan Relations Act. US supply of arms to Taiwan is rationalized on the pretext of Taiwan's defense needs, aimed at frustrating Chinese plans to reunite Taiwan by force. Yet the United States must also recognize that arms sales to Taiwan may in fact increase the prospect of a military solution from the PRC.

From the PRC's perspective, building up its military potential to take Taiwan by force if and when necessary is purely a defensive measure and an internal issue, the logic being that Taiwan is an inalienable part of China. To the extent that Chinese leaders believe it is Taiwan that is seeking to change the status quo by its efforts to acquire greater acceptance in the international community and to de-Sinonize Taiwanese society, so their behavior may be seen as reactive rather than assertive. In the PRC's view, there is no international legal basis to label the PRC's military action to prevent the emergence of an independent Taiwan as offensive aggression.

"The Chinese bottom-line goal today is not conquest but cash," remarks a UCLA scholar.[86] If not pushed to the wall, the PRC may indeed not want to conquer Taiwan. In fact, the two sides of the Taiwan Strait seem to be building a foundation for a peaceful, shared future. After all, Taiwanese companies have invested over US$100 billion in the mainland, and over 500,000 telephone calls cross the Taiwan Strait every day.[87] More than one million Taiwanese visit the mainland each year, and 500,000 Taiwanese businesspeople and their families live in greater Shanghai alone.[88] Investment in the mainland is the largest of all Taiwan's overseas investments and the third largest overseas investment received by the Chinese mainland, next only to

Hong Kong and the United States. Also, since November 2001, the Chinese mainland has become the largest export market of Taiwan.[89]

The US policy of selling advanced weapon systems to Taiwan has the potential of geopolitical irony. Even if the two sides of the Taiwan Strait claim that they are not engaged in an arms race, they have already encountered a security dilemma. The weapon sales will not improve Taiwan's security. On the contrary, the sales may well strengthen the PRC's resolve to accelerate the upgrading of its military capability and retake Taiwan sooner rather than later. So the US weapons sales to Taiwan may in fact be welcomed by those in the PRC who see a military solution as the only option.[90] In the past two decades China has de-emphasized the role of the military as part of its focus on economic construction. Ironically, the "China threat" perceptions and military pressure on the part of the United States against China may well have served as a necessary wake-up call for the PRC to review and strengthen its defensive capabilities. In reality, no amount of arms sales to Taiwan, quantitative or qualitative, can enhance the security of Taiwan. The PRC will almost certainly use force to prevent Taiwan's legal independence regardless of the level of the US military commitment. The US arms sales to Taiwan may only further prepare the PLA for a potential direct military conflict with the United States in a future Taiwan Strait crisis.

Those who believe the United States always has an ulterior motive toward China may even argue that US allegations against Chinese military prowess may be a false pretense. The gap between US and Chinese technological capabilities may in fact be increasing. What the US is actually uneasy about is China's economic growth and its uncertain regional role in the future. America's planned theater missile defense program in Asia and its continued sales of advanced weapons to Taiwan may be a plot to promote a global high-tech arms race that would bleed China of its economic potential.

From Beijing's point of view, Taiwan is the ultimate test of whether the United States is prepared to adjust to China's reemergence as a great power. An American pledge to defend Taiwan is actually an American pledge to go to war to keep China in a subordinate position, contends a leading East Asia hand.[91] The PRC's primary concern is that Taiwan does not slip away and become an independent and separate state outside China. If unified, Taiwan can negotiate with Beijing about the status of the island and its international participation. Beijing's bottom line and red line is the "one China" principle; anything else can be discussed and negotiated. Those who accuse the PRC of threatening Taiwan by deployment of missiles opposite Taiwan may be confusing cause and effect. From the PRC's perspective, the PLA's military preparedness is to deter Taiwan's further moving away from the "one China" framework. If Taiwan promises through words and deeds that it will not pursue independence from China, there will be no such kind of military "threat" to Taiwan. The priority for Taiwan is perhaps not to gradually cultivate its own non-Chinese identity, but to help modernize China and promote democracy and openness on the Chinese mainland through exchanges in all fields. Only with a democratic China can Taiwan discuss all possibilities of its future, including perhaps a separate and independent statehood if it so wishes. Taiwan's policy of creeping toward *de jure* independence is not acceptable to either the elite or the public, the military or the civilian on the Chinese mainland; its policy of restricting contacts and exchanges with the mainland is unwise and unhelpful.

Since the United States has been mired in the wars in Iraq and Afghanistan from President George W. Bush's first term, it does not wish to see another global flashpoint ready to explode, especially one that might involve another great power. For its own interests, the United States has attempted to promote stability across the Taiwan Strait. Sensing the dire consequence of Taiwan's continued slip toward de facto independence since President Chen Shui-bian came to office in 2000 and his controversial re-election in March 2004, the United States has been trying to rein in Chen's radical rhetoric and policies.[92] The United States has become more interested in consulting the Chinese side over the Taiwan issue and in urging cross-Strait dialog. During his last official visit to China in October 2004, Secretary of State Colin Powell, while reaffirming America's commitment to help Taiwan's defense, stated clearly in an interview that "Taiwan is not independent. It does not enjoy sovereignty as a nation, and that remains our policy, our firm policy."[93] In the same interview, Powell even suggested that the United States may support the actual unification of China and Taiwan. The fact that both the US State Department and the White House endorsed Powell's remarks indicates that the United States has become increasingly dissatisfied with Taipei's unilateral challenge to the status quo and that it does not support an independent Taiwan.

How to protect Taiwan's freedom and prosperity while recognizing and respecting China's vital national interests is a thorny issue for the United States. From the power transition perspective, the United States has to respect the PRC's legitimate rights and concerns on the Taiwan issue; but the United States can do more than simply attempting to maintain the status quo, especially when the status quo is becoming increasingly difficult to maintain. Instead of focusing on keeping a military balance across the Taiwan Strait, the United States should actively encourage economic, cultural, and social exchanges and integration between Taiwan and the Chinese mainland while de-emphasizing political disputes in the process. Economic integration in a globalization era may well spill over to cultural, social, and finally political spheres if both sides strive for it. A common Chinese market and eventually some form of political coalition may emerge across the Taiwan Strait. This book proposes that to avoid a showdown with China over Taiwan, the United States, sooner rather than later, should perhaps help develop a loose framework of "one China" that is acceptable to the majorities on both sides of the Taiwan Strait. Under the "one China" framework, both sides of the Taiwan Strait continue to be ruled separately while promoting cross-Strait exchanges, laying conditions for future integration and unification. The bottom line is: there can be two governments, but there can only be one country across the Taiwan Strait. A loosely formed "one China," though not the optimum outcome each side aspires for, may be the only viable solution for all three parties concerned.

In the short to medium term, the United States should also help create a situation in which no US weapons sales to Taiwan are required, with Taiwan promising to abandon policies aimed at achieving separate statehood and the PRC promising to promote unification through peaceful means only. Continued US weapons sales to Taiwan have sent the wrong message to Taiwan independence separatists and made US–China military conflict more likely over Taiwan's future. The United States has to consider where its long-term interests are in East Asia and the Pacific Region. The PRC, for its part, must reflect upon its strategies in the past decade and asks itself why Taiwan has moved further away. Since the "one country, two systems" formula is extremely unpopular in Taiwan, the PRC leadership must revise it and propose a more attractive model for reunification.

Anticipating the critics

Criticisms may be leveled against the argument that, among all potential contenders, China is most likely to challenge the US dominance in world affairs, especially in the Asia-Pacific region. Some would argue that China's future is uncertain and unpredictable. In a worst-case scenario, China may engage in civil wars and disintegrate like the former Soviet Union. This research is based on the assumption that China's domestic politics and economic growth will remain relatively stable and that both the leadership and the public wish and are working hard to raise China's great power status. That China will emerge as a great power in the twenty-first century, benign or not, is a more likely outcome than gloomier predictions about China's future. Of course, critics may speculate on other possibilities of China's development and its future, but that is not the topic of this research.

The assumption that China will challenge America's supremacy is also supported by the American government's rhetoric and actual policies that consider China the most likely challenger. China is the only country that has been labeled a "strategic competitor" by the George W. Bush administration. The US military has strengthened its forward deployment forces in the Asia-Pacific region. And in the late 1990s the United States conducted more war games with China as the presumed adversary than with any other countries, including Russia.[94] Though the 11 September 2001 incident temporarily silenced the "China threat" debate in the United States, a rising China remains a great concern for American government. Some in the United States are taking seriously the possibility that China is going to violently challenge the United States in the next power transition.

For those who believe that a future power transition is more likely to take place from the United States to the EU or any other challenger, the theoretical framework and policy prescriptions derived from this dissertation are also significant and helpful.[95] The multilevel analytical model can certainly be applied to other scenarios of potential power transitions in the future.

Inferences and summary

Some believe that China and the United States can become close friends and some predict that the two countries will eventually go to war. It may be wishful thinking for both groups. This short survey of post-Cold War Sino-American relations reveals the general trend of cooperation and competition in bilateral relations. Despite the changeable official terms used to describe the relationship such as "strategic partnership," "strategic competitors," or "constructive cooperative relations," the United States and China will most likely develop a "normal" relationship, in which they will cooperate on a wide range of bilateral, regional, and global issues but disagree and even argue over some other issues. More than 30 years after President Nixon's historic visit to China, US–China ties have strengthened and expanded into a complex relationship, often cooperative, sometimes contentious, but always vital to global stability.

The US–China relationship is a multifaceted one. In terms of economy and trade, the two countries have found common ground for closer cooperation. China's modernization provides enormous challenges and opportunities for both sides. Exchanges between private citizens are steadily increasing. On the political side, the two countries have many differences, yet neither side is enforcing its views upon the other. The future course of the relationship depends to a large extent on how the two governments and the two peoples will take advantage of globalization and interdependence and push the relationship to a new level.

The two countries are not quite friends or enemies. Sure, there are groups in both countries that perceive one another as the enemy. But even among these groups there is little support for a cutoff of normal trade and other relations. Nor do most exponents of the China threat believe that the US military should seek a direct confrontation with the armed forces of what they see as Chinese military expansionism. The China threat view reflects the interests of the powerful military–industrial complex and is frequently used as a pretext to sell more weapons to Taiwan. Unless the United States discovers another mammoth potential threat to US interests, US politicians will most likely continue to gain political points by bashing China, especially during an election year.

There are clearly both common grounds and disputes between the two countries. Generally speaking, common grounds and common interests far outweigh disputes and divergent views. On one hand, deep conflicts of interest and domestic politics often generate sharp conflict and push the two countries apart. On the other hand, countervailing imperatives that require cooperation always compel leaders of both countries to keep conflict within manageable limits and sustain a cooperative relationship. Despite the many differences between the two countries, there is no indication that they will resort to war as a means to resolve their conflicts. Since the 1995–6 military standoff near the Taiwan Strait, the United States and China have learned each side's bottom line and have become more mature in dealing with the explosive Taiwan issue. Considerable power and interdependence compel both toward mutual accommodation. Since the early 1990s, the relationship has experienced ups and downs, but every time the two countries have been able to seek common ground while reserving differences in maintaining and developing bilateral relations. There is no reason to believe why they will not be able to do so in the future.

Since 1989, successive US administrations have had difficulty in fielding a comprehensive and coordinated China policy that not only clearly defines and promulgates US national interests but also attracts widespread national and international support. To a great extent, the stage for US foreign policy difficulties was set by the 1989 Tiananmen Square crackdown, from which China has never been fully rehabilitated in the eyes of most Americans. Sixteen years later, it is time for the United States to move on.

For its part, China will have to recognize that historically the United States has had strong interests in Asia that are not going to disappear any time soon. China needs to take those interests into account in defining its new role in the region. China has to demonstrate to the world that its military modernization will not be accompanied by an aggressive foreign policy and that it does not pose a threat to its neighbors. Taiwan is, of course, a different case since Taiwan is not a foreign country. The PRC's fundamental policy toward Taiwan remains peaceful reunification. The military preparedness against potential Taiwanese independence cannot be interpreted as an indication of the PRC's aggressive foreign policy. But the PRC must understand the importance to the United States of peaceful resolution of the Taiwan issue, which is also in China's best interests.

What is noticeably absent in the US–China relationship today is a strategic foundation as solid as that during the Cold War, when the common anchor of each nation's security interest was the Soviet Union. Now each eyes the other and worries about the long term. The United States frets that China's increasing power will, in time, produce a challenge to America's regional influence. Meanwhile, the Chinese are suspicious about American intentions to restrain them and preserve what Beijing sees as a unipolar dominance. The war on terrorism has provided a welcome agenda for cooperation, but will probably not bring the two countries together strategically. In the near future, the two countries will remain cooperative on many issues but contentious on some others. In an era of economic globalization, the foreign policies of both powers are more or less constrained by conditions associated with interdependence and multilateralism.

A revisit of hypotheses

Recalling the hypotheses for this research, the following summary is made and the corresponding policy recommendations are offered.

H1: The further a rising power is incorporated into the international system, the less likely it is to challenge the status quo violently.

It may be dangerous to blindly apply historical lessons to current world politics since the international system has fundamentally changed. Nevertheless, pre-WWI Anglo-German interactions and their failure to prevent the Great War provide a useful case study of unsuccessful power transition and have policy implications for the future.

With a historical lesson in mind, this research proposes that, to avoid a potential conflict between China and the United States, the best strategy for the United States is to welcome and incorporate China into the international community such as through WTO membership. For China, membership in international organizations signifies the respect and recognition that it aspires to and deserves as a reemerging great power after humiliations by Western powers in the nineteenth and early twentieth centuries. Participation in international organizations will also expose China to international norms and practices, including democratic institutions and civil society. China's participation also ensures that China becomes a writer of new rules in a multilateral structure. It is less likely that China will challenge or attempt to violently change the rules of the game that she herself helped to write. Since it is in China's interests to play by the rules of the game in international affairs, involvement in and acceptance by the international community will more probably make China a peaceful and law-abiding power.

Supporting China's participation in the international system will not only satisfy China's needs and interests, it also conforms to America's long-term objectives to help bring about a peaceful, democratic, and prosperous China. Punishing China unilaterally will only create a dissatisfied China; incorporating China into the multilateral international arena where China's own interests hinge on abiding by international rules will be more likely to turn China into a democratic society and make China a satisfied power.

H2: The more a rising power recognizes and respects the dominant power's vital interests, the less likely it is to be perceived and treated as a threat by the dominant power.

This book suggests that China needs to become more transparent in its policy-making. It can demonstrate, through words and deeds, that its rise will not pose a threat to its neighbors and that it does not intend to replace the United States as the global power or drive the United States out of Asia. China should continue to concentrate on domestic development and seek cooperative relationships with other countries for that purpose. It is encouraging that China has proposed a free trade zone with Southeast Asian nations to boost development in the region. It has also adopted a code of conduct with regard to the disputed Spratly Islands. Although not forsaking its sovereignty over the disputed territories, China has formed constructive relations with other claimants to jointly explore and develop the rich natural resources in the region. It is helpful that China has a friendly neighbor policy and has not espoused any aggressive intentions in international affairs.

Furthermore, China must understand the importance the United States attaches to the ideals of democracy, freedom, and human rights. The United States has traditionally been a Pacific power and it is not likely to withdraw from Asia because of its vital national interests in the region. China should welcome America's positive role in preventing Japan from remilitarizing and keeping the Korean Peninsula nuclear free. And certainly China should continue to welcome America's contribution to China's economic growth through trade and investment. On the Taiwan issue, while strongly opposing Taiwanese independence for the sake of its own national interests, the PRC needs to respect the American interests of peacefully settling the cross-Strait dispute. Without doubt, US supply of weapons to Taiwan is partially linked to the PLA's military upgrading and its perceived threat to Taiwan. It may be helpful for the PLA to gradually reduce the number of short-range missiles deployed on China's southeast coast opposite Taiwan, although Taiwan needs to take corresponding measures simultaneously to demonstrate that it does not intend to seek permanent separation from China.

H3: The more the dominant power respects a challenger's vital interests, the less likely the challenger is to become dissatisfied with the international order and its relations with the dominant power.

Similarly, it is in the long-term interest of the United States to bring Taiwan and mainland China together under a loose political framework acceptable to both sides of the Taiwan Strait. This will not only guarantee Taiwan's continued autonomy, freedom, and prosperity, but will satisfy China's vital interest to keep Taiwan as part of a unified China. To support a separate and independent Taiwan, coupled with continued sales of advanced weapons to Taiwan, is an unwise choice for the United States. To accommodate the PRC on this vital issue does not mean appeasement of an aggressive China. The PRC considers the Taiwan issue as part of nation-building. It is wrong to consider Beijing's attempt for national reunification as an indication of its aggressive foreign policy in the future.

America's national missile defense (NMD) program may play the role that Britain's development of the battleship "dreadnought" played a century ago – a superweapon that upset the balance by making Germany's arsenal strategically irrelevant. The NMD will nullify China's limited nuclear deterrence and is strongly opposed by China, which argues that the program will spark an arms race in the world. What worries China more is that the overseas version of the program – theater missile defense (TMD) – may put Taiwan under American protection. From the perspective of power transition theory, placing Taiwan under the umbrella of TMD is a very unwise policy. The United States is not advised to develop any sort of formal military alliance with Taiwan.

Perhaps a loosely formed "one China" which satisfies the PRC's "one China" bottom line without sacrificing Taiwan's separate political status and way of life is the only viable solution to this thorny issue. Realistically speaking, Taiwan will never be secure if it chooses independence since it will then have to live in the shadow of a giant, hostile neighbor. What Taiwan can do is extract maximal gains from association with the Chinese mainland. This should be done first through deeper exchanges across the Taiwan Strait and then through political negotiations.

It is well understood on both sides of the Taiwan Strait that, without America's "interference," the two Chinese parties will not be able to reach any agreement on their relationship. In this sense, the United States can actively promote peaceful cross-Strait exchanges and push for some sort of political negotiations by the two Chinese parties. Without a mutually acceptable solution to Taiwan's relationship with the PRC, US–China relations will not be stable. Only when this most contentious issue is removed from US–China relations is a potential power transition likely to be peaceful.

H4: The more extensive and strong links the two societies have, the less likely there is to be war between them.

US–China relations are one of the most complicated and yet one of the strongest in the world. Cultural, educational, and social exchanges at the grassroots level are extensive and by some calculations the strongest in the world. Economic and trade ties have steadily expanded and deepened. The width and depth of such interactions help keep the relationship on track.

The weakest link is perhaps the exchange between the two militaries. Despite extensive ties and huge trade volume between the two countries, military to military exchange has been limited. The United States maintains its ban on hi-tech and military equipment and technology export to China since 1989, and military personnel exchange was also curtailed after the April 2001 military aircraft collision near Hainan Island. It is disappointing and abnormal that defense ministers from the two countries have not exchanged visits since the late 1990s. On both sides, the militaries are probably the most hawkish forces and remain suspicious of one another's intentions. Extensive exchange and mutual understanding are crucial for confidence building between the two militaries. It is encouraging that military exchanges have partially resumed following President Jiang's October 2002 visit to the United States. Exchanges and existing dialog channels such as those between the two national defense universities should be expanded and become regular.

Defense meetings and consultations at the ministerial level should be resumed as soon as possible.

US–China relations have experienced many ups and downs since normalization of diplomatic ties in the late 1970s. What makes this relationship enduring is the common interest and extensive linkage between the two countries. The two countries need to deepen and widen their exchanges in all sectors of society, especially between the two militaries, who tend to be hardliners and most suspicious of one another.

H5: The more committed national leaders are to a stable bilateral relationship, the less likely there is to be war between the two powers.

The greatest strength of the bilateral relationship lies in the common interest in expanding the already enormous economic, political, cultural, and social exchanges. Indeed, these extensive and strong links across the Pacific Ocean have helped senior officials in both countries to stabilize a relationship that sometimes threatens to spin out of control. Top-level visits and meetings occur regularly if not frequently. Every US president since Richard Nixon has visited China. Major Chinese leaders have also visited the United States since 1979. Despite a rocky start, President George W. Bush's administration has moderated its approach to China. It is truly remarkable that President Bush and President Jiang met three times within a year between October 2001 and October 2002. And in return for then Vice President Hu Jintao's April 2002 US visit, Vice President Dick Cheney visited China in April 2004. President Bush and President Hu have also planned to exchange state visits in 2005. Clearly, leaders from both sides are interested in maintaining and developing this important bilateral relationship.

For the first time in recent US presidential elections, China did not become a campaign issue in 2004. Instead both George W. Bush and John Kerry talked about strengthening relations with China in an era of globalization. China's smooth transfer of military power from Jiang Zemin to Hu Jintao in 2004 was widely hailed by the United States. Perhaps US–China relations have matured to be able to weather any change in leadership on both sides.

General hypothesis: If the government, the public, and top leaders in both the dominant power and the challenging power have positive evaluations of the bilateral relationship in a friendly international system, power transition will end in peace.

It may be an exaggeration that both China and the United States are completely satisfied with their relationship. Nevertheless, the current state of the bilateral relationship is acceptable to both sides. Issues such as Taiwan, human rights, and non-proliferation are very difficult ones and cannot be resolved any time soon. For these disputes that separate the two countries now, the two sides could seek common ground while reserving their differences so that the disputes will not become obstacles to the development of bilateral ties.

Power transition, in the strict sense, may not happen between the United States and China for decades yet. But the nature of today's interactions may determine the course of their future relationship. The future depends on how the two sides nurture this relationship at global, domestic, societal, and individual levels today. US–China interactions since 1990 have a mixed record of positive and negative elements.

Globalization at the international level is generally positive for a smooth relationship. Indeed, in the broader global context, the two great powers have much more common challenges to deal with, such as water and air pollution, AIDS, environmental degradation, global poverty, debt crisis, and international crime. It is important that the two great powers move beyond their own national interests and work together for the betterment of human beings. In the era of economic globalization and interdependence, China and the United States must seize the opportunity to expand their cooperation and become responsible players in international affairs. With increasing interdependence and mutual benefits, the two countries are expected to become more satisfied with this multifaceted relationship.

Domestically, no consensus has been reached in the United States over its conduct of China policy. In comparison, Chinese society and leaders seem to be more unified and have a common understanding of the importance of relations with the United States. Though there are hawks and doves in both societies, the majority in each society does not consider the other as an enemy, especially after the 11 September 2001 terrorist attacks. Some members of the US Congress and US media may continue to look at China negatively, and some nationalistic and hawkish Chinese may continue to demonize America, but they do not represent the mainstream views in each country. With China's further integration into the international community and its continued progress at home, and with expanded contact and exchanges between the two peoples, more favorable views of each other will be formed.

At the societal level, extensive linkages such as trade, travel, and education have developed over the past two decades. With such deep ties and potentially a security community across the Pacific, it is hard to imagine that war will be a choice for conflict resolution between the two countries. The weakest link between the two countries lies in military exchanges. Since the end of the Cold War, the two militaries have been in an awkward position vis-à-vis one another. The military establishment in each society tends to be the hardliner in bilateral relations. The delicate military relations were further strained by the 1999 embassy bombing and 2001 spy plane collision incidents. Though military exchanges had resumed to some extent by the end of 2002, the PLA and US forces remain suspicious of each other. It is uncertain whether expanded exchanges will be able to completely dispel misunderstandings between the world's largest and the world's strongest militaries. But it is hoped that after frequent contact and direct exchanges each military will better understand its counterpart and will not consider the other as the enemy.

At the individual level, in addition to the extensive cultural, educational, and personnel exchanges, commitment at the top decision-making levels is also very favorable to a cooperative and peaceful relationship. High-level exchanges are frequent and regular. In China, the fourth generation of leadership headed by Hu Jintao, like its predecessors, is fully committed to developing a constructive and cooperative relationship with the United States. In the United States, presidents from both parties since 1990 have contributed to the stabilization of bilateral relations.

This book suggests that, though the British–American style security community has not been, and probably will never be, established between China and the United States, strong ties across the Pacific have linked the two societies close together. At the beginning of the twenty-first century, they have more common ground than differences. US Secretary of State Colin Powell remarked in a speech in September 2003, "US relations with China are the best they have been since President Nixon's first visit."[96] Not everyone would agree with Mr. Powell's sanguine assessment, but the two governments seem to have recognized that together they can build a peaceful future. As a tentative conclusion, it is probably safe to say that, judging from the current state of bilateral interactions at all four levels, one can be cautiously optimistic that US–China relations will continue to be generally cooperative and a potential power transition, if managed properly, will most likely be peaceful in an era of globalization and deepening interdependence.

6 Comparisons and contrasts

This chapter summarizes the similarities and differences among the three cases discussed in the previous three chapters. Using the multilevel analytical framework, it pays particular attention to the international and domestic environments facing pre-WWI Germany and today's China. The chapter aims to answer two often asked questions: Will China's rise in the twenty-first century be peaceful? And will China challenge the international status quo violently as pre-WWI Germany did?

The international system

Historically, international stability has been episodic and often achieved through wars that engendered widespread devastation. In European history at least, there is only one period in which tension was largely absent from diplomacy – during the ascendancy of the Concert of Europe from 1818 to 1848, when great powers agreed to meet together regularly to prevent another round of Napoleonic wars. The great powers remained in general agreement with one another until their unity was ruptured by the revolutions of 1848. From then on, the common desire to avoid conflict and war was shattered, reaching its nadir in 1914.

The Concert of Europe represented the consolidation of a coalition of great powers in world politics. Such a coalition based on a balance of power, however, could not be recreated after World War I due to the isolation of the United States, the abstention of Russia, tension between France and Britain, and the pariah status of Germany. Fascism and communism created a huge divide in European politics during the interwar years. After World War II, the immediate outbreak of the Cold War and ideological conflict prevented another coalition from being constituted.

The end of the Cold War ushered in a new era in the international system. "The truly remarkable character of the period since 1991 lies in the fact that all great powers now recognize the need to keep overall peace," observes a political science scholar.[1] Indeed, a striking difference between today's international system and that of before the two world wars is the emergence and blossoming of regional and global institutions which serve as a powerful normative resource for generating cooperation among nations. The pre-WWI European status quo was maintained by the traditional, fragile balance of power with no mechanism or true incentive for cooperation. The failed League of Nations was a laudable effort by great powers to establish rules for governing their relations. The United Nations, with its many problems, is nevertheless an innovative structure upon which multilateral cooperation can be built and has become a possibility and reality. Together with other international organizations such as the WTO, the United Nations provides a truly multilateral forum to address issues and challenges common to all states. Today, great powers have reached agreement on economic growth and global stability. They also generally agree to avoid war as a resolution to conflict among them.

The information revolution and economic globalization have widened and thickened the web connecting great powers. Another difference between the present-day international system and that of late nineteenth-century Europe is that economic relations among the great powers are considerably more advanced and far reaching now than they were then. Then, each great power relied in large measure on its own sphere of states for resources, markets, and trade: Britain had its colonies; Germany was focusing on Central Europe; and Russia was mainly engaged with the small states on its borders. Now, however, not only are the trade relationships among the great powers far more developed and intertwined, but most of them have investments and production facilities in each other's territory. American, European, Japanese, and Chinese companies all have physical assets within each other's borders. China, Japan, and EU countries have also been huge buyers of US treasury bonds and other securities.[2] The unprecedented interdependence among great powers today is a substantial incentive for them to prefer cooperation to confrontation.

Rising powers tend to feel dissatisfied with the international system established by dominant powers since the rules of the game were set long before without participation by rising powers. One of the major reasons for Germany's violent challenge of the pre-WWI European system was its perceived disadvantage in the system and its ambition to gain its "place in the sun." It is sometimes assumed that, after more than a century of "national humiliation" by Western powers, China is finally going to secure the status in the world that is rightfully hers as a great power, perhaps violently as Germany did a century ago. But the trajectory of China's international behavior since 1990 suggests that China, unlike pre-WWI Germany, is reemerging in the world peacefully.

How does China fit into the current international system that is largely created and maintained by the United States? Is it a satisfied power or a revisionist power? The answers can be found from China's relations with the international community in the past three decades. Since the late 1970s China has assiduously attempted to become an active member of the international system. To a great extent, it has been successfully incorporated into the global political and economic systems as it entered the twenty-first century. The largest developing nation, China has benefited enormously from the current international political and economic structures. In return, China has been a responsible player in world politics. The PRC has basically been a positive and constructive force in the United Nations since its admission in 1971, especially since 1990. It has played a constructive role in the world since 1990, from helping financial-crisis-stricken Asian neighbors and fighting against global terrorism to promoting peace on the Korean peninsula and in the Middle East. As a new member of the WTO, the PRC has generally followed the rules of the world trading authority. China understands that it is in its interest to continue to be a stabilizing force in world politics and economics.

Today's China is far more dependent upon international technology and foreign direct investment than was pre-WWI Germany.[3] Among others, the United States is one of the largest sources of trade, investment, management, and technology needed for China's modernization. At the beginning of the twenty-first-century, China has become an engine of global economic growth. Unlike pre-WWI Germany, which was a revisionist power and attempted to break the status quo, today's China is basically a satisfied, recognized, and status quo power. By the end of the twentieth century, China had completely walked out of the Maoist isolation and had been largely integrated into the global regime. It is a member state of the United Nations, the World Bank, the International Monetary Fund, the WTO, and all other major international organizations. China maintains diplomatic ties with over 160 states across the world. China fully understands that, if it wants to assert its rightful place in the world as a respected great power, it can do so peacefully. China has become an important participant in the evolving international political and economic system, increasingly meeting and accepting more and more of that system's conventions. There is no indication that it is going to challenge or attempt to alter the system that has benefited it so much. The fourteen-year-long effort to join the WTO is a telling example of China's determination to become a member of the global system and observe global trade rules no matter how serious domestic consequences it might have to deal with.

Without doubt, many of the bilateral issues between the United States and China are rooted in the inherent tensions between a rising power trying to find its rightful place and an established hegemon seeking to define and defend the rules of the game in the international system. In general, it is fair to say that so far the two countries have dealt with these tensions maturely and satisfactorily. Though there are forces in both countries that perceive one another as the greatest potential threat, they do not represent the mainstream view in each society. China recognizes and appreciates the positive role the United States plays in maintaining global and regional order – a favorable environment that China desperately needs for its domestic development. The United States, unlike Great Britain's perception of Germany's rise and its naval buildup as a menace, welcomes the rise of a prosperous, peaceful, and more democratic China. The United States realizes that a poor, disintegrated, and aggressive China poses much greater threat to Asia and US interests globally. Like their cooperation and mutual agreement on the WTO issue and on the war against terrorism, the United States and China can work well within the framework of the current international system despite their domestic differences and disagreements over certain issues. The important thing is that, whereas it is necessary for China to abide by international rules and recognize America's national interests, China's legitimate rights and vital national interests such as in Taiwan must also be respected and recognized by the United States.

Foreign policy

In comparing pre-WWI Germany and today's China, one cannot but notice the obvious differences in their foreign policy outlooks. Germany's ambition of advancing to the level of a global power inevitably provoked at least passive hostility throughout the world. Germany had the drive to establish itself as a leading world power and its foreign policies served that purpose; China does not appear to have such a grand plan. China's only "grand strategy" is, in the words of the late leader Deng Xiaoping, to build China into a relatively wealthy society (*xiaokang shehui*) by the middle of the twenty-first century. The sixteenth National Congress of the Chinese Communist Party, which concluded in November 2002, also set a moderate blueprint for China: to build a middle-class nation with a per capita income of US$3,000 by 2020. China's foreign policy since 1990 has aimed to create a favorable international environment to serve its primary national interest: domestic development. The last thing China wants is an unstable, war-ridden world in which China cannot concentrate on economic growth. For the purpose of continued growth, China is least likely to provoke or initiate any international or regional conflict. Since the end of the Cold War, as China has focused its attentions on promoting economic development, China's foreign policy has evolved in a positive direction emphasizing regional cooperation and global diplomatic engagement rather than isolation.

Whereas Germany's *Weltpolitik* probably made world war inevitable sooner or later by provoking and targeting Britain, China's *gaige kaifang* (reform and opening) requires a peaceful domestic and international environment and is not aimed at harming any country's interests. China's foreign policy has been fundamentally defensive. It serves its fundamental interest of domestic development. China is a far more moderate power and has not pursued a policy to provoke the United States by unseating or weakening its global and regional leadership role. In comparison, pre-WWI Germany's foreign policy was aggressive, aiming to assert its "place in the sun," and its military build-up was part of the strategy and preparation for that purpose. Germany's ambitions were driven by a resentment of a perceived lack of recognition and respect, especially on the part of a haughty Britain. The high-profile German policy not only threatened Britain but also alarmed other powers at the time. As far as Great Britain was concerned, Germany contrasted sharply with the low profile and non-entangling policy of the United States, who had been swinging between isolationism and internationalism.

Despite the "Manifest Destiny" and the Monroe Doctrine, the United States had not purposely pursued a policy of becoming the dominant global power, which would challenge the British global position. To a great extent, it was pushed to the front as a global leader. That Great Britain did not regard the United States as a great menace in the late nineteenth and the early twentieth centuries is not just attributed to the great physical distance between the two nations, but also to the comparatively low profile the United States had maintained during its rise. The increasingly popular *heping jueqi* (peaceful rise) of China has become China's new strategy in the new century. Chinese leaders have repeatedly avowed that China does not intend to seek regional or global hegemony. There is no reason for the United States to block China's continued modernization and its emergence as a peaceful power in the Far East.

Of the three rising powers in the three cases studied, pre-WWI Germany was a revisionist power, seeking "justice" in the international system and determined to assert its "place in the sun." The United States and China, on the other hand, are status quo powers, seeking stability and peace of the system and keeping a low profile in international affairs during their rise. Germany chose the road of aggression and expansion, which ultimately failed; China has chosen the road to a peaceful future. The difference is obvious. Much as Great Britain did, the United States has also chosen to incorporate China into the international system and cautiously welcomed and helped China's growth.

A cursory look at the PRC's history would reveal that China's foreign policy is anything but an aggressive one. The "Five Principles of Peaceful Coexistence" have been the foundation of the PRC's foreign policy since the 1950s.[4] China adopts a friendly neighbor policy and does not espouse any aggressive intentions. It has signed an agreement with other claimants over the disputed Spratly Islands in November 2002, with all parties pledging to exercise self-restraint and to avoid activities that would complicate or escalate the dispute. This is significant since among all claimants, China has arguably the most powerful military and is the first to claim sovereignty over the resources-rich islands. It used to disregard any claims by other parties. The agreement underlies China's preference of cooperation over confrontation in its foreign policy.

Whereas Germany had been dissatisfied with the status of German–British relations since the late nineteenth century, China's view of US–China relations is more pragmatic and optimistic. When commenting on US–China relations, Chinese leaders often remark that the bilateral relationship offers more opportunities than challenges. Though there have been setbacks in the relationship, bilateral ties have been zigzagging forward (*zai quze zhong qian-*

jing). Chinese leaderships since 1990 have been generally satisfied with the international system and the state of the bilateral relations, even if they may be unhappy with the American handling of some specific issues between the two countries. For example, while pointing out the Taiwan issue as a problem between the United States and China, President Jiang Zemin told American guests in December 2002 that the two countries shared wide-ranging and vital common interests and that the bilateral relations had entered a stage of stable development.[5]

The only Chinese "aggressive" behavior most frequently cited by commentators is the PLA's missile exercises near Taiwan in 1995–6 and missile deployment aimed at Taiwan. But then Taiwan is not a foreign state, and the PRC's determination for national reunification should not be construed as an indication of its aggressive foreign policy. Indeed, the only area of potential conflict between the United States and China is Taiwan. Both countries are interested in peace and stability across the Taiwan Strait, but they sharply disagree over how the cross-Strait political dispute should be resolved. While emphasizing that peaceful reunification is China's fundamental policy, the PRC reserves the right to use military force to unify with Taiwan if Taiwan declares formal independence or if foreign powers intervene in the process. The United States, on the other hand, insists that any dispute across the Taiwan Strait must be resolved peacefully. For that purpose, the United States continues to supply advanced weapons to Taiwan for its defense – a policy the PRC vehemently opposes and denounces as a violation of the "one China" principle.

Since the early 1970s all US administrations have adhered to a "one China" policy and expressed opposition to Taiwan's *de jure* independence. Though the United States does not seem to support China's unification scheme, it does not intend to challenge the "one China" principle by supporting permanent Taiwanese separation from China now. "No unification for China, no independence for Taiwan" is probably a more accurate description of America's policy on this issue. The United States is apparently not prepared to accept either an independent Taiwan or a unified China consisting of both the PRC and Taiwan.[6] America's parallel approach to both Chinese parties – officially with the PRC and "unofficially" with Taiwan – strives for the maintenance of the status quo. Keeping the status quo across the Taiwan Strait is acceptable to the PRC right now, though it is not the PRC's ultimate objective. China's priority remains economic modernization and domestic development, to which the United States has contributed a great deal over the past two decades. A stable relationship across the Taiwan Strait under US pressure and encouragement is conducive to China's economic modernization.

After 1945, British and American interests became almost identical based on a security community between them. In comparison, the United States and China have both common interests and differences. Significantly, these differences have not hampered their cooperation on a wide range of global and regional affairs since 1990. Ties are strong, but no security community has been formed across the Pacific. True, China still has some historical grievances against Western powers for the humiliations China suffered since the Opium Wars. And in the case of the United States, the PRC correctly points out that the US intervention in the Taiwan Strait during the Korean War prevented the PRC from taking Taiwan back in the 1950s. As a regional player with its own interests, China may occasionally collide with the United States, but it has also gradually realized that its long-term interests are better served by cooperating with the United States and by observing common standards. Despite the changes in rhetoric in the United States following the change of government at the turn of the twenty-first century, China is neither a "strategic competitor" nor a "strategic partner" of the United States. Both countries seek to establish a "normal" relationship. They understand that how they manage their relations will have a major bearing on the prospects for peace and prosperity around the world. China will probably continue to complain about perceived US "hegemony," but it also wants to establish a constructive relationship with the United States. The United States also wishes to maintain a robust relationship with China through which the two countries can work together to resolve issues like North Korea's nuclear program. China appears determined to act as a responsible regional and global power. The so-called "China threat" propaganda is perhaps an inflation of China's military strength and misinterpretation of its intentions. It also results from China's sheer size and its opaque political and military policies and strategies, rather than from facts and reality.

Domestic politics

China has changed much and is still changing in a direction favorable to regional stability and prosperity. Market dynamism has replaced Maoist dogmatism. China exports computers, not communism. Over twenty years of continued development has drastically raised the living standards of most people in China. But huge problems exist such as unemployment, corruption, income inequality, and environmental degradation, and most significantly the vast gap between economic pluralism and the one-party controlled political system.

Unlike pre-WWI Germany, which sought to divert domestic tensions outwards through an ambitious foreign policy, China emphasizes the deepening of political and economic reforms as a solution to its many challenges.[7] Most members of the so-called third-generation leaders led by Jiang Zemin and fourth-generation leaders led by Hu Jintao are pragmatic, problem-solving technocrats. Most of them have been in leadership positions for a decade or so overseeing China's development, therefore there are reasons to believe that they know where problems are and how to handle domestic challenges properly.

Some people worry about the long-term stability of China. But the Chinese people themselves, after suffering from frequent political campaigns during the Mao years, perhaps treasure stability more than anybody else. Since the late 1970s China's social transformation has reached a point at which the majority of the population favors stability over chaos and continuation of reform and opening up over isolation. The Communist Party itself is reforming to accommodate the changing domestic situations. By admitting new members from social groups other than workers and peasants, the Party may eventually transform itself into a populist people's party. Village-level elections have been held in most parts of the country in the past decade and may be extended to township level in the years ahead. Most significantly, at the sixteenth Communist Party's National Congress in November 2002, the party leadership transition from Jiang Zemin to Hu Jintao was smooth, a transition claimed to be the "most orderly and peaceful" in the history of modern China by some Western media.[8] By the end of 2004, the leadership transition had been completed without any stir in Chinese politics. In the long term, the PRC regime will probably democratize as South Korea and Taiwan did. The hefty foreign exchange reserves China has accumulated over the past decade should provide a cushion in any future financial and economic crisis.

For a long period to come, China will continue to focus on domestic development. In terms of its policy toward the United States, it has been and will be nonconfrontational. In many cases, China has responded to US pressures and met US demands. For example, in October 2002, China formally established restrictions on the export of missile technology and goods that could be used to produce weapons of mass destruction, seeking to remove a perennial irritant in relations with America. The United States has also taken a less confrontational approach toward China in the early years of the twenty-first century. From 1990 to 2000, the United States had either proposed or sponsored motions harshly criticizing China's human rights record at the annual session of the UN Commission on Human Rights every year. Since 2001, the United States has chosen to abandon this strategy. Instead, it has sought serious dialog and diplomacy with China on human rights issues. In response to American pressure and its new approach, the Chinese government has agreed to allow the United Nations unconditional access to investigate claims of torture, religious persecution, and arbitrary detention.[9] And the Chinese government has accounted for the whereabouts and current conditions of political dissidents over whom the United States government has expressed concern.

As far as the domestic debate over "containment vs. engagement" of China is concerned, apparently the engagement camp has won in America. The "containment" argument reached its heyday in the early post-Cold War years until the mid-1990s. For example, the 31 July 1995 issue of *Time* magazine carried an essay by Charles Krauthammer, entitled "Why We Must Contain China." (Interestingly, *The Economist*, published in London, had a similar argument in an article entitled "Containing China" in its 29 July 1995 edition, just two days prior to the *Time* article. Is this an international scheme?) The "containment" camp had clearly weakened by the end of the twentieth century. The successful US–China negotiations over China's WTO admission and America's granting of permanent normal trade relations with China were unmistakable indications that engagement had triumphed over containment in the prolonged debate.

However, the "China Threat" argument still has a receptive audience in the United States and elsewhere. After the 11 September 2001 terrorist attacks, Americans found a more dangerous, clear, and present threat to their security. Counterterrorism has become the central focus of American foreign policy. By standing with the United States on this issue, China has become an important ally in the eyes of many Americans. But hardliners on both sides are always finding fault with the current US–China relations. In the United States, domestic politics may tempt critics of the engagement policy to reevaluate America's approach to China, including its long-standing "One China" policy.[10] As in British–German interactions, public misperceptions and sometimes open accusations still exist in today's US–China relations. Books and articles denigrating one another can be found both in the United States and China. From the sensational *The Coming Conflict with China* and *The China Threat* to the highly nationalistic and anti-American *China Can Say No*,[11] some forces in both countries attempt to create a very unhealthy atmosphere for the smooth development of this delicate relationship.

In the United States, both conservative Republicans and liberal Democrats have long been vocal of their dislike of Chinese policies regarding human rights, Taiwan, and Tibet. After the 11 September 2001 attacks, these vociferous critics have largely become silent as the United States focuses on counterterrorism. But these critics may raise their voices again should circumstances change. At the beginning of 2005, as President Bush entered his second term, the US government began upping the volume and started to openly attack China's currency regime, which the US government believed to have given China an unfair trade advantage.

In both societies, the military remains most suspicious of one another's intentions. In China, debate continues over America's long-term goals and China's security. The Chinese military is very uncomfortable about America's enhancement of its military power in Central Asia and other areas surrounding China as a result of the war on terror, its consolidation of the US–Japan security alliance, the development and deployment of its missile defense program, its increased military contacts with and arms sales to Taiwan, and its adoption of preemption as a core strategic doctrine. Chinese military spending continues to grow at a double-digit rate yearly.

The US military, on the other hand, has always considered a future war with China over Taiwan a contingency. A research report supported and released by the US Department of Defense claims that the United States and China are headed toward conflict and, by 2009, the PLA will be able to sink US aircraft carriers and cause thousands of US casualties in a war over Taiwan. The report suggests that the United States should strengthen its military cooperation with Taiwan to deal with the PLA's military modernization.[12] As a matter of fact, US military personnel have already been directly involved in the annual Taiwanese military drills.

Though the military link between China and the United States remains the weakest, it is encouraging that by the end of 2002 Chinese and American militaries had resumed some exchanges halted after the spy plane crisis of April 2001. These exchanges included, among others, a port call at Qingdao by destroyer USS Paul Foster in November 2002, the visit to Washington in early December 2002 by Lt. Gen. Xiong Guangkai, the deputy chief of staff of the PLA, and the visit to China in mid-December 2002 by Admiral Thomas Fargo, head of the US Pacific Command. In addition, partially in response to America's request for more transparency, China published in early December 2002 a white paper called "China's National Defense in 2002," which included such topics of interest to the United States as China's national defense policy, arms control and disarmament, and China's armed forces building. On the other hand, to satisfy Chinese demands, in almost all bilateral meetings, including those military exchanges, the US side has affirmed its position that it does not support Taiwanese independence.

Interestingly, and perhaps fortunately, the grievances and complaints on both sides are mostly directed at the government and politicians, not at the ordinary people. On the contrary, both Chinese and Americans have fond memories and feelings toward one another. Even though the Tiananmen Square massacre fundamentally changed Americans' view of the Chinese government, China has not been considered the most serious threat to America's national interests. A Zogby International poll found that the proportion of Americans holding favorable views of China increased from 46 percent in 1994 to 59 percent in 2004.[13]

Important for German foreign policy during 1871–1914 were the various national minorities within her border – the French in Alsace-Lorraine, the Danes in northern Schleswig, and the Poles in Prussia's eastern provinces, especially in Posen (Poznan). The annexation of Alsace-Lorraine against the clear wishes of the population into the new German Empire in 1871 turned out to be a huge liability. Alsace-Lorraine also made France a natural enemy of the Reich, and Germany always tried to isolate France as long as possible. The predominantly Catholic Poles had been one of the main factors in the launching of Bismarck's *Kulturkampf* against the Catholic Church, because by hitting Catholics in East Prussia he could also take steps against the unwanted Polish nationality. The problem of the Danish minority belongs in the same context. By refusing to hold the plebiscite in northern Schleswig on the question of whether the population preferred to belong to Denmark or to Prussian Germany – although in the 1866 Peace Treaty of Prague Prussia had promised to do so – Germany turned it into another liability.[14] The three major non-German nationalities amounted to roughly one-tenth of the Empire's population. They lived on politically sensitive borders. Although annexed to increase the power of the German Empire, in the end they weakened Germany's position morally and politically.

The United States has racial issues too, but these issues are fundamentally different since they have nothing to do with sovereignty and national unity. In comparison, China is also constantly plagued with minority issues. In addition to the difficult status of Taiwan, China has to deal with several rebellious minorities on its western and northwestern borders, especially some Tibetans and Uighurs. China's policies in the Tibet and Xinjiang autonomous regions are always scrutinized by the international community and often become issues of contention between China and the West. China has provided evidence to link some separatist groups in Xinjiang to Osama bin Laden's al-Qaeda terrorist network. Despite its initial unwillingness, the United States finally accepted China's classification of the East Turkestan Islamic Movement in Xinjiang as a terrorist group. This probably paved the way for further cooperation between the two countries in the war on terrorism, but significant disagreements over human rights and indigenous culture of minority groups, especially in Tibet, may continue to trouble US–China relations in the years ahead.

Common linkages

One of the most important contributing factors in the special Anglo-American relationship was the popular doctrine of "Anglo-Saxonism," the idea that Britons and Americans are both racial and cultural kinsmen, and that as a "race" the Anglo-Saxons are innately superior to other peoples. Many British and American leaders, including Arthur Balfour and Joseph Chamberlain, and Theodore Roosevelt and John Hay, were influenced by Anglo-Saxonist ideas in their handling of diplomacy. Britons and Germans were also friendly cousins historically and had never fought each other before World War I. That they did not enjoy a special relationship indicates that close historical ties may not be foundations strong enough to withstand the vicissitudes of international politics.

The Chinese and the Americans are two different peoples. There are almost no direct cultural or racial linkages between the two. However, as Anglo-American and Anglo-German relations indicate, racial and cultural affinities are not the only factors determining the quality of international relations. With dissimilar political systems and cultures, the United States and China have many common interests and have created a very powerful linkage between the two societies. Clearly, there is no ideological contest between China and the United States; domestic differences have not impeded their cooperation on many international and regional issues.

Despite the practical non-existence of a common racial and cultural heritage between China and the United States, there are many other encouraging signs in the bilateral linkage. One of these signs is the frequency and volume of the exchanges between the two countries. For example, today over 60,000 Chinese students are studying in the United States, including the children of some Chinese leaders and members of the elite. The Soviet Union never sent that many students to the United States in its entire 70-year history. Another such positive sign of linkage was developed before the PRC regime was established. The Chinese and the Americans joined together in the fight against the Japanese during World War II. This historical friendship and bond are treasured in both countries. The many Christian schools and hospitals Americans established in China at the end of the nineteenth century and early twentieth century are still operating, if under different names. The heroic missions of General Chennault's Flying Tigers are popular household stories in China.

Europe's great powers prior to World War I were tightly bound together economically. They nevertheless fought a long and bloody war. On the eve of 1914, Britain and Germany were each other's second largest customers for both exports and imports, and their trade accounted for a huge portion of their GNPs – 52 and 38 percent, respectively.[15] There were close economic relations between the two rival powers. The German merchant marine was insured by Lloyd's of London. Until Pearl Harbor, the United States traded with Japan. General Motors and Ford, among other major US companies, operated profitably in Germany even after Germany's declaration of war on the United States in 1941. The United States and the Soviet Union were not even loosely connected economically; they nevertheless sustained an uneasy peace for over four decades. As argued throughout this research, the most important causes of peace and war are found in a combination of international and domestic conditions. Even though strong trade ties alone may not divert war, as the German–British case illustrates, no one should ignore the pacifying effect of such a strong linkage between China and the United States in the era of increasing globalization and interdependence. Starting from less than US\$1 billion in 1978, the Sino-US trade volume has increased by over 100 times in the past 27 years. Sino-US trade had reached US\$100 billion by the end of 2003 and continues to grow. US exports to China more than doubled between 2000 and 2004, and China has become America's fifth largest export market, behind Canada, Mexico, Japan, and Britain. The United States is also expected to replace Japan by 2005 as China's biggest trade partner.

A unique feature of this linkage lies in the enormous US investment in China and a considerable US reliance on cheap Chinese labor and the huge Chinese market. Despite concerns that some of America's manufacturing jobs may have been outsourced to China, the vibrant trade is beneficial to both countries. Chinese products are affordable and of good quality, which satisfies the needs of millions of American consumers. Cultural, educational, business, social, and other exchanges continue to grow across the Pacific Ocean. This web of interaction and mutual dependence will only thicken as China's market and society further open up. The breadth and depth of interdependence between the two countries are unprecedented. Extensive links between people, trade, and information are likely to bind the two countries even closer in the twenty-first century. Once the two governments were the driving forces behind bilateral exchanges. Today it is the deepening ties among ordinary Chinese and Americans, in universities, businesses, and organizations, and elsewhere, that sustain this relationship even during the most difficult periods of official relations.

Commitment of national leaders

A great difference between today's China and pre-WWI Germany is that the Chinese leadership is fully committed to maintaining a constructive and friendly relationship with the United States. To some extent, Chinese leaders' commitment to establishing good relations with the United States is comparable to British leaders' efforts to create a special relationship with the United States during and after World War II. In the 1990s President Jiang Zemin and Prime Minister Zhu Rongji put their political life in danger by making concessions for and reaching the WTO agreement with the United States. They were sometimes blamed for being too soft toward America by hawks in the Chinese military, yet they helped US–China relations smooth over one crisis after another after 1990. The new Chinese leadership led by President Hu Jintao and Prime Minister Wen Jiabao, who came into the limelight after the November 2002 sixteenth National Congress of the Chinese Communist Party, has continued China's moderate policy toward the United States. The new leadership faces a daunting task of consolidating its power, strengthening the Chinese economy, and managing increasingly divisive social issues. On various occasions President Hu and his team have affirmed their intention to move US–China relations ahead.

On the US side, all presidents since Richard Nixon have visited China at least once and all support a strong relationship with China. Since the hotlines were established in the late 1990s, top leaders in China and the United States have maintained regular telephone conversations to exchange views and coordinate their policies, for example on the North Korea nuclear issue. Most notably, telephone exchanges between Secretary of State Colin Powell and Foreign Minister Li Zhaoxing became so frequent that the two top diplomats felt comfortable to pick up the phone any time without being bothered by the normal etiquette of 24 or even 36 hours' notice.[16] This type of high-level contact and mutual assurance was clearly absent in British–German relations prior to World War I. High-level commitment can often push the relationship to a higher level.

The differences and similarities of the three cases are summarized in Table 6.1. The table looks at the three cases from the four levels of analysis. In the British–German case, except for trade links and royal family ties, interactions between the two powers at all levels pointed to a negative relationship. Britain and Germany obviously were trapped in a security dilemma and perceived one another as the number one enemy. Unfortunately, there was no mechanism for international cooperation and the leaders on both sides were not fully committed to a friendly relationship. Economic ties were strong, but other social links were very weak, and the two militaries engaged

Table 6.1 Comparison and contrast: the three cases

	Anglo-German (1871–1914)	Anglo-American (1865–1945)	Sino-American (1990–2005)
International environment			
Agreement on international order	–	+	+/–
Common enemy/threat	–	+	+/–
International/regional cooperation	–	+	+
Domestic politics			
War as diversion of domestic crisis	–/+	–/–	–/–
Image of the other	–	–/+	m[a]
Outcome of debate	–	+	+
Societal links			
Trade links	+	+	+
Military links	–	–/+	–
Other links (cultural, educational, etc.)	–	+	+
Individual leaders			
Closeness	+/–	+	+/–
Commitment	–	+	+
Overall evaluations	–	+	+?
Outcome	*War*	*Peace*	*??*

Note
a "m" indicates "mixed". The images of China and America as perceived by each other have been mixed but steadily improving since 1990.

in a spiral arms race. With deep mutual distrust and hatred, the two great nations went on a collision course.

In contrast, interactions between Britain and the United States at all levels favor a positive relationship. It is significant that, though at domestic and societal levels some interactions were initially negative, toward the end of the period surveyed they all turned positive. This brings hope for a potential power transition in the future even between two powers with conflicting interests. What distinguishes the Anglo-American case from the Anglo-German is the fact that the two English-speaking nations established a security community across the Atlantic. With similar democratic cultures and institutions, mutual trust and responsiveness were reached between the two societies. War was ruled out as a way to resolve their differences long before the power transition took place. Coordination of policies and peaceful resolution of conflicts were expected from both sides.

US–China interactions at all four levels since 1990 have been a combination of mostly positive links and some negative ones. Compared with the two historical cases, the Sino-American relationship today bears more resemblance to the Anglo-American relationship. The current international system, characterized by economic globalization, cooperation, and multilateral institutions, is conducive for continued cooperation between the two Pacific powers. Opposition to strong ties between the two sides can be found in both countries, but it is not the mainstream in either society. What is significant in US–China relations is the ever-growing link across the Pacific and strong commitments by top leaders on both sides, key factors that were missing in British–German relations prior to World War I. With more and more transactions going on between the two Pacific powers in an era of globalization and deepening interdependence, perhaps mutual trust and responsiveness and eventually some form of security community could be built across the Pacific. This mixed yet mostly positive picture is ground for cautious optimism about a potential power transition from the United States to China in the future. Indeed, if the United States and China learn from history and consciously foster a strong relationship between them, a power transition, if it occurs, may well be peaceful.

Is war inevitable in international relations?

States make war, and war makes states, declares Columbia University sociologist Charles Tilly.[17] Wars do make states, but wars may also break states. In fact, wars had been the undoing of the British power in the twentieth century. The Boer War (1899–1902) highlighted Britain's weaknesses: first, by forcing Britain to mobilize huge resources to defeat a rather ramshackle Boer military that skillfully utilized guerilla warfare for two years; and, second, by forcing Britain to borrow from the United States to pay for its military effort. The Great War of 1914–18 severely damaged Britain's global position, with her foreign investments losing 15 percent of their value, while the American and Japanese won British markets in Latin America, India, and East Asia. In the China market for instance, Britain's share fell from 16.5 percent to 9.5 percent.[18] Britain won the Great War, but ironically it lost much of its power.

By the 1930s, Britain had lost more markets, even in Empire countries like Canada, Australia, and South Africa, to the United States. Great Britain also suffered from "the price of victory" after World War II – illusions of grandeur as a victor from a great war. Great Britain still considered itself a great power and British leaders felt it incumbent to maintain economic, imperial, and strategic positions that, in retrospect, seemed excessive and enervating. In the end, Britain was trapped in "the hegemon's dilemma" – trying to maintain a congenial international system while sapping the national power it is supposed to protect.

If wars were the unraveling of British power, they appear to have been the foundations of American power. From the Civil War (1861–5) to the Spanish–

American War (1898), the United States transformed itself into an economic powerhouse of global proportions. With a highly productive agricultural sector and world-leading corporations in almost all spheres, the United States emerged by 1900 as increasingly self-confident and assertive. The United States was almost a rival continent as far as Great Britain was concerned – not just a competitor nation. In 1901, for example, Andrew Carnegie's mills were producing more steel than the whole of England.[19] With its "Monroe Doctrine" in Latin America and its "Manifest Destiny" for the Pacific region, the United States engaged in a navy building program that, by 1914, had given it the world's third largest naval force. Before 1914, the United States had been a debtor nation; after 1918, it emerged as a creditor nation, being owed over £1,200 million by the rest of the world, excluding government loans.[20] Financially, New York was replacing London, and it was the Wall Street crash that brought about the Great Depression of the 1930s.

If America became Britain's economic challenger, another power had emerged that constituted a major military threat to the Empire: Germany. European history turned to a new page with the end of the Franco-Prussian war. Once again, it was war that made Germany a unified, powerful, and eventually aggressive nation. The great demand in Germany was for colonies. For Chancellor von Bulow, colonialism was not a choice; it was objectively necessary. German calls to build its navy and expand its army were seen as grave threats by most other powers. A rising and aggressive Germany was not welcome in the prearranged international system. But Germany's colonial expansion and its claim for a position in the great power club could only come through a redivision of the globe. Germany forced forward with such a redivision agenda, and the attempt was defeated on the battlefields of Europe. The Great War did redistribute power in Europe and elsewhere, but not to Germany's advantage. The war and subsequent power redistribution turned Germany into a vengeful nation that was going to haunt Europe in the following decades.

Wars do not just make or break states in Europe. In addition to World War I and World War II, the United States had engaged in a number of other significant wars in the twentieth century. In Asia alone, the US military involvement resulted in a unified Vietnam but a divided Korea and a separated China. War and American involvement changed all these states. The consequences of US interventions are still felt today both in the United States and in these countries.

At the beginning of the twenty-first century, the United States became engaged in a worldwide military campaign against terrorism. In 2005 it is still fighting the insurgents in Iraq and Afghanistan after introducing regime changes in both countries. Many ask if the American power will experience "imperial overstretch" and eventually decline like all previous hegemons. According to Yale scholar Immanuel Wallerstein, *Pax Americana* is already over. In fact, the United States has been fading as a global power since the 1970s. Currently, the United States has become "a lone superpower that lacks true power, a world leader nobody follows and few respect, and a nation drifting dangerously amidst a global chaos it cannot control," declares Wallerstein.[21] So the real question is not whether US hegemony is waning but whether the United States can devise a way to descend quietly, peacefully, and gracefully, with minimum damage to the world, and to itself.

Not everyone would agree. Unilateralism and resort to military forces seem to have become major US foreign policy options at the beginning of the new century. The Bush administration is determined to maintain America's military preponderance and prevent any rival at all costs from surpassing or even catching up with the United States. "The National Security Strategy of the United States" published by the Bush administration in September 2002 states that the United States will never allow its military supremacy to be challenged the way it was during the Cold War.[22] As an old Chinese saying goes, one may set a house on fire but others are not to be allowed to light a lamp. Both friends and foes have difficulty in understanding this US policy.

Chairman Mao Zedong once said, "political power grows out of the barrel of a gun." To some extent, wars also helped Chinese communists to expand and eventually gain control of the country. China's contemporary process of national unification can be traced back to the Northern Expedition of 1925–8. Although under Chiang Kai-shek's command, that campaign included many of the military and political officers who would subsequently constitute the PLA. The communist and PLA forces steadily grew during the Chinese war of resistance against Japanese invasion from 1937 to 1945. The communists came to power and established the PRC as the victor in the subsequent Chinese Civil War. The ramifications of the 1962 Sino-Indian war can still be strongly felt today, and not until very recently have the two Asian giants improved their relations. The 1969 Sino-Soviet border clash demonstrated the escalation of the ideological and political split between the two communist neighbors. China has not fought any major wars since the brief 1979 border war with Vietnam. That war marked an end to the period of radical infighting and domestic turmoil and ushered in a new era in the PRC history. Since then China has striven to improve relations with its once hostile neighbors and other major powers. Unless Taiwan declares *de jure* independence, which will almost certainly force the PLA into the battlefield again, the PLA is unlikely to fight any wars in the near future.

After investigating all wars (defined to mean conflicts among nations involving 1,000 or more battle deaths) between 1811 and 1980, Mansfield and Snyder conclude that authoritarian states in the process of modernization and democratization are much more likely to become involved in war than either autocracies or fully developed democracies.[23] If a decision for war is an operationalization of a "more assertive foreign policy," Mansfield and Snyder's study suggests that transitional, modernizing authoritarian regimes tend to adopt a more assertive foreign policy. This conclusion is reinforced by other scholars who, using Wilhelmine Germany (1871–1914) as a case, studied strategies that authoritarian regimes have adopted in their attempt to maintain power during a period of great social and political transformation. According to these scholars, authoritarian regimes have three major ruling strategies to prevent social upheavals and to legitimize power: democratization, repressive dictatorship, and a more assertive foreign policy.[24] Germany adopted the last strategy, the strategy of diversion, also known as "social imperialism."[25] Dealing with the tensions generated by the profound processes of social and political change is a difficult job. Resorting to war and assertive foreign policies that led to war had been a frequent strategy in history.

The natural question is: will a rapidly changing and modernizing China resort to war as a strategy for solving all its social, political, and economic problems? In terms of the relationship between wars and states, a larger question will be: is war inevitable between competing great powers?[26] True, there are certain similarities between pre-WWI Germany and today's China: Germany underwent and China is undergoing record-breaking rates of economic growth along with a derivative wide-ranging transformation of social relations. This transformation was and is presided over by an authoritarian regime. But there are more fundamental differences between the two countries; the most obvious of which are the global political and economic systems, the foreign policies of the two countries, and their relations with other powers. These vast differences suggest that China may well adopt a different strategy as a solution to its different challenges. As stated before, the outcome of a power transition, especially decisions for war or peace, is determined by a combination of international, domestic, societal, and individual factors. All evidence suggests that China has a basically positive evaluation of the status quo of its relations with other powers and its position in the America-led international system. There is no need for China to seek military solutions to disputes with the United States.

Perceptions in international relations

History provides clear warnings that rising powers tend to destabilize their regions and even the global power balance. This was certainly the case for Germany and Japan at the end of the nineteenth century. Will China be perceived the same way as Germany and Japan were? And how will a rising and more confident China perceive the policies of other powers?

Situated in the heart of Europe, pre-WWI Germany was surrounded by competing, hostile neighbors, whereas the insular state of Great Britain made it relatively free from invasions. In a great power competition, it should have been Germany that felt more threatened in the chaotic European continent. Similarly, China borders over a dozen countries, some of which are China's historical enemies and have even fought wars with China in the recent past. China has more nuclear neighbors than any other nation. The United States, in contrast, is flanked and protected by two huge oceans with two weak but friendly neighbors to the north and the south. This geographical feature suggests that pre-WWI Germany and present-day China would feel less secure than their competitors.

But modern technology and globalization make geographical locations less significant in state-to-state relations. Perhaps more importantly, perceptions will determine state-to-state interactions. How its neighbors and rivals treat it becomes a critical consideration in a state's foreign policy decision-making. For example, if China does not perceive any threat from its neighbors and rivals, it may continue to concentrate on domestic development without increasing its military budget; to the extent that China feels threatened by its neighbors and rivals, it may develop a second-strike capability to ensure its national safety. Policy changes in surrounding countries, such as the expanding role of Japan's Self-Defense Forces, nuclearization of South Asia and the Korean peninsula, and America's Theater Missile Defense program in East Asia, have all created great security concerns for the PRC.

By the same token, geographic location itself does not make a power a threat to its neighbor. If the power is perceived as benign, its rivals and its smaller neighbors will feel secure all the same. On the other hand, a state can be considered a threat by another state even if they do not share borders. In the German–British case, though separated from the continent by the English Channel, Great Britain still felt insecure after Germany's naval buildup since a powerful German navy would render geographic distance between them irrelevant. In the US–China case, physical distance has not been the critical factor that determines the nature of the relationship. With modern transportation, the vast Pacific Ocean can be crossed in a very short time. Modern military weapons also make geographic location of a state a less important factor in a potential war.

America's military role in East Asia after the Cold War has never been explicitly defined. It is unclear whether the US military forces in East Asia are intended to prevent Japan's re-militarization or North Korea's aggressive policy toward the South or are simply intended to contain China. And what will happen to US forces in South Korea after the Korean peninsula is reunified? These motivations and perceptions of the US military role in East Asia are important in China's decision-making. If the United States goes ahead with the Theater Missile Defense program in East Asia, especially if the program covers Taiwan, how will the United States manage its political and security relations with the PRC? Since China is still a land-based power with little projection capability, its security concerns have to be taken into consideration by the United States, which enjoys superior naval and air forces and which has forward deployment troops near China. The United States may have to address this issue in developing its military strategy toward East Asia in the twenty-first century. Similarly, the United States is unclear about the intentions of China's military modernization. Is it intended to combat US forces in the region? What kind of relationship can the PLA and US forces in Asia have? Will China attempt to drive US forces out of Asia? Transparency in Chinese defense objectives and strategies will help to alleviate US concerns.

The nature and intention of the rising power are perhaps more consequential than the systematic reconfiguration of capabilities in determining war or peace associated with power transition in the international system. Nations arm to defend themselves against what they perceive as a potential threat to their national interests. But this often creates a security dilemma, since in so doing they may become a threat to their neighbors, regardless of whether or not they have aggressive designs against their neighbors. In short, capabilities may become a threat regardless of intentions. This is particularly true in China's case, given the colossal size of China compared with its neighbors. Even though the PRC has largely been a defensive regime, some people, especially strategists in Taiwan, Japan, and the United States, still feel alarmed by any military upgrading of the PRC.

In fact, China is now further behind the United States in military power than it was in 1990. And the gap may be widening further. This is not just the Chinese perception of the reality; American political and military leaders also realize this.[27] Needless to say, China is seriously reacting to this comparative decline in military strength. The problem is that, the minute China begins to react to what it sees as an increasing gap with the United States by strengthening its military might, its neighbors and the United States begin to get worried. The United States becomes concerned that its interests in Asia may be sacrificed. At this point, the United States appropriately worries that Beijing is seeking to boost the potential costs to America of intervention on Taiwan's behalf in the event of a breakdown of peace across the Taiwan Strait. The challenge for the United States is how to dissuade China from using force in resolving cross-Taiwan Strait conflict that may involve the United States. China's problem is how to keep its poorly equipped military from falling further behind the United States without alarming Japan, India, Taiwan, and the Southeast Asian nations, and without eliciting a dramatic reaction from the United States.

Taiwan obviously feels most threatened by the PLA's military modernization, especially the deployment of short-range missiles along China's southeast coast. From Beijing's perspective, the PLA's military preparedness is defensive in nature. The missiles deployed opposite Taiwan are in response and serve as a deterrence to Taiwan's increasing unwillingness to negotiate with the mainland on terms of reunification. Taiwan's determination to expand international space and to seek wider recognition for its economic and political achievements presents a headache for the PRC leadership. As a country still growing, the PRC needs a peaceful environment for its economic development; it definitely does not want to be perceived as an aggressive power in Asia. Yet Taiwan's slipping away from the once mutually agreed upon "one China" framework leaves the PRC with few options. China has made its intentions clear that peaceful unification with Taiwan is what it pursues, but the emergence of an officially independent Taiwan is to be met with a PRC military attack. In view of this, it may be far-fetched to claim that the PRC is an aggressive power based on its resolve to unify with Taiwan simply because the PRC is reasserting an indisputable Chinese claim over part of its own territory and not setting its eye on somebody else's land. Nevertheless, it is helpful for the PRC regime to emphasize that peaceful unification is the preferred policy.

Japan also worries about growing Chinese military power. After all, the two Asian powers fought several major wars in the nineteenth and twentieth centuries. Japan has warmed up its economic and trade ties with the PRC since the 1970s, but political relations between the two countries remain volatile. Japan's own foreign policy has become more assertive since Prime Minister Junichiro Koizumi took office in 2001. In December 2004, Japan passed its "New Outline for National Defense" and a medium-term defense force development plan for 2005–9, in which China was singled out explicitly as a major threat for the first time. Whereas China and other countries have downplayed their border disputes since the mid-1990s, the Japanese government stirred up a diplomatic war with China by informing the Chinese government in early 2005 that the disputed Senkaku Islands (Diaoyu Dao) would be officially administered by the Japanese coastguard. Japan has apparently become uncomfortable with China's rising stature, since the oil sources and sea lines increasingly seen as vital by China have long been viewed the same way by Japan. In early 2005 Japan also had disputes with South Korea and Russia over territory and history. Anti-Japanese protests in Chinese cities in April 2005 plunged Sino-Japanese relations to their lowest point in 30 years. Both countries had to undertake some damage control to prevent the relationship from further deteriorating. The challenge for China and Japan is to turn these two rival tigers on the same mountain into two horses running neck-and-neck so that both will gain as a result of a friendly competition.

Interestingly, however, most other Asian nations do not seem to perceive China as dangerous. These nations, particularly in Southeast Asia, see China's rise as bringing great opportunities. They recognize China's economic and military power and even defer to China's wishes. But they apparently do not see China as a security threat.[28] Singaporean, Malaysian, Australian, and other national leaders have openly welcomed China's rise as providing development opportunities for their own economies. In Australia, according to a survey conducted in late 2004 and early 2005, 69 percent had "positive feelings" toward China, while only 58 percent had such sentiment for Australia's staunch ally, the United States. Only 16 percent were "very worried" about China's growing power, while 32 percent were "very worried" about US foreign policies.[29]

A BBC World Service poll of 22 countries found that China was viewed as playing a significantly more positive role in world affairs than either the United States or Russia. Asked about possible future trends, most were positive about China significantly increasing its economic power in the world but most were concerned about China significantly increasing its military power.[30] The poll, which was conducted between 15 November 2004 and 5 January 2005 for the BBC World Service by the international polling firm GlobeScan together with the Program on International Policy Attitudes

(PIPA) at the University of Maryland, also suggests that young people (aged from 18 to 29) worldwide are much more prone to view China positively (58 percent on average). Particularly striking is that, even in neighboring Asian countries that have historically shown substantial suspicion of China, views are relatively benign. Most notable is India, where 66 percent viewed China positively, despite decades of tensions and a history of border clashes. Positive views were also found in the Philippines (70 percent), Indonesia (68 percent), and Australia (56 percent). The challenge for China, it seems, is to persuade those who feel worried or threatened by the PLA's modernization that it is not a component or an indication of China's aggressive foreign policy. Why can't an increasingly wealthy nation upgrade its obsolete military?

Though having the most powerful military force among all claimants, China has not taken any military measures to assert its claims over the disputed Spratly Islands since 1990. China's active participation in the Association of Southeast Asian Nations (ASEAN) plus Three (Japan, South Korea, and China) regional economic and security forum and its proposed free trade agreement with the region are constructive and positively received in the region. Although geographical locations cannot be changed, what China can do, through words and deeds, is change some people's misperceptions that China is a threatening power.

Even in Taiwan, China's new leaders were developing some new strategies in 2005. Long perceived by the Taiwanese as inflexible in its insistence on the "one country, two systems" model for unification, the Chinese leadership invited opposition leaders Lien Chan and James Soong to visit the mainland and promised to continue to promote cross-Strait exchange and stability. The PRC leaders finally seem to be learning that "honey works better than vinegar" in winning the hearts and minds of the Taiwanese.[31] Whether Beijing's new "charm offensive" will be positively received and reciprocated by the Taiwanese government remains to be seen.

Globalization and power transition

What is the impact of globalization on future power transitions? What is the meaning of "power" in an age of deepening interdependence and globalization? These questions have to be answered as we predict a potential power transition in the twenty-first century. "Power" is a notoriously elusive term to define or to measure now. Even within the realist school, there is no agreement over what "power" means and how to measure it. Some scholars have taken the initiative to define "power." One of the most often cited definitions is "the ability to get others to do what they otherwise would not do."[32] But this only indicates what "power" can do without explaining what "power" really is. Another problem with this behavioral definition is how to distinguish "power" from "influence." A player, with all its capabilities, certainly can affect the actions of others. But is this "power" or "influence?" A small and not so powerful player in international relations may have big "influence" on others, as evidenced by Israel and Taiwan and their lobbying power in the United States.

Power is fungible and takes different forms. The bases of power are many and varied. Some scholars define "power" in terms of the scope and sources of power. Examples are Hart's three approaches to the measurement of power: control over resources, control over actors, and control over events and outcomes.[33] This definition identifies where power comes from and itemizes a powerful nation's capabilities, but it remains unclear what "power" itself is. Different forms of power may fundamentally change the conduct of international relations. Unlike rivals such as France or Prussia, which shared land borders with often hostile powers, Britain could shelter behind the English Channel in the nineteenth century. This did not guarantee immunity, but it did mean that normally the British did not need the sort of large standing army that became familiar on the European continent. The navy was Britain's main barrier against hostile forces crossing the Channel. Sea power alone would soon become inadequate. The use of bombers during World War II heralded the new addition to traditional military power and changed the conduct of war itself. The possession of nuclear weapons and other weapons of mass destruction has become an aspirational symbol of national greatness in the nuclear age. Likewise, in the information age, power becomes more permeating and difficult to control. A click on the button or mouse can instantly turn the world upside town. How terrifying!

Power comes from different sources. To distinguish different sources of power, some scholars have introduced the concept of "hard power" and "soft power" into the study.[34] According to Nye, the sources of hard power include population, territory, natural resources, economic size, and military forces. Sources of soft power include political leadership, morale, culture, ideology, and institutions. Hard power is linked to coercion and force in international politics, while soft power is associated with persuasion and exemplary behavior. This neorealist interpretation of power is echoed by some other scholars such as Knutsen, who defines power as a composite of military force, economic wealth, and command over public opinion, and "power transition" theorists, whose concept of power is a combination of population, economic productivity, and political effectiveness.[35] This neorealist view of power that contains a normative dimension also coincides with the "three main classes of power" proposed by Italian political philosopher Bobbio: economic, ideological, and political.[36]

Many argue that, in an era of globalization, soft power will become a more important component of national strength. But "soft power" is even more difficult to measure or define. Globalization brings about both opportunities and challenges. If the greatest threat to national security comes from terrorism, then the solution does not lie in traditional hard power; rather the answer is expanded intelligence capability, multilateral cooperation, and promotion of freedom. Historically, those states that possess predominant economic and military strengths would become powers and dominate the system, having the ability to affect the actions of other players. The military and economic dimensions of power will remain important in an interdependent world today.

In the lexicon of power transition theory, power is a combination of three elements: the number of people who can work and fight, economic productivity, and the effectiveness of the political system in extracting and pooling individual contributions to advance national goals.[37] How much power these capabilities endow a state with generates the ability to project influence beyond its borders. Politically capable governments garner relatively more resources and thereby expand national power as well as influence overseas. So power transition theorists take both "hard" and "soft" power into account when defining power. To possess power sources alone does not make a state a power. There is the question of power conversion. Power conversion is the capacity to convert potential power, as measured by resources, to realized power, as measured by the changed behavior of others or desired outcomes. Whether a state will become a power depends on the state's ability and skill to translate potential power into real power. Similarly, a state with great power does not automatically make that state a threatening one. It depends on how that nation uses that power. In this sense, it is extremely important for the international community to work together to ensure that China take advantage of its increasing power for the well-being of its citizens, not for expansive purposes.

Many international relations scholars, especially those from the realist school, have assumed that the international system is anarchic by nature, with no higher authority above independent, sovereign states. As a result, states have to compete for power in a self-help environment. For many realists, the desire for power is rooted in the nature of man. The history of international relations is the history of states competing for power, they would contend. In the measured words of Thomas Hobbes, from the eleventh chapter of *Leviathan* (1651), "I put for a general inclination of all mankind, a perpetual and restlesse desire of Power after power, that ceaseth onely in Death."[38] Neorealists, rather than viewing power as an end in itself, see power as a possibly useful means. States struggle for power in order to obtain and maintain security in an anarchic world. Realist scholars have focused on the study of states as the most important players in international politics. Those states that possess and are willing to use tangible and intangible power are considered "powers" in the international system. When a power is able to dictate, or at least dominate, the rules and arrangements by which international relations are conducted, then it becomes a hegemon. "Economic hegemony implies the ability to center the world economy around itself. Political hegemony means being able to dominate the world militarily."[39]

Power is not absolute but relative. What matters is not abstract rankings of great powers but the complex balance of forces in each particular power relationship. For example, Great Britain, in absolute terms, was much more powerful and wealthy in the mid-twentieth century than in the mid-nineteenth century, but compared with other nations, especially the United States, British power had greatly declined. No matter how power is defined or measured, an equal distribution of power among major states is impossible. The processes of uneven growth mean that some states will be growing and others declining. These transitions in the distribution of power stimulate statesmen to form alliances, to build armies, and to take risks that balance or check rising states.

However, it should be pointed out that power can also be possessed by non-state actors, especially in an era of globalization. Osama bin Laden and his terrorist network are a prime example. Though states remain the most important actors in the system, non-territorial actors such as multinational corporations, transnational social movements, international organizations, and even individuals are challenging the territorial state in controlling the resources in contemporary politics. This point is driven home by the 11 September 2001 terror attacks on the United States. And it is such a kind of power possessed by non-state actors that may fundamentally change the conduct of international relations in the twenty-first century. If Professor Rosecrance is right, states will become virtual in an information age, with more power delegated to the business world and other non-state actors. The power of a state will increasingly be based on intangibles and brainpower, and the territory-based capacity of production will drastically be downsized.[40] This change will definitely affect future power transitions.

In classical realism, most studies on the rise and fall of powers have focused on the military and economic dimensions of power of leading nations in the international system. Realists tend to be pessimistic about great power interactions since great powers fear each other and always compete with each other for power. In a study of great power politics, University of Chicago professor John Mearsheimer called the great power competition a "tragedy" in international relations. In an anarchic world, great powers that have no reason to fight each other – that are merely concerned with their own survival – nevertheless have little choice but to pursue power and to seek to dominate the other states in the system. "This situation, which no one consciously designed or intended, is genuinely tragic."[41]

Some argue that the interdependent relations among great powers before World War I failed to prevent them from drifting into deadly conflict, so globalization probably cannot do so either. The difference between today's globalization and yesterday's interdependence is not a mere matter of higher and faster economic transactions, but a qualitative one. Interdependence links states, whereas globalization integrates them, making the world like one global network. Military power may not translate into economic might, but participation in global production networks certainly does. No wonder at the turn of the twenty-first century nearly all states have proclaimed their willingness to have their economy integrated with international productions and markets.

Like Rome, Great Britain was an empire of control, while US power has been based on both material power and influence. The US position of power in the world was obtained less by design than by circumstance. A city upon the hill, the United States is often considered to command a moral high ground as it proclaims to represent the best of human potentials in a free society. While the United States continues to dominate the world militarily, economically, and technologically, its policies and practices in world affairs have been criticized by friends and foes. By taking such unilateral approaches as shying away from the Kyoto Protocol and the International Criminal Court and resorting to military options to resolve international conflicts, the United States has somewhat alienated itself from the international community at the turn of the twenty-first century. Unlike its material power, its soft power has become more vulnerable. Whether this will precipitate or accelerate the decline of the American superpower is an interesting question for students of history and international relations.

Globalization itself is a dynamic, evolving process that creates new vulnerabilities along with new opportunities. It ties states together through trade, technology, information, and interdependence. But it also is a conduit for the spread of terrorism, weapons of mass destruction, diseases, crimes, drugs, financial contagion, global climate changes, and trafficking of human beings. Such problems inevitably demand collective responses. Without partners, no country can easily or efficiently tackle problems that transcend its borders. For example, al-Qaeda operates in more than 60 countries. HIV/Aids and tuberculosis do not stop at Immigration and Customs. Industrial emissions from one country do not respect national borders. So joint efforts need to be the norm, not the exception, if we are to successfully address the transnational challenges that define this era. Globalization provides a rare opportunity for great power cooperation. It is imperative that China become a fully fledged participant in fashioning multinational solutions to global problems. When China becomes one of the makers of the new rules in a globalized world, it is not likely to seek a change in the international regime violently.

China seems to understand that, in the era of globalization and interdependence, national strength comes not just from pure military and economic power, but also from its international behavior and policies. The fact that China has attempted to charm its neighbors and other powers with policies of cooperation and mutual development suggests that China is also slowly building its "soft" power.

Is China a threat?

Is today's China like pre-WWI Germany? In studying perceptions in international politics, an international relations scholar maintains that decision makers often rely "too quickly" and mistakenly on perceived historical lessons in making policies to avoid repeating past failures, with the assumption that "the contemporary situation resembled the past one so closely that the same sequence would occur."[42] In the current strategic debate over China, those raising the historical analogy of pre-WWI Germany simply use history as an anecdote without bothering to systematically examine the truthfulness of what is implied: that China is or will become like Wilhelmine Germany. True, like Germany in the late nineteenth century, China is also an authoritarian regime and is growing rapidly and uncertainly into a global system in which it feels it deserves more respect from the dominant power. But Wilhelmine Germany and today's China are fundamentally different in their foreign policy strategies, domestic development, international linkage, and leadership. And it is exactly these factors that will largely determine a country's future course of development.

Today's China, in relation to the wider international system, is neither the militarist Japan of the 1930s nor the ideologically and strategically threatening Soviet Union of the 1950s to 1970s. Its record since 1990 indicates that China does not pose a direct security or ideological threat to the United States. It is not regionally destabilizing and is in fact behaving internationally in a responsible fashion. China acted responsibly during the 1998 Asian financial crisis, for which it was internationally applauded. China has also steadfastly cooperated in the America-led campaign against global terrorism.

Whereas pre-WWI Germany was a revisionist power, unsatisfied with the international status quo and determined to change it to its advantage, today's China is a satisfied, status quo power, enjoying benefits from the current international political and economic systems and working to preserve these systems. Whereas Germany was seeking "justice" for its "place in the sun," China is striving for peace and stability in the world and the region so that it can concentrate on domestic development. Even in dealing with Japan, a country that invaded China and inflicted heavy Chinese casualties and loss, the Chinese government's position is not seeking justice. To placate anti-Japanese sentiments that are still strong in China especially among the older generations, the Chinese government may occasionally criticize Japan and ask Japan to reflect upon history and apologize for its war guilt, but Chinese leaders have emphasized cooperation between the two neighbors and the importance of peace in the region. In a speech commemorating the thirtieth anniversary of the normalization of Sino-Japanese relations in 2002, the then Vice President Hu Jintao remarked that the two countries should look ahead to the future and push forward mutually beneficial cooperative relations. They should expand their cooperation and efforts to promote peace and prosperity in Asia, he added.[43] After Sino-Japanese relations soured in early 2005 because of disputes over a Japanese textbook and Japan's ambitious foreign policies, President Hu and Japanese Prime Minister Junichiro Koizumi met during the Asia–Africa summit in Jakarta, Indonesia, in April 2005 and vowed to improve bilateral ties. Today's China is future oriented and is mature enough to have walked out of its past century of humiliation.

During the Cold War, US–China relations were built upon what they were against; today they are increasingly based upon what they stand for: peace, stability, growth, and freedom. US–China relations have moved from an anti-Soviet dependence to a modern partnership appropriate to the challenges of a global age. China does not have the capability or intention to challenge the American supremacy. Neither does it show an interest in doing so in the future. While China should continue its economic and political reforms and improve its images overseas, the United States government and public need also to learn more about China's rapid changes and look at China in a more realistic and positive light. In the end, people on both sides of the Pacific will realize that they have more in common and that they are not enemies of each other.

Thus far, the United States and countries in Asia have welcomed China's rise and benefited from the growing trade and investment ties that have accompanied China's rapid economic development and emergence as a major global trading country. Skillful Chinese diplomacy has also eased regional concerns about an incipient China threat, commented J. Stapleton Roy, former US ambassador to China.[44] The Chinese have recognized the potential dangers that a rising power can create and have advanced concepts such as *heping jueqi* (peaceful rise) and *heping fazhan* (peaceful development) to demonstrate that China intends to avoid the mistakes made by other rising powers, especially Germany and Japan. The most daunting task for the United States is to recognize the importance of adjusting its foreign policy and contemplating a global system in which there is room at the table for a stronger and more prosperous China.

China's surge in the past two decades has arguably been the most colossal political, economic, and social transformation in peacetime in all of human history. Can a quarter of the world's population move from an agrarian society to an industrial and information one peacefully and eventually become a benevolent global power without a major war? No one can answer this question with absolute certainty. This book, based on China's domestic and international conditions and China's role in international and regional affairs since 1990, argues that China's rise is very likely to be peaceful in the twenty-first century. States do not have to make wars, and wars do not have to accompany states during their ascendancy. This conclusion is supported by the summary of the comparisons and contrasts of the three cases in this book.

Preventive war

In discussing the future course of US–China relations, some people focus on the unpredictability of the Chinese regime and tend to conclude that China would be the troublemaker or war initiator if deadly conflict were to break out between China and the United States. The diversionary theory of war also suggests that a state plagued with tremendous domestic problems may decide to shift domestic attentions elsewhere by initiating a war overseas. Though there is no indication that China is ready to do that, this proposition may have some truth. However, it will be naïve, if not completely wrong, to rule out the possibility that the United States would launch a preventive war in the next couple of decades before China becomes too powerful.

Since the United States remains the only superpower with unmatched military predominance after the Cold War, some American political leaders have been tempted to rely on military solutions in international conflict. This is evidenced in America's military campaigns in Iraq, Afghanistan, the former Yugoslavia, Somalia, and Afghanistan, and its readiness to use force to rein in North Korea and Iran.

The George W. Bush administration published its first National Security Strategy in September 2002. The document outlines doctrines of striking foes first and shifts American military strategy toward preemptive action against hostile states and terrorist groups developing weapons of mass destruction. The document also states, for the first time, that the United States will never allow its military supremacy to be challenged the way it was during the Cold War. Dismissing growing criticism of America's unilateralism in international affairs, the document calls the American muscle-flexing "a distinctly American internationalism." "Our forces will be strong enough," Mr. Bush's document states, "to dissuade potential adversaries from pursuing a military buildup in hopes of surpassing, or equaling, the power of the United States."[45] With Russia so financially hobbled that it can no longer come close to matching American military spending, the doctrine seemed aimed at rising powers like China.

Certainly the United States will face a much tougher decision on whether it should go to war with China than with Iraq or Afghanistan, yet it is not completely inconceivable that the United States may use Taiwan as a pretext to launch a preemptive attack on China if the United States perceives China's rise as a threat to its regional and global interests. One such scenario may be like this: the United States, while still nominally sticking to the "one China" policy, may secretly encourage Taiwan to move toward official declaration of independence, thus invoking the PLA's attack on the island. In the name of defending freedom, democracy, and a loyal friend, the US military will directly clash with the PLA in and near the Taiwan Straits. If this were to occur within the next two decades, the United States would probably win and China's development would be drastically slowed. The United States would be able to continue to dominate world affairs for a much longer time before a potential new challenger could rise again. So a potential war between China and the United States may well be initiated by Taiwan or the United States itself, not by China as some of the "China threat" alarmists have claimed.

"Every war between Great Powers started out as a preventive war," concluded A. J. P. Taylor after a survey of European diplomacy between 1848 and 1918.[46] Indeed, preventive logic is a ubiquitous motive for war. Thucydides argued that the Peloponnesian War was at root preventive: "What made war inevitable was the growth of Athenian power and the fear that this caused in Sparta."[47] The Roman Marcus Cato favored destroying the weakened Carthage as a preventive measure, otherwise Carthage might rise again to threaten Rome. Frederick the Great attacked Austria in 1740 in part to exploit Austria's temporary weakness after the death of Emperor Charles VI.

He attacked Austria again in 1756 to interrupt Austrian preparations for a war of revenge. In 1904 Japan felt compelled to attack Russia by the daily growth of Russian military power in the Far East. Japan's general staff advised war because "the present is the most favorable time for this purpose . . . If we let today's favorable opportunity slip by, it will never come again." German hawks offered preventive arguments for war in 1914. General Moltke declared during the July crisis that "we shall never hit it again so well as we do now with France's and Russia's expansion of their armies incomplete." Reflecting on the war's origins in early 1918, German Chancellor Bethmann-Hollweg explained that "Lord yes, in a certain sense it was preventive war," motivated by "the constant threat of attack . . . and by the military's claim: today war is still possible without defeat, but not in two years!" On the eve of war in 1939, Hitler told his generals that Germany should fight to exploit "favorable circumstances [that] will no longer prevail in two or three years' time."[48] Preventive motives were evident in wars in history.

The growth of Chinese power has already caused some concerns in the United States. It is not impossible that the United States may launch a preventive war against a perceived hostile China before the latter becomes too powerful. The key lies in the perceptions of each other. While the Chinese views of America have been relatively constant and positive, Americans tend to view China through glasses of a different color. Before the 11 September 2001 terrorist attacks, the US government, especially the Bush administration, considered China a potential strategic rival capable of harming US interests in the Asia-Pacific region. The US campaign against terrorism and China's political and intelligence cooperation have temporarily reduced the market for the "China threat" propaganda in the United States. But the "China threat" view is deep-rooted in some quarters of American society, including some government officials – both Republican and Democrat – scholars, members of Congress, and conservative media as well as some misinformed or misguided members of the public. If China does not improve its international image through internal political reform and external public relations, and if some forces in the United States continue to consider and treat China as a hostile rival, there will always be the danger of a military conflict between the two countries based on the preemptive doctrine.

Most people would agree that the Taiwan Strait is the most likely venue for American–Chinese military conflict. Some people point to the PLA's missile deployment in Fujian and Jiangxi provinces opposite Taiwan as indication that the PRC's policy toward Taiwan is aggressive and should be contained. But the PRC's Taiwan policy has been consistent since the late 1970s when it dropped the militaristic slogan of "liberating Taiwan." Though the "one country, two systems" formula is unpopular in Taiwan, the PRC's fundamental policy toward Taiwan has been peaceful reunification. The PLA's military preparation, from the PRC's perspective, is defensive and an insurance policy to prevent Taiwan from officially declaring independence. The PRC's primary goal in the near future remains economic modernization. So it can be argued that instead of worrying about the PRC's intention of provoking a Taiwan Strait war, one may pay due attention to the scenario in which the United States plans to launch a preventive war against the PRC by explicitly or implicitly encouraging Taiwan to move further toward independence and thus provoking the PLA into a direct conflict with the United States. A crisis in the Taiwan Strait will provide an ideal window for the United States to launch a preemptive war if the United States makes such a choice.

Since the end of the Cold War, the United States has pursued a two-pronged strategy toward China. On one hand, the United States has sought to engage China, hoping that China will eventually become a peaceful democracy through extensive contact with the West. On the other hand, the United States has purchased an insurance against a revisionist China by strengthening its alliance ties in East Asia. A Taiwan Strait crisis has always been a contingency for the US military. In other words, the United States military is prepared to fight against the Chinese over Taiwan if it decides to do so.

The US's intentions toward China are also reflected in its nuclear strategy. The classified US Nuclear Posture Review delivered to Congress on 8 January 2002 and leaked to the press on 9 March 2002 revealed that China is one of the striking targets of US nuclear weapons.[49] This and the American determination to develop the national missile defense and the theater missile defense in Asia clearly indicate that the United States is actively preparing for the contingency of a future war with China. President George W. Bush's statement that the United States would do whatever it takes to defend Taiwan is another indication that the United States is prepared to fight with the PRC over Taiwan. While much attention has been paid to the military budget increase in China and China's missile deployment on the coast near Taiwan, America's development of new nuclear weapons and its secret war plans in Asia have largely gone by unnoticed.

Establishing stable US–China relations in the twenty-first century

Whether the United States and China are locked into a long-term path of escalating security conflict is unknown. At present, both governments appear to agree on the need for short-term economic and political cooperation based on each nation's own interests. However, bilateral cooperation on global and regional issues such as the war against terror and peace on the Korean Peninsula may collapse when circumstances change. For example, if US–Taiwan relations drastically warm up and Taiwan's president officially visits Washington, DC, US–China relations will undoubtedly plummet and the PRC is expected to cool down or suspend its cooperation with the United States on global and regional issues.

Norman Angell wrote a book called *The Great Illusion* in 1910, saying there would never again be a European war because it would be economic madness.[50] He was right about the consequence, but underestimated mankind's potential for suicidal behavior. To avoid the repetition of historical tragedies, the United States and China need to develop a more healthy and comprehensive bilateral relationship beyond the domain of economy and trade. Though trade and economic cooperation themselves cannot prevent war, the breadth and depth of interdependence between the United States and China are unprecedented. With a bilateral trade that tops US$100 billion annually, the two countries will hopefully delete war from their menu of choice. How to avoid or deescalate security conflicts in an era of globalization and deepening interdependence will be a great challenge facing political leaders in both China and the United States.

The good news about today's China and the United States is that they do not have the same simmering nationalism as Europe in 1914. Germany was a relatively new nation-state after it fought a war with France in 1871. It was allied to a declining multi-ethnic empire, Austria-Hungary, which was primarily concerned about the upsurge of Serbian and Slavic nationalism. This resulted, in turn, from the decline of the Ottoman Empire and the rise of a more economically dynamic Russia. The combination of rising nationalism, declining empires, and a European tradition of interstate warfare going back hundreds of years greatly eroded the potential for economic integration to contain the threat of renewed military conflict.

After the terrorist attacks on 11 September 2001, American nationalism has run high. But the aggressive foreign policy is somewhat balanced by the government's and the public's desire and determination to bring the declining domestic economy back to normal. In comparison, China is still a country with powerful nationalist instincts. But nationalism is also balanced by the necessity of the Communist Party to maintain legitimacy through continued economic prosperity. There is little doubt that China will increasingly regard itself as a great power. As such, it will expect more deference and respect from other countries. But such ambitions need not provoke conflicts if China continues to pursue internationally oriented economic and trade policies rather than expansionist foreign policies. There is no compelling reason or evidence to indicate that China is going to emerge as another dangerous superpower comparable to Germany prior to 1914.

Germans before World War I viewed themselves as victims of an international campaign to keep them from taking their rightful place in world affairs. Some Chinese hold a similar view due to China's humiliating history of Western domination and its perceptions of American obstruction of its great power status on certain issues. But there are many differences between the Germany of around 1900 and the China of today: land size, population, levels of development relative to Britain and the United States respectively, domestic and foreign policies, participation in international organizations, international environment, national leaders, etc. Most importantly, pre-WWI Germany was a revisionist power seeking "justice" from an unfair international system; today's China is basically a satisfied status quo power seeking peace and stability in the system. To a great extent, China today feels already an accepted and respected power. These differences underscore the importance of the core policy question the United States faces today: how will it bring a potential rival peacefully into the globalized world economy?

Political scientist Bruce M. Russett used "community and contention" to describe the close but complicated relationship between Great Britain and the United States during the first half of the twentieth century.[51] Today, "cooperation and competition" characterize US–China relations. The United States and China cooperate on a wide range of regional and global issues, but the two countries also have vast disagreements, especially over America's unilateral approach in world affairs and its Taiwan policy. Despite improvements in bilateral relations since the 11 September 2001 terrorist attacks, China felt deeply uncomfortable with America's unilateral approach to foreign affairs. While China supported the global campaign against terror in principle, it did not agree with the US policies in Iraq, Iran, North Korea, and elsewhere. And the Taiwan issue is both hopeful and treacherous, as rapidly growing economic ties across the Taiwan Strait are being matched by political stalemate and an escalating arms race. America's national interests require that it support the maintenance of Taiwan's democratic freedom, prosperity, and security, but the United States also has long-standing commitments, affirmed by all administrations since the 1970s, not to support a Taiwanese bid for independence. Instead of continuing to supply advanced weapons to Taiwan, which makes a military conflict more likely, the United States must be more creative and take the initiative to increase the chances of a peaceful resolution of cross-Strait issues.

As a historical power in Asia, the United States maintains vital national interests in the region. Some of these interests converge with those of China, such as ensuring stability on the Korean Peninsula and peace across the Taiwan Strait. As a global hegemon, the United States will not so easily give up its leading role in Asia, though there are speculations that the United States may reduce or even withdraw its forces from Asia after Korean unification. If the purpose of continued US presence in Asia is to serve as a balancer and to maintain peace in the region, then its role is welcomed by China. If its true intention is to contain China or prevent China from becoming a regional power, then conflict will inevitably develop between the two countries.

In the war with Germany, Britain was not only fighting for her safety, but fighting in fulfillment of her treaty obligations and in defense of her honor.[52] In comparison, when talking about defending Taiwan, some American officials and scholars argue that the United States has to come to Taiwan's help in fulfillment of America's obligations as written in the Taiwan Relations Act and in defense of America's credibility among allies and friends. But the United States has not specified under what conditions the United States will get directly involved in a conflict with China. If a Taiwan Strait conflict is initiated by a Taiwanese declaration of independence, is it worthwhile for the

United States to honor its "credibility" at the risk of engaging in a large-scale war with China?

In addition, the Taiwan Relations Act is a US domestic law. Some in America argue that the Taiwan Relations Act is "the law of the land" in the United States, while the three joint communiqués between the United States and China are just policy statements by the two countries. But can one country use a domestic law to justify its objectionable foreign policies to another party to the joint agreement? If every country were to justify its policies based on its own laws while disregarding international agreements, what kind of world would we live in?

On 4 August 1914, when the German troops, violating Belgian neutrality, marched through Belgium in response to the alleged French intention of invading Belgium, the British, who had determined to keep Belgium a free and independent state since the Congress of Vienna in 1815, finally decided to enter the war against Germany. Britain's interest, quite as much as Britain's honor, compelled her to take sides in the Great War.[53] If Britain had bargained away her obligation to defend Belgium, she would have lost her credibility and would one day have had to withstand unaided the attack of a Germany that would have become more powerful, more aggressive than the Germany of 1914. Today, similar arguments can be heard when some people in the United States talk about defending Taiwan from a possible Chinese attack. However, there are many significant differences between the two situations. First of all, it is very unlikely that the PRC will launch an unprovoked attack on Taiwan since it is in the PRC's best interests to maintain the strong economic interdependence and stability across the Taiwan Strait; second, Taiwan, whose future political relationship with the PRC has yet to be negotiated, is not a recognized independent and separate state; third, the PRC's policy toward Taiwan is not necessarily a barometer of its foreign policy. Even if the worst scenario happens in which the PRC takes Taiwan by force, either provoked or unprovoked, it should not be taken for granted that the PRC's foreign policy will become aggressive. Instead of defending Taiwanese independence, the United States has the obligation to ensure that China's national sovereignty and territorial integrity not be violated and that peace across the Taiwan Strait be maintained. This would require that the United States help to prevent Taiwan from moving toward *de jure* independence. Defending Taiwan's independence from China cannot and should not become an American obligation.

For the Taiwan issue to be resolved, wisdom, patience, and respect for the vital interests of each party are needed. Both the United States and China have to work hard to ensure that Taiwan does not dominate their bilateral agendas and that it does not obstruct their cooperation on a wide range of other issues. With deepening economic interdependence, perhaps a certain form of political association will emerge across the Taiwan Strait. If economic prosperity and political stability are the objectives for all, then the United

States, the PRC and Taiwan should all work together to achieve these goals. It is encouraging that in April and May of 2005, two major Taiwan opposition leaders, Lien Chan and James Soong, accepted Chinese President Hu Jintao's invitations and visited the Chinese mainland. They all reaffirmed their opposition to Taiwanese independence and their wish to seek peace and development across the Taiwan Strait. While welcoming such exchanges, the US government has also asked the Beijing leadership to talk to Taiwan's ruling party directly.

Historical lessons can and must be learned. With political wisdom from national leaders and active participation by citizens, helped by an increasingly globalized and interdependent international system, the United States and China are expected to form a smooth and cooperative relationship in the twenty-first century. The two great powers hold the key to continued prosperity and stability in the Asia-Pacific region; only through working together can they make a peaceful twenty-first century a reality.

7 US–China relations in the 21st century

US–China relations are arguably the most important and consequential bilateral ties in the twenty-first century. Since 1990, the bilateral relationship has experienced many ups and downs. What is the status of US–China relations now? What can we learn about the future trajectory of the bilateral relations from their interactions in the past and from other power transitions in history? This chapter summarizes the theoretical and empirical discussions of previous chapters and explores how a potential power transition from the United States to China will take place peacefully in the future.

Toward a comprehensive theory of power transition and great power relations

Ever since A. F. K. Organski first formulated it as a competing theory to counter traditional balance-of-power theory (for example Morgenthau, 1948; Kissinger, 1957), power transition theory has undergone various modifications and expansions. The original basic statement of the power transition perspective is found in Organski's *World Politics* (1958), with extensions to the nuclear era in the second edition (1968). The fundamental test of the theory is found in Organski and Kugler's *The War Ledger* (1980). More theoretical testing and extensions are done by other scholars such as Bueno de Mesquita (1981), Kim (1992), Kim and Morrow (1992), Bueno de Mesquita and Lalman (1992), Kugler and Lemke (1996, 2000), Lemke (1997), DiCicco and Levy (1999), and Tammen *et al.* (2000), who have all contributed to the clarification and improvement of the theory.[1] But the power transition perspective remains far from satisfactory as a theory when used to explain and predict great power relations both at the global and regional levels.

Whereas balance-of-power theory is based upon the assumptions that the international system is anarchic in structure, that the power of each national unit is relatively fixed in relation to other units, and that nations can enhance their power through flexible alliance politics, power transition theory postulates that the international system is a hierarchical one led by a dominant country, that alliance politics is rigid and fixed rather than flexible (i.e., a nation is either satisfied or dissatisfied with the status quo), and that domestic power increases are the major sources of the greatest disturbances in the international system. Significantly, power transition theory identifies rapid domestic growth and change as the most important factors for a rising power to challenge the international order. It is the rise and fall of great powers and the growth differential that led to violent systemic changes in international history. Put simply, balance-of-power is a theory of statics, power transition is a theory of dynamics. The two competing theories provide alternative descriptions and explanations of the international system and about peace and war.

Power transition theorists do not completely dismiss the balance-of-power perspective. In fact, the balance-of-power theory has a longer history and still enjoys widespread acceptance among scholars of international relations. These scholars believe that under a power equilibrium decision makers tend to preserve peace, whereas a preponderant country or group of countries will choose to engage in war. The balance-of-power paradigm retains its influence in international politics in the modern era mainly because it provides a comprehensive framework for the preservation of national security in the nuclear age with weapons of mass destruction. Some reviews of the evidence on balance-of-power and power transition and their relation to war were inconclusive with respect to both.[2] The two rival theories may continue to find acceptance among different scholars, though both have explanatory and empirical limitations.

Even power transition theorists themselves realize the limitations of their theory and suggest that "power transition should be superseded by a more comprehensive perspective focusing on power parity as a correlate of war, rather than on intersections of power trends."[3] Is there a better theory? Certainly some other theories in international politics can also help explain the power transition phenomenon. The democratic peace theory, for instance, can help explain why Great Britain and the United States managed their power transition peacefully from the late nineteenth century until the end of World War II. Since Britain and America share democratic institutions and culture, they are expected to resolve their conflicts peacefully. In the past decade or so, expected utility theory has quickly emerged as a rigorously formulated, elaborately tested, and frequently used theory in economics and international relations. Whatever its advantages, nevertheless, the expected utility perspective has been a more or less static theory, not making much allowance for the dynamic structure of the relationships in the international system. It identifies friends and foes at any one point and makes predictions about the outcomes of conflict situations based on the calculation of the "expected utility" or costs and benefits, but it hardly captures the fluid domestic and international environments in which political leaders make their decisions, and it is not able to make any statement about what might happen in the international system in the future. What is known is well dealt with, but the theory is agnostic with respect to the direction of political tendency in the world.

A good international relations theory should have both explanatory and predictive strengths. A great challenge in the study of power transition is to connect power parity with alternative war and peace perspectives and develop a more comprehensive theory. The original power transition theory does not consider conscious policy intervention or decision-making as important variables. As an effort to take on the challenge, this book argues that power parity (or power preponderancy, for that matter) and status quo dissatisfaction only provide a window for war. Decisions for war or peace are not made by national leaders in a vacuum but are made under certain international and domestic conditions. In this respect, the two-level games logic, rational choice, and expected utility models may provide some insights to the complexity of decision-making. The Organskian power transition perspective only offers a structural explanation and leaves out important variables such as decision environments, perceptions, personality, and other factors affecting decision-making. The new framework developed and tested in this research is an agent–structure model. It treats power transition as a dynamic process and adds decision-making, statesmanship, and diplomacy to the discussion. The major thrust of the new model is that the outcome of a power transition is not pre-decided; rather, it is determined by a combination of war opportunity and political considerations. The process of a power transition and political decisions are molded by interactions of international environment, domestic politics, and societal factors. A multilevel analysis at the international, domestic, societal, and individual levels that takes the changing international and domestic conditions into consideration offers a better and more comprehensive framework for explaining and predicting great power interactions in the international system.

This new framework (Figure 7.1) can not only explain why a power transition led to war or peace in history, but also predict what is going to happen and therefore provides pertinent policy recommendations in order to avoid war during a future power transition. Through this framework, better explanations are offered with regard to why the Anglo-German power rivalry ended violently and why the Anglo-American power transition resulted in peace. Judging from all four levels of bilateral interactions, one can conclude that Great Britain and Germany (1871–1914) were trapped in a classic security dilemma with mutual mistrust, poisoned social relations, and a spiral arms race; whereas the United States and Great Britain (1865–1945) succeeded in establishing a Deutschian security community with mutual confidence, responsiveness, and expectations of peaceful solution of bilateral conflicts. Using the new framework, one can also find that interactions at all four levels between the United States and China since 1990 have been mostly positive or moving toward positive directions, but problems exist at all levels. The research suggests that the two countries need to further develop their relationship, build mutual trust, and prevent contentious issues from dominating their agendas. It is further argued that, with prudent statesmanship and popular support, the United States and China can manage their rela-

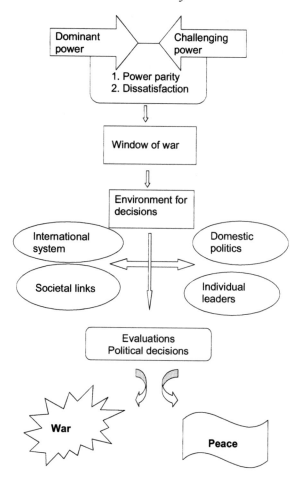

Figure 7.1 Power transition and great power relations: a multilevel analysis.

tionship peacefully and smoothly in an era of globalization and deepening interdependence.

The new framework modifies Organski's original power transition theory in that it incorporates the vigor of other relevant international relations theories into the study of power transition. It provides a clearer and more comprehensive model than the original power transition theory and complements similar perspectives. Among others, the two-level games theory, democratic peace theory, deterrence theory, international regime theory, security dilemma theory, expected utility theory, and security community theory can all be used to offer part of the explanations. This book acknowledges the vitality of these theories. Yet the framework developed in this book is a better model and provides more complete explanations than some of the competing theories. The democratic peace theory, for example, may explain why Britain and the United States did not fight each other during the period surveyed; it cannot be used to satisfactorily explain the British–German case or predict the American-Chinese case since they are not democratic dyads. And it cannot be used to explain why Great Britain and the United States engaged in a war in 1812. The two-level games theory links international and domestic factors, but it is deficient in analyzing the roles of individuals in decision-making. Similarly, deterrence may explain why the two superpowers did not go to war during the Cold War, but the dynamics of decision-making on either side are not fully accounted for.

An important contribution of the new framework to the study of international relations is that it stresses the role of statesmanship and diplomacy. The original power transition theory is basically a historical–structural interpretation, rendering decision makers powerless and irrelevant. This new framework offers an agent–structural interpretation, recognizing the importance of perceptions, individual personalities, decision-making, and diplomacy. Instead of being a prisoner of the international and domestic structure, a decision-maker is an agent in the structure capable of influencing the outcome of power transition. Decisions are made based on the overall evaluations of bilateral interactions at all four levels surveyed. If the government, the public, and top leaders in both the dominant power and the challenging power have positive evaluations of the bilateral relationship in a friendly international system, the two countries will be satisfied with their coexistence and power transition will end in peace.

In the British–American case, although initially some conditions at all four levels were negative, especially at societal and individual levels, toward the end of the period surveyed all conditions turned or were becoming positive, heralding the most successful and peaceful power transition in history. This observation is significant in that it provides hope for a peaceful power transition even between two powers with diverse and conflicting interests so long as they can control the negative aspects and settle their differences peacefully while accentuating the positive aspects of the relationship. Of course this requires prudent statesmanship and diplomacy. The new framework can better predict what would happen if a power transition were to occur from the United States to China or any other challenger. Accordingly, policy recommendations are significant for the United States, China, or any other power or group of powers in order to manage their interactions constructively before a potential power transition takes place some time in the twenty-first century.

Power transition can happen at both international and regional levels. This research framework could also be used to explain and predict regional power rivalry in, for example, South Asia between India and Pakistan, East Asia between Japan and China, South America between Brazil and Argentina, and the Middle East between Israelis and Palestinians and between Iran and Iraq.

US–China relations and power transition in the twenty-first century

Though the basic pattern of great power competition and cooperation remains unchanged, international politics has undergone some tremendous transformations as a result of economic globalization and deepening inter-dependence. Even the nature of power has dramatically changed. While the traditional material power – economic and military power – continues to be an important indicator of national strength, the so-called soft power that derives from cultural and ideological appeal and the capability to muster multilateral cooperation aimed at tackling global issues has become increasingly significant for nation-states today. In predicting future power transition, one cannot ignore the new conditions of globalization and multilateral institutions and the changed concept of power in international politics.

At the beginning of the twenty-first century, the United States remains the only superpower in international relations. Its preponderant military, economic, and technological edge is likely to remain unrivaled for at least another couple of decades. But other powers have grown rapidly and are quickly catching up. If the cycle of the rise and fall of great powers continues, American supremacy will gradually decline and America's global leadership position will weaken and probably be replaced by another major power sooner or later. How will the world's sole superpower deal with potential rivals in the international system? Should they be contained by powerful military alliances or engaged through exchanges and agreements? In particular, how should the United States cope with an emerging People's Republic of China? And how can the United States help to ensure the peaceful surge of China in the twenty-first century? These are important foreign policy and security questions for the United States and the international community today.

How power will be distributed in the twenty-first century remains an issue that invites debate, and forecasting the future of world politics over the next few decades is problematic since, among other things, international relations and national units are not constant, but change over time. Of all potential challengers, however, an increasingly powerful and confident China is becoming the most credible rival to US dominance in world affairs in the future, especially in the Asia-Pacific region. A potential power transition from the United States to China is based upon the assumptions that the existing national units, like the United States and China, will remain, that great powers will continue to rise and decline, and that the current trend of social, political, and economic transformation will continue around the world.

For those who do not agree with the prediction that the next power transition is most likely to take place from the United States to China, this book is also significant. The theoretical framework and policy recommendations developed from study of historical cases and analysis of contemporary US–China relations are generic and will be useful in predicting and managing a potential power transition from the United States to another power or group of powers as well as power transitions at the regional level.

Looking at the global political and security map at the beginning of the twenty-first century, it is not hard for one to assume that the United States is much more likely to go to war with China than it is with any other major powers. In fact, hardliners in both countries perceive one another as the most dangerous potential enemy and have prepared for the possible contingency near the Taiwan Strait. Other current or emerging great powers are aligned with the United States (EU and Japan), are struggling against crippling decline (Russia), or, while having occasional tense diplomatic relations with America, have no plausible reason for war with the latter (India). By all accounts, China's rise as both an economic and a military power is probably the greatest challenge for US foreign policy in the twenty-first century.

That causes of war exist does not mean deadly conflict will necessarily take place. It is hardly inevitable that China will challenge American leadership violently and that the two countries will embark on a collision course. The solution lies in how the two powers manage their relations during the uncertain period of China's rise and America's relative decline in the early decades of the twenty-first century. From the power transition perspective, the two nations have to remove contentious issues from their bilateral relationship. Good policy requires good judgment. Good judgment is "the ability to assess a situation accurately and, where applicable, prescribe a course of feasible policy that does the most to advance recognized interests and bring about desirable outcomes at the lowest possible direct and indirect costs."[4] Prudent statesmanship and diplomacy on both sides are the key. As in the Anglo-American case, mutual trust and responsiveness could be consciously fostered. It will be a great challenge for both powers to turn the currently most contentious and explosive issue – Taiwan – into an opportunity. Both China and the United States desire peace and prosperity across the Taiwan Strait. This provides a good foundation for the two sides to have serious dialogs and find the best available option for Taiwan's future.

Challengers to the existing international system are usually those powerful and dissatisfied great nations who have grown in power after the imposition of the existing international order. This book suggests that, although China's economic and military power continues to grow and its international influence continues to expand, it is hardly a dissatisfied revisionist power. Rather, it is a basically satisfied status quo power, eager to be part of the international community. China has benefited enormously from the international political and economic system since the late 1970s. China's development is shaped by the international system and, most significantly, as an important and active participant China is also helping to shape the changing international system at the beginning of the twenty-first century.

Because of its historical grievances against Western activities in China and unresolved issues such as Taiwan, perhaps the PRC will not become a fully satisfied great power. But the Beijing regime is pragmatic and has been taking advantage of the existing international order for its own benefit. Today's China is not a revisionist or revolutionary power that exports any ideology or attempts to alter the international system like pre-WWI Germany. By most accounts, China has behaved responsibly in international and regional affairs since 1990 and is not, as some have charged, a destabilizing force in Asia and the world. Its responsible policies during the 1998 Asian financial crisis were widely applauded; its pivotal role in defusing tensions on the Korean peninsula and South Asia was much appreciated and respected; and its cooperation and support for the war against global terrorism remain important for the United States and the international community. China's charm offensive in Asia, Africa, and Latin America has resulted in some concrete benefits in terms of trade and international image. While some people in some countries have expressed concerns about China's future development, surveys conducted in many countries after 2000 suggested that the majority in most countries seemed to have favorable views of a growing China. In addition to being the host of the 2008 Olympic Games, China has hosted several Fortune Global Forums as of 2005. The global "China rush" shows no sign of slowing down in trade and investment. China now feels accepted as a major, respected, and even envied actor in the international arena. It is actively pursuing multilateral approaches to trade and security issues and is rapidly opening its economy and society to increased foreign investment and influence. As a basically satisfied status quo power, China continues to contribute to and benefit from the existing international system and is not likely to challenge it violently.

A major difference between today's China and pre-WWI Germany is that China has proclaimed a policy of *heping jueqi* (peaceful rise) as a national strategy and objective.[5] This peaceful ascent will be beneficial and stabilizing to the region and the world, a view increasingly accepted by China's neighbors and other states. People in most countries view China's rise as a rare historical opportunity, rather than a threat. The so-called "China threat" is most likely to be heard in some quarters of Japan, Taiwan, and the United States and perhaps only there. Almost everybody else is talking about grasping the opportunities of China's growth for their own development.

Within China, the cliché term *zhonghua minzu de weida fuxing* (great rejuvenation of the Chinese nation) has quietly been replaced by the phrase *heping jueqi* (peaceful rise) since the word "rejuvenation" often makes neighboring countries suspicious that China might attempt to restore the imperial system. China has reassured the nations of East Asia, Southeast Asia, and the United States that China's rise in military and economic prominence will not be a threat to peace and stability, and that other nations will benefit from China's rise. Explicit in the *heping jueqi* doctrine is the notion that China's economic and military development is not a zero-sum game and that China represents less of an economic competitor than a source of economic opportunities. The doctrine emphasizes the importance of soft power and is based in part on the premise that good relations with its neighbors will enhance rather than diminish Chinese comprehensive national power. In diplomacy, the doctrine emphasizes multilateral cooperation through institutions such as the six-party talks concerning North Korea's nuclear program and the Shanghai Cooperation Organization. It also calls for less assertiveness in border disputes such as the Spratly Islands with Southeast Asian nations, Diaoyutai/Senkaku with Japan, and Aksai Chin with India. In addition, this doctrine seeks to avoid confrontation with the United States, acknowledging that trade with the United States is essential for China's economic modernization.

That history is replete with confrontations between incumbent dominant powers and rising aspirant powers does not preclude a peaceful power transition in the future. From its interactions with the dominant power – the United States – at all four levels of analysis, one can conclude that today's China is entering the international stage steadily and satisfactorily. The PRC regime harbors no ambitious or aggressive foreign policy objectives. Some people in the United States, Taiwan, Japan, and elsewhere may think that the PRC poses a threat to its neighbors, but China's military modernization is perhaps a natural outcome of China's economic modernization. There is no evidence that it is part of preparation for an expansionist foreign policy; rather it is a passive policy for defensive purposes. Why is it wrong for a military to modernize itself after its country's economy has been growing for decades? After all, China's military sophistication is decades behind that of the United States. To worry about China's long overdue military upgrading is probably an overreaction.

Granted, the PRC wants unification with Taiwan, peacefully for preference but militarily if necessary. At least in the near future, the PRC can live with the status quo of "no independence, no unification" of Taiwan. While some claim that the PLA's modernization and especially its deployment of short-range missiles near Taiwan threaten peace across the Taiwan Strait, the PRC argues, perhaps correctly, that the Taiwanese independence movement is the real source of instability in the region. There will be no need for the PRC to deploy any military facilities or forces to intimidate Taiwan if the latter does not forsake its Chinese links and move toward independence. So long as Taiwan does not officially declare independence or unilaterally alter the status quo across the Taiwan Strait, the PRC is not likely to conquer the island by military means. The military buildup is used to deter ultra-independence forces in Taiwan. One may note that crises and tensions between Taiwan and the PRC in recent years have largely been initiated and caused by provocative statements and actions of pro-independence Taiwan leaders, such as Lee Teng-hui's 1999 statement of a "special state-to-state relationship" across the Taiwan Strait and Chen Shui-bian's 2002 pronouncement of "one country on each side of the Taiwan Strait." Without the Taiwanese independence movement, which unnecessarily impairs China's core national interests, there would be no so-called PLA threat to Taiwan. The cause should not be confused with the effect.

China's preoccupation with domestic development issues and its good neighbor policy also make it unlikely to resolve territorial disputes with

Japan and Southeast Asian nations through military options. China's modernization is both a challenge and an opportunity for its neighbors as many Asian leaders and businesses have suggested; it need not become a threat. Most Asian countries are seeking cooperative relations with China, taking advantage of China's economic expansion to promote their own growth.

That China is not a dissatisfied power does not mean a peaceful power transition is guaranteed in the future. China's current political, financial, and social systems are not well equipped to deal with all the challenges and problems associated with its modernization and participation in economic globalization. The future of China is not predetermined, with many unpredictable developments and potential problems. Because of this, China's rise presents both challenges and opportunities for the United States and thus has to be handled cautiously by the United States. Policy makers in an established power are always faced with a dilemma: should they welcome the arrival of a strong competitor, or should they try to blunt it by restricting its economic and military expansion? The debate is far from over in the United States regarding the best strategy toward a rising China: engage and welcome it or contain and blunt it? The hawks in the United States must realize that, instead of blocking China's rise, the United States can shape China's development positively. Containment simply does not work.

Though overall US policy toward China since 1990 has been engagement, there are several aspects of containment strategies in America's China policy, such as forbidding technology transfer to China, selling weapons to Taiwan but preventing others from selling weapons to China, and firming up the US–Japan military alliance.[6] The US policy of engagement is based on the assumptions that China's national interests and intentions can change and that it can become a responsible and peaceful power thanks to domestic liberalization, external pressure, and internationally induced assimilation. But to bring China into the international system peacefully requires China's proper response. The current US engagement discourse tends to fixate on how the United States should deal with a rising China without giving adequate attention to how China will respond. This one-sidedness contains a major policy flaw: unilateral fixation tempts one to set preconditions for China to meet while ignoring China's concerns and demands, thereby fueling Chinese fear of containment and suspicion about US intentions.

China, like any other major power, has legitimate national interests and concerns. In the current US debate over China, whether or not China's legitimate concerns and demands need to be addressed is often unclear. The "China threat" proponents tend to focus on and often exaggerate China's potential capability but negate China's national interests. "An effective engagement policy entails a recognition and accommodation of China's preeminent security interest in maintaining regime survival and integrity, prohibiting Taiwan independence and other vital regional security concerns," contend two Chinese-American scholars.[7] To the extent that engagement implies change only on the part of China, it is doubtful that it will work well.

Hence, it is imperative for the United States to treat China as an equal partner whose interests should be recognized. Engagement without considering
rightful Chinese concerns and interests could be interpreted by the Chinese
as a comprehensive containment strategy aiming to belittle, destabilize,
and hold back China. The United States is advised to continue to encourage China toward participation in the open, global, market-based economic
order and rules-based political system and to avoid transforming it into a
power bent on overturning that order, as earlier emerging powers in history
have frequently tried to do. At the same time, China's concerns over political stability, national unity, and state sovereignty have to be recognized and
respected.

For some pessimists in both countries, China and the United States are
destined to be adversaries as China's power continues to grow. Some in both
countries predict daily a US–China conflict; they either propose wrong prescriptions or do not undertake diplomacy and statecraft to head it off. According to a popular book in China, "the fundamental conflicts between the
national interests of China and the United States that rouse deep passions in
both countries" might make a confrontation unavoidable. The basic problem
confronted by China is that the United States and other Western nations
are not willing to accept China as a major power, declare the authors.[8] This
kind of misinterpretation of intentions is also reflected in the "China threat"
argument in the United States. History reveals that misperceptions and misunderstandings are harmful to bilateral relations. And enemy images may be
self-fulfilling. Lack of mutual trust between the two powers is worrisome and
should be seriously addressed by political leaders, media, and the public.

In the United States some people believe that a policy of engagement of
China is doomed to fail. It does not matter whether China is a democracy or
not since great powers always head toward competition and conflict. So the
United States has "a profound interest in seeing Chinese economic growth
slow considerably in the years ahead," suggests University of Chicago political scientist John Mearsheimer.[9] This sounds like a rather wrong-headed and
naïve proposition. First of all, whether China's growth can be obstructed or
slowed "considerably" is a big question. Few outside America's hawkish camp
look at China so negatively. The Europeans and Japanese, for example, have
great interests in maintaining mutually beneficial relations with China and
helping with China's modernization. Second, even if the United States could
blunt China's development for a while, would it not be simply postponing a
conflict with China instead of defusing it? If future conflicts are inevitable,
then why not attempt to eliminate or at least decrease the sources of potential clashes now? States have different interests, yet states also cooperate
whether they are allies or not. The brief history of post-Cold War US–China
relations illustrates that the two countries can cooperate well on many international and regional issues while agreeing to disagree on several difficult
issues. The argument from the "containment" camp does not make much
sense in an increasingly interdependent world. A policy of containing China

is really a nonstarter. It could not be effectively implemented even if the United States sought to do so today; no other major powers will willingly join the United States in this useless effort. At the beginning of 2005, EU countries were planning to lift the arms ban on China that was imposed after the 1989 Tiananmen tragedy. This not only demonstrated the EU's confidence in a prosperous and peaceful China, but also suggested that any unilateral effort by the United States to contain China was unlikely to be supported even by its key allies.

More than 30 years after Nixon's historic visit to China, US–China relations have become robust enough to withstand major shocks. Despite some unresolved issues such as China's growing trade surplus with the United States and North Korea's nuclear program, as well as the issue of Taiwan-PRC relations, the bilateral relationship is not so fragile anymore.[10] Part of the reason is that the two governments have elevated the relationship to a strategic level. In addition to frequent phone conversations and meetings between the presidents and between the Chinese foreign minister and US secretary of state, the two governments started to engage in strategic dialogs at the ministerial level in early 2005. Although there were still differences, the relationship seemed to be getting "institutionalized."[11] The two countries have grown mature enough to resolve their differences through *duihua yu jiaoliu* (dialogs and exchanges). If such trend continues, direct military conflict will not become an option for either side.

Diplomacy and statesmanship

As the theoretical framework in this book indicates, war or peace decisions associated with power transition are made by political leaders after evaluations of the conditions of bilateral interactions at global, domestic, societal, and individual levels. Clearly, political will and perceptions are as important as the international and domestic structures. This agent–structure model emphasizes the role of leadership, diplomacy, and statesmanship. As the British–American case shows, national leaders committed to a strong relationship can make a difference. If the United States and China want to avoid future conflicts, national leaders on both sides need to consciously foster and develop a strong linkage across the Pacific Ocean. As the British–German case reveals, a bilateral relationship without strong popular support cannot endure. With huge sums of transactions going back and forth between the United States and China, the two societies are increasingly linked. Some sort of Deutschian security community could hopefully be formed between the two Pacific powers in the future. But this calls for prudent diplomacy and active public participation and support.

The original Organskian power transition theory emphasizes the importance of vital interests to a state's evaluations of status quo. If the vital interests of either the dominant power or the challenger are not respected and accommodated, a power transition tends to be violent. The pre-1914 relationship between Britain and Germany reminds us of what can happen when a dominant state refuses to accord a rising power the prestige and status to which it is entitled. This research suggests that both the dominant power and the challenger need to recognize and respect one another's core national interests. Only when both powers are relatively satisfied will a peaceful power transition become likely. It is unfortunate that pre-WWI Germany's legitimate rights as a rising great power were denied by the British determination to maintain its global leadership, and Germany had to go its own way. It is equally unfortunate that British Prime Minister Chamberlain and French Premier Daladier's appeasement policy at the Munich Conference failed to pacify Adolf Hitler before World War II.

However, accommodation and adjustment are part of statesmanship and diplomacy. They are fundamentally different from "appeasement" in the Munich sense. Prior to the late 1930s, "appeasement" did not mean feeding the appetite and power of an aggressor, but pacifying through compromise and concessions a conflict that threatened to erupt into war. Gracefully giving and taking remains the art of diplomacy and international relations, though a line has to be drawn to convince the opponent where it must stop if it becomes aggressive. As if Britain and its allies had learned a tragic lesson from World War I or they felt guilty of their harsh treatment of Germany after World War I, they chose to appease and defer to Nazi Germany's. They failed to halt Hitler's outright aggressions in the Rhineland, Czechoslovakia, and Poland. They did not know that an aggressor's appetite cannot be satisfied. On the other hand, if Great Britain had refused to adjust to America's rising power and its interests through a series of concessions, the two countries would probably have fought another war.

From the brief survey of China's foreign policy practices since 1990, one can see that today's China is totally different from either Wilhelmine or Nazi Germany, which harbored aggressive intentions and adopted aggressive policies. True, China has been assertive toward Taiwan in response to Taiwan's words and deeds that smack of independence, but China is not pursing aggressive policies toward other countries. This is demonstrated in its handling since 1990 of territorial disputes with Japan, some ASEAN nations, India, and Russia. In all cases, China has emphasized the importance of cooperation and mutual development. The PRC's Taiwan policy is not necessarily a barometer of its foreign policy. From the PRC's perspective, the Taiwan issue concerns China's core interests such as national unity, territorial integrity, and regime legitimacy. It is part of China's nation-building. The bottom line is that the PRC's unification ambition with Taiwan is not an aggressive policy designed to annex a foreign country.

The outcome of power transitions is not automatic and predetermined. Power transitions are socially constructed, and the ways to manage power transitions can be learned from history and from prudent judgment. Whether a power transition is peaceful or violent depends not only on the powers' material capabilities, their quantity and quality, and their intrinsic attributes, but also on interactive processes through which the identities and interests of the rising and the declining powers become established, and on the context of their interaction. To a large extent, therefore, peaceful transitions will depend on the ability and willingness of leaders and the public in both the rising and the declining powers jointly to discredit, delegitimate, and disempower domestic societal actors who play a role in constructing reciprocally conflicting images, identities, and interests.

The difficult relations between rival powers are structural at the international systems level, but domestic politics clearly sets the agenda of a power's foreign policy, as illustrated by Putnam's two-level games theory. For the United States and China, perhaps the greatest challenge is to rebuild and sustain a domestic consensus for maintaining a healthy relationship with each other. Politicians, media, opinion leaders, academics, and private citizens are all responsible for creating such an atmosphere in both countries. To better understand each other's intentions, *duihua yu jiaoliu* (dialogs and exchanges) between the two countries at all levels and in all issue areas need to be strengthened and expanded. The two countries must respect each other's core national interests and learn to coexist peacefully in an interdependent world.

Reinhold Niebuhr, philosopher, theologian, and commentator on American–European relations, once labeled Americans as "awkward imperialists," trying unsuccessfully to manage their wealth and the world with the same informal economic methods which had created their riches. This limited, awkward dominion aggravated world instability. Yet Niebuhr was optimistic that, if the United States could avoid this fatal error in the future, eventually "a world community" would emerge from the American empire. America had only to "prevent the wedding of economic and military power . . . since the more our economic power is supported by military strength, the more we shall be inclined to solve our problems by intransigence and defiance of world opinion, and the more shall we multiply animosities against us."[12] Since the late 1990s, the United States has largely abandoned the restraint urged by Niebuhr and others. It has often resorted to the unilateral approach in its foreign relations. The 11 September 2001 tragedy hardened the Bush administration's determination to go it alone if need be. President George W. Bush's tough rhetoric, such as "you are either with us or against us," leaves many nations with no choice. It seems encouraging that as President Bush started his second term in early 2005, he and his foreign policy team were emphasizing multilateral cooperation and diplomacy on issues such as Iraq's reconstruction and Iran and North Korea's nuclear programs. Diplomacy and statesmanship are also required to resolve differences between China and the United States.

While the United States maintains its military, economic, and technological advantages, its unilateral approach in international affairs has eroded its "soft power" to a great extent. While people around the world still look up to the United States as a haven of ultimate freedom and would agree with

America's assertion that human rights and democratic values are universal, how many of them would admire and support its behavior in the world? Fortunately, there are debates between the doves and the hawks within the United States, and the doves often push the hawks to adopt a more moderate foreign policy. As far as China is concerned, the doves and the engagement camp seem to have a much wider support base in the United States in the early twenty-first century. This is important since a stable relationship requires solid societal support.

If it is not possible to prevent China from becoming a future global leader, it is still possible to influence future relations between China and the United States by actions today. This research suggests that if the United States accommodates China's legitimate interests and further incorporates China into the multilateral international community, then a cooperative and friendly relationship could be established between the two major powers. The research also indicates that the changed conditions of globalization and interdependence in the international system provide the best opportunity for a peaceful power transition in the twenty-first century. Interdependence and extensive contacts between China and the United States already make the bilateral relationship one of the strongest in the world. Continued expansion and deepening of linkages between the two societies are likely to discourage national leaders on both sides from taking drastic actions in dealing with each other.

The "unsinkable" Taiwan issue

China has already been incorporated into the international system, including its admission into the WTO, thanks to a large extent to US support and cooperation. But the two countries still have several areas of disagreement. One major dispute is over Taiwan's future, although the disagreement on the issue is perhaps narrower today than three decades ago. Compared with other issues in the bilateral relationship such as trade imbalances, China's currency regime, intellectual property rights, human rights, and Tibet, only the Taiwan issue has the potential to bring the two powers into actual military conflict.

The American debate over the relative merits of engagement versus containment seemingly treats China as a static entity that will simply have to adjust to whatever policy the other nations pursue. What is not being discussed is how the United States should "adjust to" the reemergence of China as a peaceful great power. From the power transition perspective, whether and how the United States recognizes and respects China's vital interests is critical to the future course of Sino-American relations. To adjust to the PRC's legitimate interests in Taiwan does not necessarily mean to endorse the PRC's "one country, two systems" policy (though the PRC would hope so); but it does mean, at the minimum, to understand the PRC's legitimate concerns and side with the PRC in preventing Taiwanese independence, an outcome that would certainly be disastrous for Taiwan, the PRC, and the United States. Some in the United States tend to view Taiwan as a bargaining chip in dealing with the PRC, or as an "unsinkable submarine" that could be used to block the PRC's power projection. Few have explored the benefits to the United States of peaceful unification between the two Chinese parties.[13] Even fewer have ever thought about how to turn Taiwan into an opportunity, such as taking advantage of the expanding economic and social interactions across the Taiwan Strait to narrow the political gap between the two sides.

Since the Nixon administration, the US government has adopted the "one China" policy and has refrained from supporting a separate and independent Taiwan. The US government recognizes the Beijing regime as the sole legitimate government of China and acknowledges the Chinese position that there is only one China and Taiwan is part of China. This basic principle has been adhered to by all administrations. But America's treatment of Taiwan as a de facto nation-state, based on the Taiwan Relations Act, and its gradual upgrading of "unofficial relations" with Taiwan, particularly its increasingly robust sale of advanced weapons to Taiwan, have added elements of uncertainty to US–China relations and made a US–China conflict over Taiwan ever more likely. In power transition analysis, ways have to be found to prevent contentious issues from dominating bilateral agendas. Perhaps one solution to the Taiwan issue is for the PRC and Taiwan to form a loosely framed "one China" that is ruled by two separate entities, with Taiwan maintaining its political autonomy but not becoming an outright independent state. This framework would also give Taiwan much more freedom and autonomy than Hong Kong and Macao are enjoying under the "one country, two systems" formula.

Realistically, Taiwan's future lies in China both economically and politically. Instead of moving away from China, Taiwan should, as former Democratic Progressive Party chairman Hsu Hsin-liang has suggested, boldly go westward and cooperate with China during the latter's *heping jueqi*. Taiwan can set an example for the mainland to gradually democratize as its economy continues to expand. A more prosperous and democratic China with which Taiwan is closely associated serves the best interests of the 23 million residents in Taiwan.

To maintain stability and prosperity in East Asia is in America's national interests. The United States can definitely do more to promote cross-Strait exchanges and integration. Most importantly, if the United States helps in the process of China's peaceful unification, the accommodating gesture will be appreciated by the PRC, removing the largest hurdle in relations between the two countries, making a smooth relationship and a peaceful power transition most likely. Encircling or separating China with military alliances and using Taiwan as a pawn will only create a resentful and revengeful China. The United States welcomed the visits to the mainland by Taiwan's opposition leaders in 2005; it can do more to encourage the PRC and the ruling party in Taiwan to be more flexible in their positions and to talk directly.

Both China and the United States can contribute to the reduction of tensions in the bilateral relations over Taiwan. Many officials and scholars in the United States and Taiwan argue that the PLA's missiles aimed at Taiwan pose a great security threat to the island, which also constitutes a basis for the United States to provide military hardware for Taiwan's defense. Realizing this rationale, the PRC is well advised to withdraw some, if not all, of its short-range missiles from locations too close to Taiwan. Missile deployment near Taiwan has more political significance than military. This political gesture can also generate goodwill both on Taiwan and in the United States and may invalidate the basis for US weapons sales to Taiwan. As a political strategy, the PRC should be flexible in this regard. And since the "one country, two systems" model is unlikely to be accepted by Taiwan, the PRC must be more creative in directly addressing major concerns of the Taiwanese, including Taiwan's international participation and Taiwan's security.

As for whether the PRC should renounce the use of force in handling the cross-Strait conflict, it is another issue and can be discussed and resolved by both sides of the Taiwan Strait. An ideal solution would be simultaneous declarations by Taiwan that it will not pursue formal independence unilaterally but will strive for future unification, and by the PRC that it will not force the island into a union by military means but will strive for peaceful unification gradually. This is a feasible solution and is consistent with proposals suggested by scholars and former US government officials such as Kenneth Lieberthal. The PRC should also be flexible in permitting Taiwan to participate in some international activities such as international organizations that do not require statehood for memberships. And in organizations that are composed of sovereign states, the PRC government should consider how to invite Taiwan to participate as part of the Chinese delegation. In some cases such as at the World Health Organization, a "one mission, two delegations" model could also be considered to ensure that Taiwan's voice can be heard. Diplomatic isolation for Taiwan has long been hated and condemned by the Taiwanese public. It is up to the PRC whether and how it will accommodate the desire of the Taiwanese people to be represented internationally.

Conclusion

There are basically two ways to prevent war: by eliminating the sources of conflict that would lead a nation to resort to the use of arms, and by rendering the use of arms so unattractive that a nation would rather not start a war.[14] Britain and Germany failed to achieve either a century ago. Today globalization and deepening interdependence have linked China and the United States inextricably together. Military conflict can be avoided if prudence and sense prevail on both sides. With political wisdom and will from national leaders and public support on both sides, the United States and China can peacefully manage this multifaceted relationship and avoid another human tragedy associated with a potential power transition. Great powers are increasingly united by common interests, instead of being divided by conflicting ideologies. The twenty-first century holds extraordinary opportunities for the United States and China to form coalitions against new global challenges such as terrorism and environmental degradation. Properly managing this relationship will be an essential twenty-first-century undertaking for both countries.

Many in the United States are already aware of the importance of China's growing power and its great impact. This awareness, however, has not yet been translated into preparedness. For example, the workforce at the US embassy in China numbers approximately 1,000, which is half the employees planned for the new embassy in Iraq.[15] Training in Asian languages for US government officials has been increased only marginally. And only a few thousand American students are studying in China now, compared with the more than 60,000 Chinese who are studying in American schools. Despite the engagement policy embraced by all US administrations since President Richard Nixon, hardliners within the United States have attempted to jeopardize the policy, especially during election years. Clearly, much remains to be done to move the relationship to a higher level.

In China, people are discovering that economic development is the only lasting source of national wealth. But economic prosperity alone will not make China a great power. In time, more and more people will realize that social and political freedom is the only true source of national greatness. Ultimately, how China uses its increasing wealth at home and growing influence abroad are matters for the Chinese to decide. What the United States can do is to work closely with the Chinese to encourage China's peaceful transformation. The best option for the United States is not to inhibit the rise of Chinese power but to influence and adjust to it. Both countries have to learn to coexist peacefully and respect each other's vital national interests. Neither China nor the United States wishes to repeat the tragic mistakes the established powers made during the late nineteenth and early twentieth centuries.

In addition to the Taiwan dispute, both the United States and China also need to address other areas of disagreement such as human rights and nonproliferation. It is important for the PRC to understand the core values of democracy and human rights for Americans. Democratic principles are held so dearly in America that China simply cannot evade the issue of democracy and democratization in its future dealings with America. To become a more respectable great power, China has to improve its human rights record, support a free press, and promote political pluralism. This is in the long-term interests of China itself.

Since Immanuel Kant first proposed his tripod of peace in 1795, people have hoped that perpetual peace could be achieved in the world based on mutually accepted norms of democracy, commercial interdependence, and international law.[16] As we look at US–China relations in the early years of the twenty-first century, we cannot but notice that extensive economic, trade, and social links have pushed the two nations inextricably closer; both countries are major players in international organizations; and China is moving, albeit very slowly, toward a more liberal and democratic society. There are hope and reason to believe that peace will prevail between the two Pacific powers in the future.

Globalization, deepening interdependence, and modern communications afford a rare opportunity to learn from history, anticipate the pending profound changes in the world order that will result from China's *heping jueqi*, and fashion a strategy for dealing with this eventuality. Reviewing the interactions between the United States and China at all levels between 1990 and 2005, one can be cautiously optimistic about the future of US–China relations and a peaceful potential power transition in the twenty-first century. Although US–China ties since 1990 have gone through cyclical progressions, the overall movement has always been forward. If both the United States and China take on the historic challenge and exercise statesmanship and creativity, the two powers can not only cooperate well in global and regional issues, but also manage a potential power transition peacefully in the future.

Notes

1 Introduction

1 "Is China the World's Next Superpower?," Special Report, *Newsweek*, 9 May 2005, 26–47; Robert D. Kaplan, "How We Would Fight China," *Atlantic Monthly*, June 2005, 49–64.
2 Robert Gilpin, *War and Change in World Politics* (New York: Cambridge University Press, 1981), p. 15: "Although . . . peaceful adjustment of the systemic disequilibrium is possible, the principal mechanism of change throughout history has been war, or what we shall call hegemonic war (i.e., a war that determines which state or states will be dominant and will govern the system)."
3 A. F. K. Organski first stated the power transition theory in his book *World Politics* (New York: Knopf, 1958). Further discussion of the theory can be found in Chapter 2.
4 For Kenneth N. Waltz's "three images," see his *Man, the State, and War* (New York: Columbia University Press, 1959).
5 Jack S. Levy, "Too Important to Leave to the Other: History and Political Science in the Study of International Relations," *International Security* 22(1) (Summer 1997), 22–33.

2 Rethinking theories of power transition

1 For a fascinating account of the rise and fall of great powers, see Paul Kennedy, *The Rise and Fall of the Great Powers* (New York: Random House, 1987).
2 E. H. Carr, *The Twenty Years Crisis, 1919–1939: An Introduction to the Study of International Relations* (New York: Harper and Row, 1964), pp. 208–23.
3 Torbjorn L. Knutsen, *The Rise and Fall of World Orders* (Manchester: Manchester University Press, 1999), p. 21.
4 Arnold Toynbee, *War and Civilization* (New York: Oxford University Press, 1950).
5 Quincy Wright, *A Study of War* (Chicago: University of Chicago Press, 1965).
6 Immanuel Wallerstein, "The United States and the World 'Crisis,'" in Terry Boswell and Albert Bergesen, eds., *America's Changing Role in the World System* (New York: Praeger, 1987), p. 17.
7 George Modelski, *Long Cycles in World Politics* (London: Macmillan, 1987).
8 Nikolai Kondratieff. *The Long Wave Cycle*, new edition by G. Daniels and J. Snyder (New York: Richardson and Snyder, 1984).
9 George Modelski and William Thompson, *Leading Sectors and World Powers* (Columbia, SC: University of South Carolina Press, 1996).
10 Italics added by this author.

11 Jacek Kugler and Douglas Lemke, *Parity and War* (Ann Arbor: University of Michigan Press, 1996), p. 4, italics original.
12 Ronald L. Tammen *et al.*, eds., *Power Transitions: Strategies for the 21st Century* (New York: Seven Bridges Press, 2000), p. 21.
13 A. F. K. Organski, *World Politics* (New York: Alfred A. Knopf, 1958), p. 333; A. F. K. Organski and Jacek Kugler, *The War Ledger* (Chicago: University of Chicago Press, 1980), p. 59.
14 Jacek Kugler and Douglas Lemke, "The Power Transition Research Program," in Manus I. Midlarsky, ed., *Handbook of War Studies II* (Ann Arbor, MI: University of Michigan Press, 2000), pp. 130–1. Italics original.
15 Organski, *World Politics*, pp. 300–6.
16 Kugler and Lemke, "The Power Transition Research Program," pp. 132–3.
17 Democratic peace theorists argue that democracies or dominant states in the system are usually satisfied with the status quo. They tend to have a favorable evaluation of their status quo – one of the major reasons why democracies do not fight fellow democracies. For democratic peace theory, see, for example, Steve Chan, "Mirror, Mirror on the Wall ... Are the Freer Countries More Pacific?" *Journal of Conflict Resolution* 28 (1984), pp. 617–48; Bruce M. Russett, *Grasping the Democratic Peace: Principles for a Post-Cold War World* (Princeton, NJ: Princeton University Press, 1993); William Dixon, "Democracy and the Peaceful Settlement of International Conflict," *American Political Science Review* 88 (1994), pp. 14–32; and James Lee Ray, *Democracy and International Conflict: An Evaluation of the Democratic Peace Proposition* (Columbia, SC: University of South Carolina Press, 1995).
18 Kugler and Lemke, "The Power Transition Research Program," pp. 135–40.
19 Ibid., p. 130.
20 Bruce Bueno de Mesquita and David Lalman make this argument in their *War and Reason: Domestic and International Imperatives* (New Haven, CT: Yale University Press, 1992), see Chapter 6.
21 There is plenty of literature that deals with causes of war. See, for example, Kenneth Waltz, *Man, the State, and War* (New York: Columbia University Press, 1959); Greg Cashman, *What Causes War?* (New York: Macmillan, 1993); Nazli Choucri and Robert C. North, *Nations in Conflict: National Growth and International Violence* (San Francisco: Freeman, 1975); Stephen Van Evera, *Causes of War: Power and the Roots of Conflict* (Ithaca, NY: Cornell University Press, 1999); and Dale C. Copeland, *The Origins of Major War* (Ithaca, NY: Cornell University Press, 2000).
22 Organski and Kugler, *The War Ledger*, p. 51.
23 Bruce Bueno de Mesquita, "The War Trap Revisited: A Revised Expected Utility Model," *American Political Science Review* 79 (1985), pp. 156–77.
24 For the linkage of domestic and international politics, see Robert D. Putnam, "Diplomacy and Domestic Politics: The Logic of Two-Level Games," *International Organization* 42 (1988), pp. 427–60; and Bueno de Mesquita and Lalman, *War and Reason*.
25 Waltz, *Man, the State, and War*, p. 238.
26 Putnam, "Diplomacy and Domestic Politics."
27 For theory of deterrence, see, for example, Glenn H. Snyder, *Deterrence and Defense: Toward a Theory of National Security* (Princeton, NJ: Princeton University Press, 1961).
28 See Charles A. Kupchan, "Introduction: Explaining peaceful power transition" in Charles A. Kupchan *et al.* (eds.), *Power in Transition: The Peaceful Change of International Order* (New York: United Nations University Press, 2001).
29 Organski, *World Politics*, p. 366.
30 Midlarsky first proposed this argument. See Manus I. Midlarsky, *On War: Political Violence in the International System* (New York: Free Press, 1975).

31 See, for instance, Gerritt W. Gong, *The Standard of "Civilization" in International Society* (Oxford: Oxford University Press, 1984), Chapter 6.
32 Karl W. Deutsch, *et al.*, *Political Community and the North Atlantic Area* (Princeton, NJ: Princeton University Press, 1957).
33 Paul Papayoanou, *Power Ties: Economic Interdependence, Balancing, and War* (Ann Arbor, MI: University of Michigan Press, 1999), p. 156.

3 British–German relations, 1871–1914

1 For general causes of WWI, see, for example, James Joll, *The Origins of the First World War* (London: Longman, 1992); Gordon Martel, *The Origins of the First World War* (London: Longman, 1996); and Luigi Albertini, *The Origins of the War of 1914* (London: Oxford University Press, 1952). For Britain's and Germany's roles respectively, see Zara S. Steiner, *Britain and the Origins of the First World War* (London: Macmillan, 1977) and Fritz Fischer, *Griff nach der Weltmacht* (Dusseldorf: Bertelsmann Universitätsverlag, 1961). For an argument emphasizing ideological conflict as the cause of war, see Charles Sarolea, *The Anglo-German Problem* (London: Thomas Nelson and Sons, 1912), and Charlie W. Eliot, *British and German Ideals: the Meaning of the War* (London: Macmillan, 1915).
2 Paul Kennedy, *The Rise of the Anglo-German Antagonism: 1860–1914* (London: George Allen & Unwin, 1980), p. 5.
3 Stephan Richter, "Repeating History: In Dealing with China, the United States Can Learn a Great Deal from British–German Relations in 1880," *Globalist,* 11 July 2000, http://www.theglobalist.com/nor/news/2000/07-11-00.shtml.
4 Aaron L. Friedberg, *The Weary Titan* (Princeton, NJ: Princeton University Press, 1988), p. 41.
5 A. J. P. Taylor, *The Struggle for Mastery in Europe: 1848–1918* (London: Oxford University Press, 1957), pp. xxvii–xxxi.
6 Edward Cook, *How Britain Strove for Peace: Record of Anglo-German Negotiations 1898–1914* (London: Macmillan, 1914), p. 13.
7 Raymond James Sontag, *Germany and England: Background of Conflict 1848–1898* (New York: D. Appleton-Century Company, 1938), p. 302.
8 Sean M. Lynn-Jones, "Détente and Deterrence: Anglo-German Relations 1911–1914," *International Security* 11(2) (Fall 1986), pp. 149.
9 Joll, *The Origins of the First World War*, p. 50.
10 George Monger, *The End of Isolation: British Foreign Policy 1900–1907* (London: T. Nelson, 1963), pp. 329–31.
11 Pierre Renouvin, "Britain and the Continent: The Lessons of History," *Foreign Affairs* 17 (October 1938), pp. 111–27.
12 Cook, *Why Britain is at War*, p. 16.
13 Friedberg, *The Weary Titan*, p. 302.
14 Martel, *The Origins of the First World War*, p. 52.
15 H. H. Asquith, *The Genesis of the War* (New York: Books for Libraries Press, 1923), pp. 43, 23.
16 Imanuel Geiss, *German Foreign Policy 1871–1914* (London: Routledge & Kegan Paul, 1976), p. 85.
17 Cook, *How Britain Strove for Peace*, p. 17.
18 Cook, *Why Britain is at War*, p. 17.
19 Joll, *The Origins of the First World War*, pp. 148, 164.
20 Friedberg, *The Weary Titan*, p. 295.
21 Michael R. Gordon, "Domestic Conflict and the Origins of the First World War: the British and the German Cases," *Journal of Modern History* 46(2) (June 1974), pp. 195, 198, 199.

22 Gordon, "Domestic Conflict and the Origins of the First World War," 200.
23 Ibid., pp. 210–12.
24 Geiss, *German Foreign Policy 1871–1914*, p. 15.
25 Gordon, "Domestic Conflict and the Origins of the First World War," pp. 199–200.
26 Friedberg, *The Weary Titan*, p. 79.
27 Ibid., p. 79.
28 Quoted in Friedberg, *The Weary Titan*, p. 70.
29 Friedberg, *The Weary Titan*, pp. 57–9.
30 Ibid., p. 87.
31 Ibid., p. 294.
32 Gordon, "Domestic Conflict and the Origins of the First World War," pp. 197–8.
33 B. E. Schmitt, *England and Germany 1740–1914* (Princeton, NJ: Princeton University Press, 1918), Chapter 9, "The Mood of 1914."
34 Ibid., pp. 227–8.
35 Geiss, *German Foreign Policy 1871–1914*, p. 85.
36 Quoted in Schmitt, *England and Germany*, p. 155.
37 Matthew Stibbe, *German Anglophobia and the Great War, 1914–1918* (Cambridge University Press, 2001).
38 J. A. Cramb, *Germany and England* (New York: E. P. Dutton & Co., 1914), p. 26.
39 Cramb, *Germany and England*, p. 118.
40 Schmitt, *England and Germany*, p. 159.
41 Cramb, *Germany and England*, p. 1.
42 Schmitt, *England and Germany*, p. 6.
43 Ibid., p. 10. Also Cramb, *Germany and England*, p. 39.
44 Quoted in Fritz Fischer, *War of Illusions: German Policies from 1911 to 1914* (New York: W. W. Norton, 1975), p. 30.
45 Geiss, *German Foreign Policy 1871–1914*, p. 80.
46 Cramb, *Germany and England*, pp. vi–vii.
47 Schmitt, *England and Germany*, pp. 92–5.
48 Cramb, *Germany and England*, p. viii.
49 Geiss, *German Foreign Policy 1871–1914*, p. 16.
50 Peter Padfield, *The Great Naval Race* (London: Hart-Davis, MacGibbon, 1974), p. 16.
51 Schmitt, *England and Germany*, pp. 59–60.
52 Ibid., p. 68.
53 Cramb, *Germany and England*, p. 51.
54 Taylor, *The Struggle for Mastery in Europe 1848–1918*, p. 324.
55 Geiss, *German Foreign Policy 1871–1914*, p. 58.
56 Quoted in Martel, *The Origins of the First World War*, p. 11.
57 Geiss, *German Foreign Policy 1871–1914*, p. 76.
58 Padfield, *The Great Naval Race*, p. 36.
59 Cook, *How Britain Strove for Peace*, p. 7.
60 Friedberg, *The Weary Titan*, p. 168.
61 Quoted in Cook, *How Britain Strove for Peace*, p. 8.
62 Cook, *How Britain Strove for Peace*, p. 8.
63 Ibid., pp. 20–1.
64 Kennedy, *The Rise of the Anglo-German Antagonism*, p. 465.
65 Cook, *How Britain Strove for Peace*, p. 9.
66 Ibid., p. 28.
67 The previous two paragraphs are based on Friedberg, *The Weary Titan*, pp. 169–72.
68 Cook, *How Britain Strove for Peace*, pp. 38–9.
69 Kennedy, *The Rise of the Anglo-German Antagonism*, p. 466.
70 Cramb, *Germany and England*, p. vi.

4 Anglo-American relations, 1865–1945

1 Quoted in David Reynolds, *Britannia Overruled: British Policy and World Power in the Twentieth Century* (London: Longman, 1991), p. 10.
2 B. J. C. McKercher, *Transition of Power: Britain's Loss of Global Pre-eminence to the United States, 1930–1945* (London: Cambridge University Press, 1999), p. 3. Also, Paul Kennedy, *The Rise and Fall of the Great Powers* (New York: Vintage, 1987), p. 149.
3 A. C. Turner. *The Unique Partnership: Britain and the United States* (New York: Bobbs-Merrill, 1971). pp. 146–7.
4 Robert M. Hathaway, *Great Britain and the United States: Special Relations since World War II* (Boston: Twayne Publishers, 1990), p. 1.
5 Quoted in H. G. Nicholas, *The United States and Britain* (Chicago: University of Chicago Press, 1975), p. 9.
6 Ibid., p. 2.
7 Charles S. Campbell, *From Revolution to Rapprochement: The United States and Great Britain, 1783–1900* (New York: John Wiley & Sons, 1974), p. 95.
8 David Dimbleby and David Reynolds, *An Ocean Apart* (New York: Random House, 1988), p. 26.
9 Ibid., p. 32.
10 Campbell, *From Revolution to Rapprochement*, pp. 134–5.
11 Nicholas, *The United States and Britain*, p. 43.
12 Dimbleby and Reynolds, *An Ocean Apart*, p. 36.
13 Nicholas, *The United States and Britain*, p. 53.
14 Dimbleby and Reynolds, *An Ocean Apart*, p. 35.
15 Bruce M. Russett, *Community and Contention: Britain and America in the Twentieth Century* (Cambridge, MA: MIT Press, 1963), p. 7.
16 Ritchie Ovendale, *Anglo-American Relations in the Twentieth Century* (New York: St. Martin's Press, 1998), p. 159.
17 Hathaway, *Great Britain and the United States*, p. 7.
18 Ibid., p. 10.
19 Ovendale, *Anglo-American Relations in the Twentieth Century*, p. 37.
20 See Kupchan *et al.*, *Power in Transition*, p. 22.
21 See Russett, *Community and Contention*.
22 Kupchan *et al.*, *Power in Transition*, pp. 106–7.
23 Alex Danchev, *On Specialness: Essays in Anglo-American Relations* (New York: St. Martin's Press, 1998), pp. 2–3.
24 This paragraph is based on Frank Costigliola, *Awkward Dominion: American Political, Economic, and Cultural Relations with Europe, 1919–1933* (Ithaca, NY: Cornell University Press, 1984), pp. 34–5.
25 Quoted in Costigliola, *Awkward Dominion*, p. 263.
26 Ibid.
27 Quoted in Costigliola, *Awkward Dominion*, p. 264.
28 This is the view of McKercher. See his *Transition of Power*, p. 343.
29 Geoffrey Warner, "The Anglo-American Special Relationship," *Diplomatic History* 13(4) (Fall 1989), p. 479.
30 Chamberlain to Hilda Chamberlain, 17 December 1937, Chamberlain Papers, NC 18/1/1032, Birmingham University Library. Quoted in Danchev, p. 12.
31 Turner, p. 56.
32 John Callaghan, *Great Power Complex: British Imperialism, International Crises and National Decline, 1914–51* (London: Pluto Press, 1997), p. 44.
33 John E. Moser, *Twisting the Lion's Tail: American Anglophobia between the World Wars* (New York: New York University Press, 1999), p. 4.
34 Ibid., p. xvii.

35 Unsigned memorandum, 21 March 1944, Record Class FO 371/38523/AN1538, PRO. Quoted in Geoffrey Warner, "The Anglo-American Special Relationship", p. 480.

36 F. S. Northedge, "Britain as a Second-Rank Power," *International Affairs* 46 (1970), p. 40.

37 Quoted in Moser, *Twisting the Lion's Tail*, p. 173.

38 Ibid., pp. 187–8.

39 Ibid., pp. 177–8.

40 Ibid., p. 179.

41 Ibid., p. 181.

42 The quotes in this paragraph are cited in Kupchan *et al.*, *Power in Transition*, p. 108.

43 Ovendale, *Anglo-American Relations in the Twentieth Century*, p. 9.

44 Ibid., pp. 7–8.

45 Quoted in Campbell. *From Revolution to Rapprochement*, p. 203.

46 For a detailed discussion of these three division of ideas, see B. J. C. McKercher (ed.), *Anglo-American Relations in the 1920s* (Edmonton, Alberta: The University of Alberta Press, 1990), Chapter 7, "'The Deep and Latent Distrust': The British Official Mind and the United States, 1919–1929."

47 McKercher, *Anglo-American Relations in the 1920s*, p. 220.

48 Quoted in C. J. Bartlett. *The Special Relationship: A Political History of Anglo-American Relations since 1945* (London: Longman, 1992), p. 12.

49 Winston S. Churchill, *Their Finest Hour*, vol. 2 of *The World War II* (Boston: Houghton Mifflin, 1949), p. 409. Quoted in Hathaway, p. 5.

50 Dimbleby and Reynolds, *An Ocean Apart*, p. 135.

51 Turner, p. 87.

52 Hathaway, p. 11.

53 Keith Alldritt, *The Greatest of Friends* (New York: St. Martin's Press, 1995), p. 213.

54 Vital Speeches of the Day 12 (15 March 1946), pp. 329–32. Quoted in Hathaway, p. 12.

55 Moser, *Twisting the Lion's Tail*, p. 1.

56 Commager, *Britain Through American Eyes*, p. xxiii.

57 Turner, pp. 32–3.

58 Turner, p. 35.

59 Emerson, *English Traits* (Boston, 1856), quoted in Commager, *Britain Through American Eyes*, p. xxxiv.

60 See Commager, *Britain Through American Eyes*, pp. 749–59.

61 Ibid..

62 A. Nevins (ed.), *America Through British Eyes* (New York: Oxford University Press, 1948), p. 82.

63 Ibid., p. 500.

64 Quoted in Costigliola, *Awkward Dominion*, p. 20.

65 Cited in Kupchan *et al.*, *Power in Transition*, p. 23.

66 Moser, *Twisting the Lion's Tail*, p. 4.

67 Dimbleby and Reynolds, *An Ocean Apart*, pp. 115–16.

68 Costigliola, *Awkward Dominion*, p. 176.

69 Dimbleby and Reynolds, *An Ocean Apart*, p. 124.

70 The Ethics of Aristotle, trans. J. A. K. Thomson (London: Penguin Books, 1976), pp. 263–4.

71 Ovendale, *Anglo-American Relations in the Twentieth Century*, p. 8.

72 Turner, pp. 20, 23.

73 Ibid., p. 38.

74 Nicholas, *The United States and Britain*, p. 24.

75 H. C. Allen, *The Anglo-American Relationship Since 1783* (London: Adam & Charles Black, 1959), p. 129.
76 Turner, p. 27.
77 Commager, *Britain Through American Eyes*, p. xxii.
78 Quoted in Commager, *Britain Through American Eyes*, p. xxiv.
79 These men include Joseph Chamberlain, Lord Playfair, Sir William Harcourt (leader of the Liberal Party), Lord Randolph Churchill, and George Curzon, a future Foreign Secretary. See Campbell, p. 203.
80 Hathaway, p. 6.
81 Ibid., p. 23.
82 Turner, p. 29.
83 Nevins, *America Through British Eyes*, p. 402.
84 Campbell, pp. 201–2.
85 Ibid., p. 200.
86 Quoted in McKercher, *Transition of Power*, p, 308.
87 Clement R. Attlee, "Britain and America: Common Aims, Different Opinions," *Foreign Affairs* 32 (1954), p. 190.
88 F. S. Northedge, "Britain as a Second-Rank Power," p. 47.
89 Dimbleby and Reynolds, pp. 38–9.
90 Ibid., p. 81.
91 Callaghan, pp. 44–5.
92 Turner. *The Unique Partnership*, p. 58.
93 Turner, pp. 61–2.
94 Hathaway, p. 16.
95 Robert V. Roosa, "Where is Britain Heading?" *Foreign Affairs* 46 (1968), p. 503.
96 Nicholas, *The United States and Britain*, pp. 14–20.
97 J. B. Brebner, *The North Atlantic Triangle* (New Haven, CT: Yale University Press, 1945), p. 251; quoted in Russett, *Community and Contention*, p. 5.

5 Sino-American relations, 1990–2005

1 For a good historical survey and analysis of Sino-American relations up to 1990, see Warren I. Cohen, *America's Response to China: A History of Sino-American Relations* (New York: Columbia University Press, 2000). Also see Nancy Tucker, "China and America: 1941–1991," *Foreign Affairs*, 70(5) (Winter 1991/92), pp. 75–93.
2 John Diamond, "Prediction: India, China Will Be Economic Giants," *USA Today*, 13 January 2005, accessed online the same day at www.usatoday.com/news.
3 Oded Shenkar, *The Chinese Century: The Rising Chinese Economy and Its Impact on the Global Economy, the Balance of Power, and Your Job* (Philadelphia: Wharton School Publishing, 2004).
4 Robert D. Kaplan, a senior correspondent for the Atlantic Monthly, discussed the importance and urgency for US Military to prepare for a war with China. See Kaplan, "How We Would Fight China," *Atlantic Monthly*, June 2005, pp. 49–64.
5 Charlotte Denny, "China is No Threat to America – for Now," *Guardian*, 8 April 2002.
6 "China Races to Replace U.S. as Economic Power in Asia," *New York Times* (online edition), 28 June 2002.
7 "China's Comprehensive National Strength is a Quarter that of the United States," *Lianhe Zaobao* (Singapore), 15 July 2002. In comparison, the report says that Japan, the second most powerful nation, possesses 60 percent of America's national strength, while France, Germany and Britain tie one another with half of America's national strength each. Russia's national strength is about 40 percent that of the United States.

8　Willy Wo-Lap Lam, "Hu's New Deal," CNN News Analysis at www.cnn.com, accessed on 3 December 2002.

9　"President: China Targets US\$4 Trillion GDP by 2020," *China Daily*, 16 May 2005, accessed online from www.chinadaily.com.cn/english the same day.

10　Former Senator Warren B. Rudman, "Homeland Defense: Issues and Challenges," Nixon Center, Washington, DC, 19 June 2002.

11　Quoted in "Jiang Looks to US for Unlikely Final Legacy," *CNN News* at www.cnn.com, accessed on 22 October 2002.

12　The US–China Security Review Commission report, published on 15 July 2002, claims China presents "an increasing threat to U.S. security interests, in the Middle East and Asia in particular." See the highlights of the report on the Commission's webpage at www.uscc.gov/pr7_15.htm. The Department of Defense's report, published three days earlier, considers China's missiles along the southeast China coast not only a threat to Taiwan, but a direct threat to the United States and US interests in Japan and the Philippines. The full text of the Department of Defense report can be accessed at www.defenselink.mil/news/Jul2002/d20020712china.pdf.

13　Constitution of the People's Republic of China, 3rd edn. (Beijing: Foreign Languages Press, 1994), p. 6.

14　"Pentagon to Renew Ties with China," *CNN News* at www.cnn.com, accessed on 22 June 2002.

15　See John Pomfret, "China Sees Interests Tied to U.S.," *Washington Post*, 2 February 2002, p. A1.

16　Asian countries increasingly perceive a rising China as peaceful and friendly. See for example Jane Perlez, "Asian Leaders Find China a More Cordial Neighbor," *New York Times*, 18 October 2003.

17　Quoted in Nicholas R. Lardy, *Integrating China into the Global Economy* (Washington, DC: Brookings Institution Press, 2002), p. 155.

18　"Main Characteristics of China's Foreign Policy," excerpts of Premier Li Peng's speech at the 96th Inter-Parliamentary Conference on 19 September 1996. From the website of the PRC's Embassy in Washington, DC, at http://www.china-embassy.org/eng/7005.html, accessed on 5 July 2002.

19　"Zhu Advocates Continued Independent Foreign Policy of Peace in 2002," *Xinhua* news dispatch, 5 March 2002.

20　David E. Sanger, "Bush Lauds China Leader As 'Partner' in Diplomacy," *New York Times*, 10 December 2003, p. A6.

21　Putnam, "Diplomacy and Domestic Politics."

22　Zhiqun Zhu, "To Support or Not To Support: the American Debate on China's WTO Membership," *Journal of Chinese Political Science*, 6(2) (Fall 2000), pp. 77–101.

23　Robert G. Sutter, "The U.S. Congress: Personal, Partisan, Political," in Ramon H. Myers, *et al* (eds.), *Making China Policy: Lessons from the Bush and Clinton Administration* (New York: Rowman & Littlefield, 2001), p. 89.

24　Quoted in Laurence J. Brahm (ed.), *China's Century: The Awakening of the Next Economic Powerhouse* (Singapore: John Wiley & Sons, 2001), p. 63.

25　Sutter, "The U.S. Congress: Personal, Partisan, Political," p. 91.

26　"New Pentagon Report Sees Rapid Buildup by China," *New York Times*, 13 July 2002. Accessed online the same day at http://www.nytimes.com.

27　The transcript of the 11 July 2002 joint press conference can be found on the website of the Embassy of Australia in Washington, D.C. at http://www.austemb.org. Interestingly, the same transcript cannot be found at the US State Department website, which has reports about the Australian prime minister's visit to the United States.

28 Jim Lobe, "US Hawks Unhappy at Improving Beijing Ties," *Asia Times* (online), 13 July 2002, at http://www.atimes.com.
29 These enormous challenges prompt some people to think that China is going to fail in the next twenty years or so. See, for example, Gordon G. Chang's *The Coming Collapse of China* (New York: Random House, 2001). This author does not take such a pessimistic view.
30 "President: China Targets US$4 Trillion GDP by 2020."
31 From Scott Barbour, "China's Aging Population Will Cause Serious Problems" in James D. Torr (ed.), *China: Opposing Viewpoints* (San Diego: Greenhaven Press, 2001), p. 19.
32 Ibid., p. 21.
33 David R. Francis, "To Stay Out of the Red, China Needs To Go Green," *Christian Science Monitor*, 29 April 2004.
34 Lardy, *Integrating China into the Global Economy*, p. vii.
35 John W. Garver, "Sino-American Relations in 2001: the difficult accommodation of two great powers," *International Journal* (Spring 2002), p. 309.
36 "US–China Relationship: Not Quite Friends or Enemies," *Christian Science Monitor*, 1 April 2002, p. 7.
37 "China–United States Sustained Dialog," *Program Brief* 8(4), Nixon Center, Washington, DC, 19 March 2002.
38 Maxine S. Thomas, and Zhao Mei (eds.), *China–United States Sustained Dialog 1986–2001* (New York: Kettering Foundation, 2001), p. 31.
39 The People's Daily maintains an online discussion website where Chinese web users can comment on the news they read. See http://www.people.com.cn for sample comments on international events and US–China relations.
40 "Year after Spy Plane Crisis, China–US Ties Face New Uncertainty," *AFP* news from Yahoo! Singapore at http://sg.search.yahoo.com/search/news, accessed on 1 April 2002.
41 "China–United States Sustained Dialog." Many of these surveys were conducted between 1 April and 11 September 2001. The terrorist attacks on America may have influenced some of these perceptions about America.
42 Richard Bernstein, and Ross H. Munro, *The Coming Conflict with China* (New York: Alfred A. Knopf, 1997). Humphrey Hawksley and Simon Holberton, *Dragon Strike: A Novel of the Coming War with China* (New York: St. Martin's Press, 1999).
43 Kaplan, "How We Would Fight China."
44 Song Qiang *et al.*, *Zhongguo keyi shuo bu* (China Can Say No) (Beijing: Chinese Industrial & Commercial Joint Publishing House, 1996).
45 Fang Ning *et al.*, *Quanqiuhua yinmou xia de Zhongguo zhi lu* (China's Road: Under the Conspiracy of Globalization) (Beijing: Chinese Social Sciences Publishing House, 1999).
46 John W. Garver, "More From the 'Say No Club,'" *China Journal*, 45 (January 2001), p. 154.
47 Zhang Zeqing, *America, Why Are You Powerful?* (Beijing: China City Publishing House, 1999).
48 Thomas and Zhao (eds.), *China–United States Sustained Dialog 1986–2001*, p. 25.
49 Orville Schell, "Prisoner of Its Past," *Salon Magazine*, 8 June 1999.
50 Thomas and Zhao (eds.), *China-United States Sustained Dialog 1986–2001*, pp. 35–6.
51 Quoted in "US–China Relationship: Not Quite Friends or Enemies," p. 7.
52 "China–United States Sustained Dialog."
53 Chicago Council on Foreign Relations, "Global Views 2004: American Public Opinion and Foreign Policy" (Chicago: Chicago Council on Foreign Relations, 2004), p. 12.
54 "Committee of 100 Study Reveals Improved American Attitudes Toward China

While Raising New Concerns," Committee of 100, New York, 13 January 2005. Accessed from www.committee100.org the same day.

55 "U.S.–China Dialog Research Report, October 2000" in Thomas and Zhao (eds.), *China–United States Sustained Dialog 1986–2001*, pp. 2–21.

56 For an evaluation of Bush's China policy, see for example, Robert S. Ross, "The Bush Administration: the Origins of Engagement," in Ramon H. Myers *et al.* (eds.), *Making China Policy: Lessons from the Bush and Clinton Administrations* (New York: Rowman & Littlefield, 2001), pp. 21–44.

57 Nancy Bernkopf Tucker, "The Clinton Years: The Problem of Coherence" in Myers *et al.* (eds.), *Making China Policy*, p. 52.

58 In June 1998 President Clinton expressed the US administration's policy as follows: "We don't support independence for Taiwan, or two Chinas, or one Taiwan, one China. And we don't believe that Taiwan should be a member of any organization for which statehood is a requirement." The "three nos" usually means no support for two Chinas, one China and one Taiwan, or Taiwanese independence.

59 Richard C. Bush, "Taiwan Policy Making since Tiananmen: Navigating through Shifting Waters," in Myers *et al.* (eds.), *Making China Policy*, p. 197.

60 David M. Lampton, "The Danger of Writing Taiwan a Blank Security Check," Nixon Center, 15 August 2002, accessed the same day at www.nixoncenter.org.

61 "US–China Relationship: Not Quite Friends or Enemies."

62 Jay Taylor, "Bush Scraps China Policy of Six Presidents," *Los Angeles Times* online edition at www.latimes.com, 28 April 2002.

63 "Bush Sr.'s Glad Tidings for Beijing," *Business Week* online edition, 10 May 2002.

64 Author's interview with an official from Shanghai Foreign Affairs Office on 15 June 2002.

65 "The U.S. Reiterates It Does Not Support Taiwan Independence," *Lian He Zao Bao* (Singapore), 9 August 2002.

66 Deputy Secretary of Defense Paul Wolfowitz at the Foreign Press Club, Washington, DC, 29 May 2002. News Transcripts from the Department of Defense's website at http://www.dod.gov/news/May2002/briefings.html.

67 James G. Lakely, "Bush Warns Taiwan Against Separation," *Washington Times*, 10 December 2003.

68 Robert M. Hathaway, "George Bush's Unfinished Asian Agenda," *Foreign Policy Research Institute* E-notes, Philadelphia, 13 May 2005.

69 "Cheney: US–China Relations in Good Shape," *China Daily*, 14 April 2004, accessed from http://www.chinadaily.com.cn/english the same day.

70 "US Willing to Cooperate with China in Many Fields: Rumsfeld," *Xinhua News*, 5 June 2004, accessed from www.chinaview.cn the same day.

71 Garver, "Sino-American Relations in 2001: the Difficult Accommodation of Two Great Powers," *International Journal*, Spring 2002, p. 284.

72 Quoted in Brahm (ed.), *China's Century: The Awakening of the Next Economic Powerhouse*, p. 64.

73 Gary Klintworth, "China, Taiwan, and the United States," *Pacific Review* 13(1) (February 2001), p. 51.

74 Vice President Hu Jintao's speech at a dinner in Washington, DC, 1 May 2002, accessed from the Chinese Embassy website at http://www.china-embassy.org/eng/29640.html.

75 "Bush to Hu: US Opposes Independence for Taiwan," *Straits Times*, 30 May 2004, accessed from http://straitstimes.asia1.com the same day.

76 "Remarks by President Bush and Chinese President Hu Jintao After Bilateral Meeting," Hyatt Regency Hotel, Santiago, Chile, 20 November 2004. Released by the Office of the Press Secretary, the White House the same day.

77 Domke argues that decisions for war are constrained by internal political struc-

ture, foreign trade, and participation in international organizations. See William Domke, *War and the Changing Global System* (New Haven, CT: Yale University Press, 1988).

78 Quoted in "Jiang Sets off for Final U.S. Tour," *CNN News*, 20 October 2002, accessed from http://www.cnn.com the same day.

79 Robert J. Samuelson, "Economics as Statecraft," *Newsweek*, 29 November 1999, p. 58.

80 Hu Jintao, "Enhanced Mutual Understanding and Trust Toward a Constructive and Cooperative Relationship between China and the United States," speech in Washington, DC, 1 May 2002.

81 "Highlights from Open Doors 2001" at IIE's website at www.opendoorsweb.org.

82 "U.S.–China Ties Still Strong," *Associated Press*, 31 May 2001 at http://dailynews. yahoo.com/htx/ap/20010531/pl/us_china_life_goes_on_3.html.

83 Based on a talk given at Yale University by Weihang Chen, Executive Director of China Department of the Alliance for Children, Inc., on 12 November 2004.

84 "U.S.–China Flights to Increase," *USA Today*, 20 June 2004, accessed online 21 June 2004.

85 From "White Paper – The Taiwan Question and Reunification of China," Taiwan Affairs Office and Information Office of the State Council, August 1993, Beijing, China. The PRC issued a second white paper on Taiwan in 2000, called "White Paper – The One-China Principle and the Taiwan Issue," Taiwan Affairs Office and Information Office of the State Council, 21 February 2000, Beijing, China. The two white papers explain the origin and current state of the Taiwan question as well as official PRC policy on Taiwan. The two documents can be accessed from the website of the PRC embassy in Washington at http://www.china-embassy.org/eng/c2865.html.

86 Tom Plate, "The Virtue of Keeping Mum on Taiwan," *Japan Times*, 29 April 2002, accessed from www.japantimes.co.jp the same day.

87 Colin L. Powell, Remarks at Asia Society annual dinner, New York, 10 June 2002, accessed from http://www.state.gov/secretary/rm/2002/10983.htm.

88 Taylor, "Bush Scraps China Policy of Six Presidents."

89 Vincent Shao, "Trojan Horse or Peace Bridge: Trade across the Taiwan Straits," *China Times*, 22 October 2002, accessed from http://news.chinatimes.com the same day.

90 Henry C. K. Liu, "U.S., China: The Politics of Ambiguity," *Asia Times Online*, 24 April 2002, accessed from http://www.atimes.com/china/DD24Ad02.html the same day.

91 Chalmers Johnson, "The United States Should Not Try to Control China," in James D. Torr, ed., *China: Opposing Viewpoints* (San Diego: Greenhaven Press, 2001), p. 184.

92 Chen Shui-bian won the 2000 Taiwan presidential election largely because the longtime ruling Kuomintang split and the popular Taiwan governor James Soong formed his own People First Party. Supporters of the status quo had to divide their votes between Soong and Kuomintang's Lien Chan, giving Chen an easy victory. Chen was re-elected with a paper-thin margin in 2004. On 19 March 2004, the eve of the election, both Chen and his running mate, Annette Lu, were mysteriously shot and apparently injured, winning them some sympathy votes. The opposition Kuomintang and the People First Party have since charged that Chen and Lu staged the assassination attempt and won the re-election disgracefully.

93 "Powell Speaks of China, Taiwan 'Reunification,'" *Reuters*, 25 October 2004.

94 Jim Mann, "Fears of Chinese Spying Only Deepens U.S. Mistrust," *Los Angeles Times*, 20 May 1999, accessed from http://www.latimes.com the same day.

95 Some scholars do believe that the greatest challenge to US primacy in the

twenty-first century will not come from China. In his provocative book, *The End of the American Era: U.S. Foreign Policy and the Geopolitics of the Twenty-first Century* (New York: Alfred A Knopf, 2002), Charles Kupchan, Professor of International Relations at Georgetown University and Director of European Studies at the Council on Foreign Relations, contends that Europe, not China, will be America's greatest challenge because the EU, whose economy already rivals America's, will inevitably rise as a counterweight to the United States.
96 Colin L. Powell, Remarks at the Elliott School of International Affairs, George Washington University, Washington, DC, 5 September 2003.

6 Comparisons and contrasts

1 Arthur A. Stein, "Introduction" in Richard Rosecrance (ed.), *The New Great Power Coalition: Toward a World Concert of Nations* (Lanham, MD: Rowman & Littlefield, 2001), p. 2.
2 According to some estimates, the Chinese central bank bought more than US$250 billion US securities in 2004 alone. See Edmund L. Andrews, "US Warns China on Currency Policies and Hints at Retaliation," *New York Times*, 17 May 2005.
3 China's official statistics indicate that by the end of 2004 China had attracted a total of US$562.1 billion in foreign direct investment and approved the establishment of over 500,000 foreign-funded enterprises. In addition, the number of R&D centers set up by foreign investors in China had exceeded 700, and over 400 firms out of the Fortune 500 had invested in China. See "President: China Targets US$4 Trillion GDP by 2020," *China Daily*, 16 May 2005, accessed online from http://www.chinadaily.com.cn/english the same day.
4 The Five Principles are mutual respect for sovereignty and territorial integrity, mutual non-aggression, non-interference in each other's internal affairs, equality and mutual benefit, and peaceful coexistence. They were first set forth by Premier Zhou Enlai in his talk to the Indian delegation at the start of the negotiations that took place in Beijing from December 1953 to April 1954 between representatives of the Chinese and Indian governments on relations between the two countries. Later, the Five Principles were formally written into the preface to the "Agreement between the People's Republic of China and the Republic of India on Trade and Intercourse Between the Tibet Region of China and India" (http://meaindia.nic.in/treatiesagreement/1954/chap94.htm). Since June 1954, when the Five Principles were included in the joint communique issued by Premier Zhou Enlai and Prime Minister Jawaharlal Nehru, they have been adopted in many other international documents and have become widely accepted as norms for relations between countries. At the first Asian–African Conference (the Bandung Conference) held in April 1955, Zhou Enlai reiterated these principles, the spirit of which was incorporated into the declarations of the Conference. In 1982 these Five Principles were written into the Constitution of the People's Republic of China.
5 President Jiang made these remarks when meeting with Henry J. Hyde, chairman of the International Relations Committee of the US House of Representatives, and Carly Fiorina, CEO of Hewlett-Packard Co. *Xinhua* news, 10 and 11 December 2002.
6 The United States has reportedly warned Taiwan that the island may have to deal with the consequences itself if it declares independence. Meanwhile, through continuous and robust advanced weapons sales to Taiwan, the United States either intentionally or unintentionally promotes the arms race across the Taiwan Strait and perpetuates the separate status of Taiwan from the PRC. If

the United States were interested in China's unification, its policy would have been different. The US's unpreparedness to deal with a unified China is reflected in Nancy Bernkopf Tucker, "If Taiwan Chooses Unification, Should the United States Care?," *Washington Quarterly* 25(3) (Summer 2002), pp. 15–28.

7 See, for example, Jiang Zemin, *Political Report at the sixteenth National Congress of the Chinese Communist Party*, Beijing, November 2002.

8 "New Leader Chosen in China," *Washington Post*, 15 November 2002, p. A1.

9 "Breakthrough in China Human Rights," *CNN news*, 17 December 2002, accessed online at http://www.cnn.com the same day.

10 In the 2004 annual report to Congress by the US–China Economic and Security Review Commission, submitted on 15 June 2004 (http://www.uscc.gov/researchpapers/2004/04annual_report.htm), the bipartisan group cited "troubling trends" in US–China relations for the long-term economic and national security interests of the United States. It recommended a series of measures to address issues perceived as problems, including suggestions to reexamine America's "One China" policy.

11 Bernstein and Munro, *The Coming Conflict with China*; Bill Gertz, *The China Threat: How the People's Republic Targets America* (Washington, DC: Regnery Publishing, 2000); Song Qiang *et al.*, *China Can Say No*.

12 Chinese language news at http://www6.chinesenewsnet.com, 18 December 2002. The news is based on the US Department of Defense's publication "Defense News". The English source of the news was not available.

13 Vanessa Hua, "U.S. Poll Finds More View China Approvingly," *San Francisco Chronicle*, 13 January 2005, p. A12.

14 Geiss, *German Foreign Policy 1871–1914*, p. 11.

15 Kenneth N. Waltz, "Globalization and American Power," *National Interest* 59 (Spring 2000), pp. 46–56.

16 "Powell: I Can Call Chinese Foreign Minister Directly," *Lianhe Zaobao* (Singapore), 8 November 2003, accessed online the same day from http://www.zaobao.com.

17 Charles Tilly, *Coercion, Capital, and European States, AD 990–1990* (Cambridge: Basil Blackwell, 1990).

18 Reynolds, *Britannia Overruled*, pp. 74, 105.

19 Kennedy, *The Rise and Fall of the Great Powers*, pp. 313–14.

20 Inderjeet Parmar, *Special Interests, the State and the Anglo-American Alliance, 1939–1945* (London: Frank Cass, 1995), p. 24.

21 Immanuel Wallerstein, "The Eagle Has Crash Landed," *Foreign Policy* (July/August 2002).

22 "Bush Outlines Doctrine of Striking Foes First," *New York Times*, 20 September 2002, p. A1.

23 Edward D. Mansfield and Jack Snyder, "Democratization and War," *Foreign Affairs*, 74(3) (May–June 1995), pp. 79–87; Mansfield and Snyder, "Democratization and the Danger of War," *International Security* 20(1) (Summer 1995), pp. 5–38.

24 See the summary of these ruling strategies in John W. Garver, "Will China Be Another Germany?," paper prepared for the Conference on China into the Twenty-first Century: Strategic Partner and/or Peer Competitor, US Army War College, Carlisle Barracks, PA, 23–25 April 1996. Also Richard J. Evans, "Introduction: Wilhelm II's Germany and the Historians," in *Society and Politics in Wilhelmine Germany* (New York: Barnes and Noble, 1978), pp. 11–23.

25 On "social imperialism," see for example, Geoff Eley, "Defining Social Imperialism: Use and Abuse of an Idea," *Social History* 1(3) (1976), pp. 265–90.

26 This is a question also asked by James Lee Ray. In his article "Does Interstate War Have A Future?," *Conflict Management and Peace Science*, 19(1) (Spring 2002), pp. 53–80, Ray argues that interstate wars between independent nation-states

are likely to occur with some frequency in the first decades of the twenty-first century, especially in Africa, the Middle East, and parts of Asia. But he categorically rejects the danger of war between China and the United States. He thinks that the analysis of US–China relations and their dispute over Taiwan may have exaggerated the dangers of interstate wars and is thus misleading.

27 Carolyn W. Pumphrey (ed.), *The Rise of China in Asia: Security Implications* (Carlisle, PA: Strategic Studies Institute, 2002), p. 295.
28 Ibid, pp. 7–9.
29 "Australians Speak 2005: Public Opinion and Foreign Policy," The Lowy Institute for International Policy, Australia, 2005.
30 "China's Influence Seen Positive," *BBC News*, 5 March 2005.
31 "A Rising China," editorial, *New York Times*, 6 May 2005.
32 Robert Dahl, "The Concept of Power," *Behavioral Science* 2 (July 1957), p. 202.
33 Jeffrey Hart, "Three Approaches to the Measurement of Power in International Relations," *International Organization*, 30(2) (Spring 1976), pp. 289–305.
34 For example, see Joseph Nye, *Bound to Lead* (New York: Basic Books, 1990), Chapter 1.
35 Knutsen. *The Rise and Fall of World Orders*; Tammen *et al.* (eds.), *Power Transitions*.
36 Cited in Gianfranco Poggi, *The State: Its Nature, Development, and Prospects* (Stanford, CA: Stanford University Press, 1990), p. 4.
37 Tammen *et al.*, *Power Transitions*, pp. 8–9.
38 Hobbes, T., *Leviathan* (London: Oxford University Press), p. 49.
39 Joshua Goldstein, *Long Cycles: Prosperity and War in the Modern Age* (New Haven, CT: Yale University Press, 1988), p. 281.
40 Richard Rosecrance, *The Rise of the Virtual State: Wealth and Power in the Coming Century* (New York: Basic Books, 1999).
41 John J. Mearsheimer, *The Tragedy of Great Power Politics* (New York: W. W. Norton & Company, 2001), p. 3.
42 Robert Jervis, *Perception and Misperception in International Politics* (Princeton, NJ: Princeton University Press, 1976), pp. 274–8.
43 "China, Japan Share Responsibility to Push Forward Bilateral Ties: Vice President," *People's Daily*, 29 September 2002.
44 J. Stapleton Roy, "The Rise of China and the Outlook for US–China Relations," National Committee on United States–China Relations Notes, Winter/Spring 2005, p. 17.
45 See report and comments by David E. Sanger, "Bush Outlines Doctrine of Striking Foes First," *New York Times*, 20 September 2002, p. 1.
46 Taylor, *The Struggle for Mastery in Europe, 1848–1918*, p. 166.
47 Thucydides, *History of the Peloponnesian War*, trans. Rex Warner (Harmondsworth: Penguin, 1954), p. 49.
48 This paragraph is based on Stephen Van Evera, *Causes of War: Power and the Roots of Conflict* (Ithaca, NY: Cornell University Press, 1999), pp. 76–9.
49 "U.S. Works Up Plan for Using Nuclear Arms," *Los Angeles Times*, 9 March 2002, p. 1. Also, "U.S. Nuclear Plan Sees New Weapons and New Targets," *New York Times*, 10 March 2002, p. 1. The other targets are Russia, Iraq, North Korea, Iran, Libya, and Syria.
50 See Norman Angell, *The Great Illusion: A Study of the Relation of Military Power in Nations to Their Economic and Social Advantage*, New York: G. P. Putnam's Sons, 1911.
51 See Russett, *Community and Contention*.
52 Cook, *How Britain Strove for Peace*, p. 5.
53 Schmitt, *England and Germany 1740–1914*, p. 496.

7 US–China relations in the 21st century

1 Bruce Bueno de Mesquita, "Risk, Power Distributions, and the Likelihood of War," *International Studies Quarterly*, December 1981, pp. 541–68; Woosang Kim, "Power Transitions and Great Power War from Westphalia to Waterloo," *World Politics*, 45(1), October 1992, pp. 153–72; Woosang Kim and James D. Morrow, "When Do Power Shifts Lead to War?," *American Journal of Political Science*, 36(4), November 1992, pp. 896–922; Bueno de Mesquita and Lalman, *War and Reason*; Kugler and Lemke, "The Power Transition Research Program"; Kugler and Lemke, *Parity and War*; Douglas Lemke, "The Continuation of History: Power Transition Theory and the End of the Cold War," *Journal of Peace Research*, 34(1), 1997, pp. 23–36; Jonathan M. DiCicco and Jack S. Levy, "Power Shifts and Problem Shifts: The Evolution of the Power Transition Research Program," *Journal of Conflict Resolution*, 43(6), 1999, pp. 657–704; and Tammen *et al.*, *Power Transition*.

2 Randolph M. Siverson and Michael P. Sullivan, "The Distribution of Power and the Onset of War," *Journal of Conflict Resolution*, 27, 1983, pp. 473–94.

3 Douglas Lemke and Jacek Kugler, "The Evolution of the Power Transition Perspective," in Kugler and Lemke (eds.), *Parity and War*, p. 29.

4 Richard N. Haass, "Why Foreign Policy (When It Comes to Judgment, at Least) Is Not Pornography," in Stanley A. Renshon and Deborah Welch Larson (eds.), *Good Judgment in Foreign Policy: Theory and Application* (Lanham, MD: Rowman & Littlefield, 2003), p. 247–58.

5 China's peaceful rise *(heping jueqi)* is a foreign policy doctrine mentioned increasingly by the People's Republic of China in the early twenty-first century. The term was first used in a speech given by the former Vice Principal of the Central Party School of the Chinese Communist Party, Zheng Bijian, in late 2003 during the Boao Forum for Asia. It was introduced to the world by Chinese President Hu Jintao on his tour of Southeast Asia in October 2003, and was then reiterated by Chinese Prime Minister Wen Jiabao in an ASEAN meeting as well as his visit to the United States in December 2003. It appears to be one of the first initiatives by the fourth generation of Chinese leaders headed by Hu and Wen. Other alternative names for the new policy include "peaceful development *(heping fazhan)*," "peaceful coexistence *(heping gongchu)*," and "peaceful ascendancy *(heping shengqi)*."

6 China scholar Thomas J. Christensen seems to hold similar views. In his talk on US–China relations at Yale University on 22 April 2005, Christensen discussed several containment strategies by the United States in the context of an overall engagement policy toward China.

7 Yong Deng and Fei-Ling Wang, "Introduction: Toward an Understanding of China's Worldview," in Yong Deng and Fei-Ling Wang (eds.), *In the Eyes of the Dragon: China Views the World* (New York: Rowman & Littlefield, 1999), p. 10.

8 Fang Ning, Wang Xiaodong, and Song Qiang, *China's Road: Under the Conspiracy of Globalization (Quanqiuhua yinmou xia de Zhongguo zhi lu)* (Beijing: Chinese Social Sciences Publishing House, 1999), p. 13

9 Mearsheimer, *The Tragedy of Great Power Politics*, p. 402.

10 Harry Harding considered the bilateral relationship as "fragile" in his survey of US–China relations between 1972 and 1990. See his *A Fragile Relationship: The United States and China since 1972* (Washington, DC: Brookings Institution), 1992.

11 This is the observation of China scholar David M. Lampton. See Stan Crock, "The Coming US–China Summits," *BusinessWeek Online*, 3 May 2005, accessed online at http://www.businessweek.com the same day.

12 Reinhold Niebuhr, "Awkward Imperialists," *Atlantic Monthly*, 145, June 1930, pp. 670–5; Niebuhr, "Perils of American Power," *Atlantic Monthly* 149, January 1932, p. 95.

13 One of the articles exploring the potential benefits of PRC–Taiwan unification is Nancy Bernkopf Tucker, "If Taiwan Chooses Unification, Should the United States Care?"

14 Fred Charles Ikle, *Every War Must End* (New York: Columbia University Press, 1991), p. 108.

15 James F. Hoge, Jr., "A Global Power Shift in the Making," *Foreign Affairs* 83(4), July/August 2004.

16 For a more recent study of Kantian peace, see John R. Oneal and Bruce M. Russett, *Triangulating Peace: Democracy, Interdependence, and International Organizations* (New York: W. W. Norton & Company, 2001).

Bibliography

"Agreement between the People's Republic of China and the Republic of India on Trade and Intercourse between the Tibet Region of China and India," Beijing, China, 29 April 1954. The text of the agreement can be found on the website of India's Ministry of External Affairs at http://meaindia.nic.in/treatiesagreement/1954/chap94.htm.

Albertini, L., *The Origins of the War of 1914*, London: Oxford University Press, 1952.

Alldritt, K., *The Greatest of Friends: Franklin D. Roosevelt and Winston Churchill 1941–1945*, New York: St. Martin's Press, 1995.

Allen, H. C., *Great Britain and the United States*, London: Odhams Press, 1954.

——, *The Anglo-American Relationship Since 1783*, London: Adam & Charles Black, 1959.

Allen, M., and B. Gellman, "Preemptive Strikes Part of U.S. Strategic Doctrine," *Washington Post*, 11 December 2002, p. A1.

Allison, G. T., A. Carnesale, and J. S. Nye Jr. (eds.), *Hawks, Doves, and Owls: An Agenda for Avoiding Nuclear War*, New York: W. W. Norton, 1985.

Andrews, E. L., "US Warns China on Currency Policies and Hints at Retaliation," *New York Times*, 17 May 2005, accessed online from www.nytimes.com the same day.

Angell, N., *The Great Illusion: A Study of the Relation of Military Power in Nations to Their Economic and Social Advantage*, New York: G. P. Putnam's Sons, 1911.

Aristotle. *See* Thomson, J. A. K.

Asquith, H. H., *The Genesis of the War*, New York: Books for Libraries Press, 1923.

Attlee, C. R. "Britain and America: Common Aims, Different Opinions," *Foreign Affairs* 32 (January 1954), pp. 190–202.

"Australians Speak 2005: Public Opinion and Foreign Policy," Lowy Institute for International Policy, Australia, 2005.

Barbour, S., "China's Aging Population Will Cause Serious Problems," in James D. Torr (ed.), *China: Opposing Viewpoints*, San Diego: Greenhaven Press, 2001, pp. 1–5.

Bartlett, C. J., *The Special Relationship: A Political History of Anglo-American Relations since 1945*, London: Longman, 1992.

Bernstein, R., and R. H. Munro, *The Coming Conflict with China*, New York: Alfred A. Knopf, 1997.

Betts, R. K., and T. J. Christensen, "China: Getting the Questions Right," *National Interest* 62 (Winter 2000/01), pp. 17–30.

Borrus, A., "The Best Way to Change China is from the Inside," *Business Week*, 17 May 1993, p. 69.

Brahm, L. J. (ed.), *China's Century: The Awakening of the Next Economic Powerhouse*, Singapore: John Wiley & Sons, 2001.

"Breakthrough in China Human Rights," *CNN News*, 17 December 2002, accessed online from www.cnn.com the same day.

Brookes, P. T. R., "Strategic Realism: The Future of U.S.–Sino Security Relations," *Strategic Review*, Summer 1999, pp. 53–6.

Brzezinski, Z., *The Grand Chessboard: American Primacy and Its Geostrategic Imperatives*, New York: Basic Books, 1997.

——, "Living with China," *National Interest* 59 (Spring 2000), pp. 5–21.

Bueno de Mesquita, B., "Risk, Power Distributions, and the Likelihood of War," *International Studies Quarterly*, December 1981, pp. 541–68.

——, "The War Trap Revisited: A Revised Expected Utility Model," *American Political Science Review* 79 (1985), pp. 156–77.

Bueno de Mesquita, B., and D. Lalman, *War and Reason: Domestic and International Imperatives*, New Haven, CT: Yale University Press, 1992.

"Bush Outlines Doctrine of Striking Foes First," *New York Times*, 20 September 2002, p. A1.

Bush, R. C., "Taiwan Policy Making Since Tiananmen: Navigating through Shifting Waters," in Ramon H. Myers *et al.* (eds.), *Making China Policy: Lessons from the Bush and Clinton Administrations*, New York: Rowman & Littlefield, 2001.

"Bush Sr.'s Glad Tidings for Beijing," *Business Week* online edition, 10 May 2002.

"Bush to Hu: US Opposes Independence for Taiwan," *Straits Times*, 30 May 2004.

Callaghan, J., *Great Power Complex: British Imperialism, International Crises and National Decline, 1914–51*, London: Pluto Press, 1997.

Campbell, C. S., *From Revolution to Rapprochement: The United States and Great Britain 1783–1900*, New York: John Wiley & Sons, 1974.

Campbell, K. M., "The Challenges Ahead for U.S. Policy in Asia," E-Notes from Foreign Policy Research Institute, 30 March 2001, accessed online from http://www.fpri.org/enotes/asia.20010330.campbell.challengesahead.html.

Carpenter, T. G., "U.S. Goes Too Far with Visit of Taiwan Official," Cato report, 25 March 2002, accessed online from http://www.cato.org/cgi-bin/scripts/printtech.cgi on 10 April 2002.

Carr, E. H., *The Twenty Years Crisis, 1919–1939: An Introduction to the Study of International Relations*, New York: Harper and Row, 1964.

Cashman, G., *What Causes War?* New York: Macmillan, 1993.

Chan, S., "Mirror, Mirror on the Wall . . . Are the Freer Countries More Pacific?" *Journal of Conflict Resolution* 28 (1984), pp. 617–48.

——, "Democracy and War: Some Thoughts on a Future Research Agenda," *International Interactions* 18 (1993), pp. 205–13.

Chang, G. G., *The Coming Collapse of China*, New York: Random House, 2001.

Chang, M. H., *Return of the Dragon: China's Wounded Nationalism*, Boulder, CO: Westview Press, 2001.

Chen, Weihang, "American Adoptions of Chinese Children," talk given at Yale University, 12 November 2004.

"Cheney: US–China Relations in Good Shape," *China Daily*, 14 April 2004, accessed online from http://www.chinadaily.com.cn/english the same day.

"China, Japan Share Responsibility to Push Forward Bilateral Ties: Vice President," *People's Daily*, 29 September 2002, p. 1.

"China Races to Replace U.S. as Economic Power in Asia," *New York Times* online edition, 28 June 2002.

"China's Century," Special Report, *Newsweek*, 9 May 2005, pp. 26–47.

"China's Comprehensive National Strength is a Quarter that of the United States," *Lianhe Zaobao* (Singapore), 15 July 2002.

"China's Influence Seen Positive," *BBC News*, 5 March 2005.

"China–United States Sustained Dialog," *Program Brief* 8(4), Nixon Center, Washington, DC, 19 March 2002.

Ching, F., "China Puts Growth before 'Reunification,'" *Japan Times*, 19 April 2002, accessed online from http://www.japantimes.co.jp the same day.

Choucri, N., and R. C. North, *Nations in Conflict: National Growth and International Violence*, San Francisco: Freeman, 1975.

Christensen, T. J., "Posing Problems Without Catching Up: China's Rise and Challenges for U.S. Security Policy," *International Security* 25(4) (2001), pp. 5–40.

——, "US–China Relations," talk given at Yale University, 22 April 2005.

Chu, S. L., "US–China Relations after the Iraq War," talk given at Colgate University, USA, 18 November 2003.

"CIA Warns of Chinese Plans for Cyber-Attacks on U.S.," *Los Angeles Times*, 25 April 2002, accessed online from http://latimes.com/la-042502china.story the same day.

Clifford, M., "Bush Sr.'s Glad Tidings for Beijing," *Business Week*, 10 May 2002, accessed online from www.businessweek.com the same day.

Cohen, W. I., *America's Response to China: A History of Sino-American Relations*, 4th edition, New York: Columbia University Press, 2000.

Commager, H. S. (ed.), *Britain Through American Eyes*, New York: McGraw-Hill, 1974.

"Committee of 100 Study Reveals Improved American Attitudes Toward China While Raising New Concerns," Committee of 100, New York, 13 January 2005, accessed online from www.committee100.org the same day.

Constitution of the People's Republic of China, 3rd edition, Beijing: Foreign Languages Press, 1994.

"Containing China," Editorial, *The Economist*, 29 July 1995, p. 11.

Cook, E., *How Britain Strove for Peace: Record of Anglo-German Negotiations 1898–1914*, London: Macmillan, 1914.

——, *Why Britain is at War: the Causes and the Issues*, London: Macmillan, 1914.

Copeland, D., *The Origins of Major War*, Ithaca, NY: Cornell University Press, 2000.

Costigliola, F., *Awkward Dominion: American Political, Economic, and Cultural Relations with Europe 1919–1933*, Ithaca, NY: Cornell University Press, 1984.

Cramb, J. A., *Germany and England*, New York: E. P. Dutton, 1914.

Crock, Stan, "The Coming U.S.–China Summits," *Business Week* online edition, 3 May 2005, accessed online from http://www.businessweek.com the same day.

Dahl, R., "The Concept of Power," *Behavioral Science* 2 (July 1957), p. 202.

Danchev, A., *On Specialness: Essays in Anglo-American Relations*, New York: St. Martin's Press, 1998.

Dawson, R., and R. Rosecrance, "Theory and Reality in the Anglo-American Alliance," *World Politics* 19(4) (1966), pp. 21–51.

Deng, Y., and F. L. Wang (eds.), *In the Eyes of the Dragon: China Views the World*, New York: Rowman & Littlefield, 1999.

Denny, C., "China is No Threat to America – for Now," *Guardian*, 8 April 2002, accessed online from http://www.guardian.co.uk the same day.

Deutsch, K. W. *et al., Political Community and the North Atlantic Area*, Princeton, NJ: Princeton University Press, 1957.

Diamond, J., "Prediction: India, China Will Be Economic Giants," *USA Today*, 13 January 2005, accessed online from www.usatoday.com/news the same day.

DiCicco, J. M., and J. S. Levy, "Power Shifts and Problem Shifts: The Evolution of the Power Transition Research Program," *Journal of Conflict Resolution* 43(6) (1999), pp. 657–704.

Diehl, P. F., and G. Goertz, *War and Peace in International Rivalry*, Ann Arbor, MI: University of Michigan Press, 2000.

Dimbleby, D., and D. Reynolds, *An Ocean Apart: The Relationship Between Britain and America in the Twentieth Century*, New York: Random House, 1988.

Dixon, W. J., "Democracy and the Peaceful Settlement of International Conflict," *American Political Science Review* 88 (1994), pp. 14–32.

Domke, W., *War and the Changing Global System*, New Haven, CT: Yale University Press, 1988.

Doran, C. F., *The Politics of Assimilation: Hegemony and Its Aftermath*, Baltimore: Johns Hopkins University Press, 1971.

———, *Systems in Crisis: New Imperatives of High Politics at Century's End*, Cambridge: Cambridge University Press, 1991.

Doran, C. F., and W. Parsons, "War and the Cycle of Relative Power," *American Political Science Review* 74(4) (December 1980), pp. 947–65.

Economy, E., "Take a New Look at a Changing China," *International Herald Tribune*, 30 April 2002, accessed online from http://www.iht.com on 3 May 2002.

Eley, G., "Defining Social Imperialism: Use and Abuse of an Idea," *Social History* 1(3) (1976), pp. 265–90.

Eliot, C. W., *British and German Ideals: The Meaning of the War*, London: Macmillan, 1915.

Ellis, J. D., and T. M. Koca, "China Rising: New Challenges to the U.S. Security Posture," *Strategic Forum* 175 (October 2000), pp. 1–4.

Evans, R. J., "Introduction: Wilhelm II's Germany and the Historians," in *Society and Politics in Wilhelmine Germany*, New York: Barnes and Noble, 1978, pp. 11–23.

Fang Ning *et al., Quanqiuhua yinmou xia de Zhongguo zhi lu* (China's Road: Under the Conspiracy of Globalization), Beijing: Chinese Social Sciences Publishing House, 1999.

Fischer, F., *Griff nach der Weltmacht*, Dusseldorf: Bertelsmann Universitätsverlag, 1961.

———, *War of Illusions: German Policies from 1911 to 1914*, New York: W. W. Norton, 1975.

Francis, D. R., "To Stay Out of the Red, China Needs To Go Green," *Christian Science Monitor*, 29 April 2004.

Freytag-Loringhoven, B., *Deductions from the World War*, London: Constable, 1918.

Friedberg, A. L., *The Weary Titan: Britain and the Experience of Relative Decline, 1895–1905*, Princeton, NJ: Princeton University Press, 1988.

Friedman, T. L., *The Lexus and the Olive Tree*, New York: Farrar Straus Giroux, 1999.

Funabashi, Y., *et al., An Emerging China in a World of Interdependence*, New York: Trilateral Commission, 1994.

Garver, J. W., "Will China be Another Germany?," paper prepared for the Conference on China into the Twenty-first Century: strategic partner and/or peer competitor, US Army War College, 23–25 April 1996.

——, "More From the 'Say No Club,'" *China Journal* 45 (January 2001), pp. 154–8.

——, "Sino-American Relations in 2001: The Difficult Accommodation of Two Great Powers," *International Journal,* Spring 2002, pp. 283–310.

Geiss, I., *German Foreign Policy 1871–1914,* London: Routledge & Kegan Paul, 1976.

Geller, D., "Power Transition and Conflict Initiation," *Conflict Management and Peace Science* 12(1) (1992), pp. 1–16.

Gertz, B., *The China Threat: How the People's Republic Targets America,* Washington, DC: Regnery Publishing, 2000.

Gilpin, R., *War and Change in World Politics,* New York: Cambridge University Press, 1981.

——, *The Challenge of Global Capitalism: The World Economy in the 21st Century,* Princeton, NJ: Princeton University Press, 2000.

"Global Views 2004: American Public Opinion and Foreign Policy," Chicago Council on Foreign Relations, Chicago, 2004.

Goldstein, J., *Long Cycles: Prosperity and War in the Modern Age,* New Haven, CT: Yale University Press, 1988.

Gong, G. W., *The Standard of "Civilization" in International Society,* Oxford: Oxford University Press, 1984.

Gordon, M., "Domestic Conflict and the Origins of the First World War: The British and German Cases," *Journal of Modern History* 46(2) (June 1974), pp. 191–226.

Haass, R. N., *The Reluctant Sheriff: the United States after the Cold War,* New York: Council on Foreign Relations Press, 1997.

——, "Why Foreign Policy (When It Comes to Judgment, at Least) Is Not Pornography," in Stanley A. Renshon and Deborah Welch Larson (eds.), *Good Judgment in Foreign Policy: Theory and Application,* Lanham, MD: Rowman & Littlefield, 2003, pp. 247–58.

Haass, R. N., and S. Stein Jr., "What to Do with American Primacy," *Foreign Affairs* 78(5) (September/October 1999), pp. 37–49.

Hamilton, L., "Keeping Peace With Rising China," *Indianapolis Star,* 25 April 2005, accessed online from http://www.indystar.com the same day.

Harding, H., *A Fragile Relationship: The United States and China since 1972,* Washington, DC: Brookings Institution, 1992.

——, "Tough and Smart on China," *Brookings Review* 11(46) (Winter 1993), p. 46.

Hart, J., "Three Approaches to the Measurement of Power in International Relations," *International Organization* 30(2) (Spring 1976), pp. 289–305.

Hathaway, R. M., *Great Britain and the United States: Special Relations since World War II,* Boston: Twayne Publishers, 1990.

——, "George Bush's Unfinished Asian Agenda," *Foreign Policy Research Institute* E-notes, Philadelphia, 13 May 2005.

Hawksley, H., and S. Holberton, *Dragon Strike: A Novel of the Coming War with China,* New York: St. Martin's Press, 1999.

"Highlights from Open Doors 2001," IIE website at www.opendoorsweb.org.

Hobbes, T., *Leviathan,* London: Oxford University Press, 1998.

Hoffman, R. J. S., *Great Britain and the German Trade Rivalry, 1875–1914,* New York: Russell & Russell, 1933, 1964.

Hoge, J. F., Jr., "A Global Power Shift in the Making," *Foreign Affairs* 83(4) (July/August 2004), pp. 2–7.

Holbrooke, R., "A Defining Moment with China," *Washington Post*, 2 January 2002, p. A13.

Holt, P. M., "The US–China Frame of Mind: Both Nations Need to Put Aside Paranoia and Talk Straight," *Christian Science Monitor*, 14 September 1995, p. 19.

"Homeland Defense: Issues and Challenges," *Program Brief* 8(10) (19 June 2002), Nixon Center, Washington, DC.

Houweling, H., and J. Siccama, "Power Transitions as a Cause of War," *Journal of Conflict Resolution* 32(1) (1998), pp. 87–102.

"Howard Steers Between Giants," *Australian*, 12 February 2005, accessed online from http://www.theaustralian.news.com.au the same day.

Hu Jintao, "Enhanced Mutual Understanding and Trust Toward a Constructive and Cooperative Relationship between China and the United States," speech in Washington, DC, 1 May 2002. Official translation from the Embassy of the People's Republic of China website at http://www.china-embassy.org/eng/29640.html.

Hua, V., "U.S. Poll Finds More View China Approvingly," *San Francisco Chronicle*, 13 January 2005, p. A12.

Huntington, S., *The Clash of Civilizations and the Remaking of World Order*, New York: Simon & Schuster, 1996.

——, "The Lonely Superpower," *Foreign Affairs* 78(2) (March/April 1999), pp. 35–49.

Ikle, F. C., *Every War Must End*, New York: Columbia University Press, 1991.

"It's Unambiguous: 'Strategic Ambiguity' is Dead," *Far Eastern Economic Review*, 25 April 2002.

Jervis, R., *Perception and Misperception in International Politics*, Princeton, NJ: Princeton University Press, 1976.

"Jiang Looks to US for Unlikely Final Legacy," *CNN News* at www.cnn.com, accessed on 22 October 2002.

"Jiang Sets off for Final US Tour," *CNN News* at www.cnn.com, accessed on 20 October 2002.

Jiang Zemin, *Political Report at the sixteenth National Congress of the Chinese Communist Party*, Beijing, November 2002.

Johnson, C., "The United States Should Not Try to Control China," in J. D. Torr (ed.), *China: Opposing Viewpoints*, San Diego: Greenhaven Press, 2001, pp. 184–9.

Joll, J., *The Origins of the First World War*, London: Longman, 1992.

Kahn, J., "Hands Across Pacific: U.S.–China Ties Grow," *New York Times*, 15 November 2002, accessed online from www.nytimes.com the same day.

Kantorowicz, H., *The Spirit of British Policy and the Myth of the Encirclement of Germany*, New York: Oxford University Press, 1932.

Kaplan, R. D., "How We Would Fight China," *Atlantic Monthly*, June 2005, pp. 49–64.

Kazmin, A., "ASEAN Leaders and China Sign Deal for Free Trade Area," *Financial Times*, 5 November 2002, p. 6.

Kegley, C. W., Jr., and G. A. Raymond, *A Multipolar Peace? Great-Power Politics in the Twenty-first Century*, New York: St. Martin's Press, 1994.

Kennedy, P., *The Rise of the Anglo-German Antagonism: 1860–1914*, London: George Allen & Unwin, 1980.

——, *The Rise and Fall of the Great Powers: Economic Change and Military Conflict from 1500 to 2000*, New York: Random House, 1987.

——, *Preparing for the Twenty-first Century*, New York: Random House, 1993.

Kennedy, S. (ed.), *China Cross Talk: The American Debate Over China Policy Since Normalization, A Reader*, Lanham, MD: Rowman & Littlefield, 2002.

Keohane, R., "The Theory of Hegemonic Stability and Changes in International Economic Regimes, 1967–1977," Cisa Working Paper Series no. 12, Los Angeles: UCLA Center for International Relations, 1980.

Keohane, R. O., and J. S. Nye Jr., "Power and Interdependence in the Information Age," *Foreign Affairs* 77(5) (September/October 1998), pp. 81–94.

Kim, W., "Power Transition and Great Power War from Westphalia to Waterloo," *World Politics* 45 (October 1992), pp. 153–72.

Kim, W., and James D. Morrow, "When Do Power Shifts Lead to War?" *American Journal of Political Science* 36(4) (November 1992), pp. 896–922.

Kissinger, H., *Nuclear Weapons and Foreign Policy*, New York: Harper, 1957.

——, *Diplomacy*, New York: Simon & Schuster, 1995.

——, *Does America Need a Foreign Policy? Toward A Diplomacy for the 21st Century*, New York: Simon & Schuster, 2001.

Klintworth, G., "China, Taiwan, and the United States," *Pacific Review* 13(1) (February 2001), pp. 41–60.

Knutsen, T. L., *The Rise and Fall of World Orders*, Manchester: Manchester University Press, 1999.

Kondratieff, N., *The Long Wave Cycle*, new edition by G. Daniels and J. Snyder, New York: Richardson and Snyder, 1984.

Krauthammer, C., "Beyond the Cold War," *New Republic* 199 (19 December 1988), pp. 14–19.

——, "Why We Must Contain China," *Time*, 31 July 1995, p. 72.

Kristof, N., "The Rise of China," *Foreign Affairs* 72(6) (November/December 1993), pp. 59–74.

Kristof, N., and S. WuDunn, *Thunder from the East: Portrait of a Rising Asia*, New York: Alfred A. Knopf, 2000.

Kugler, J., R. Tammen, and S. Swaminathan, "The Asian Century," paper presented at the International Studies Association Convention, Hong Kong, China, 26–28 July 2001.

Kugler, J., and D. Lemke, *Parity and War: Evaluations and Extensions of the War Ledger*, Ann Arbor, MI: University of Michigan Press, 1996.

——, "The Power Transition Research Program: Assessing Theoretical and Empirical Advances," in Manus I. Midlarsky (ed.), *Handbook of War Studies II*, Ann Arbor, MI: University of Michigan Press, 2000, pp. 129–63.

Kupchan, C. A., et al., *Power in Transition: The Peaceful Change of International Order*, Tokyo: United Nations University Press, 2001.

Kupchan, C., *The End of the American Era: U.S. Foreign Policy and the Geopolitics of the Twenty-first Century*, New York: Alfred A. Knopf, 2002.

Kurlantzick, J., "China's Influence Waxes as Washington's Wanes," *Washington Times*, 4 December 2000, accessed online from www.washtimes.com the same day.

Kynge, J., and J. Harding, "Jiang Zemin in Crawford: Why Beijing Is Eager to Please, and Washington Less Keen to Reciprocate," *Financial Times*, 22 October 2002, p. 13.

Lakely, J. G., "Bush Warns Taiwan Against Separation," *Washington Times*, 10 December 2003, p. 1.

Lam, W. W., "Hu's New Deal," CNN News Analysis at www.cnn.com, accessed on 3 December 2002.

Lampton, D. M., and K. Lieberthal, "Heading Off the Next War," *Washington Post*, 12 April 2004, p. A19.

Lampton, D. M., *Same Bed, Different Dreams: Managing U.S.–China Relations 1989–2000*, Berkeley, CA: University of California Press, 2001.

——, "The Danger of Writing Taiwan a Blank Security Check," Nixon Center, 15 August 2002.

Lapid, Y., and F. Kratochwil (eds.), *The Return of Culture and Identity in IR Theory*, Boulder, CO: Lynne Rienner Publishers, 1997.

Lardy, N. R., *China's Unfinished Economic Revolution*, Washington, DC: Brookings Institution Press, 1998.

——, *Integrating China into the Global Economy*, Washington, DC: Brookings Institution Press, 2002.

Lasater, M. L., *The Taiwan Conundrum in U.S. China Policy*, Boulder, CO: Westview Press, 2000.

Layne, C., "The Unipolar Illusion: Why New Great Powers Will Rise," *International Security* 17(4) (Spring 1993), pp. 5–51.

LeFeber, W., *The American Age: United States Foreign Policy at Home and Abroad since 1750*, New York: W. W. Norton, 1994.

Lemke, D., "The Continuation of History: Power Transition Theory and the End of the Cold War," *Journal of Peace Research* 34(1) (1997), pp. 23–36.

Lemke, D., and Kugler, J., "The Evolution of the Power Transition Perspective," in Kugler and Lemke (eds.), *Parity and War*, Ann Arbor, MI: University of Michigan Press, 1996, pp. 3–34.

Levy, J. S., "Too Important to Leave to the Other: History and Political Science in the Study of International Relations," *International Security* 22(1) (Summer 1997), pp. 22–33.

Li Peng, "Main Characteristics of China's Foreign Policy," speech at the 96th Inter-Parliamentary Conference on 19 September 1996, accessed online from http://www.china-embassy.org/eng/7005.html on 5 July 2002.

Lichtblau, E., "CIA Warns of Chinese Plans for Cyber-attacks on U.S.," *Los Angeles Times*, 25 April 2002, accessed online from http://latimes.com/la-042502china.sotry the same day.

Lieberthal, K., "Has China Become an Ally?," *New York Times*, 25 October 2002, accessed online from www.nytimes.com the same day.

——, "Dire Strait: The Risks on Taiwan," *Washington Post*, 8 January 2004, p. A23.

——, *Governing China: From Revolution Through Reform*, 2nd edition, New York: W. W. Norton, 2004.

Lilley, J. R., and W. L. Willkie II (eds.), *Beyond MFN: Trade with China and American Interests*, Washington, DC: AEI Press, 1994.

Liu, H. C. K., "How the US will Play China in the New Cold War," *Asia Times Online*, 19 April 2002, accessed online from http://www.atimes.com the same day.

——, "US, China: The Politics of Ambiguity," *Asia Times Online*, 24 April 2002, accessed online from http://www.atimes.com the same day.

Liu, J., "Will the 21st Century Belong to China or the United States?," *Beijing Review*, 27 March 2000, pp. 13–15.

Liu, M., and J. Barry, "Soft Power, Hard Choices: China is emerging as a major economic power, but will that translate into a military threat? Taiwan will be test," *MSNBC* and *Newsweek*, 7 March 2005, accessed online from http://www.msnbc.msn.com/id/7037845/site/newsweek/.

Lobe, J., "US Hawks Unhappy at Improving Beijing Ties," *Asia Times Online*, 13 July 2002 at www.atimes.com.

Lynn-Jones, S. M., *Germany and England: Background of Conflict 1848–1898*, New York: D. Appleton-Century Company, 1938.

McKercher, B. J. C., *Transition of Power: Britain's Loss of Global Pre-eminence to the United States, 1930–1945*, London: Cambridge University Press, 1999.

——, (ed.), *Anglo-American Relations in the 1920s*, Edmonton, AB: University of Alberta Press, 1990.

McNaugher, T. L., "A Strong China: Is the United States Ready?," *Brookings Review*, Fall 1994, pp. 15–19.

Mander, J., *Our German Cousins: Anglo-German Relations in the 19th and 20th Century*, London: John Murray, 1974.

Mann, J., *About Face: A History of America's Curious Relationship with China, from Nixon to Clinton*, New York: Alfred A. Knopf, 1999.

——, "Fears of Chinese Spying Only Deepens U.S. Mistrust," *Los Angeles Times*, 20 May 1999, accessed online from http://www.latimes.com the same day.

Mansfield, E. D., *Power, Trade, and War*, Princeton, NJ: Princeton University Press, 1994.

Mansfield, E. D., and J. Snyder, "Democratization and War," *Foreign Affairs* 74(3) (May–June 1995), pp. 79–87.

——, "Democratization and the Danger of War," *International Security* 20(1) (Summer 1995), pp. 5–38

Marquand, R., "US–China Relationship: not quite friends or enemies," *Christian Science Monitor*, 1 April 2002, accessed online from http://www.csmonitor.com/2002/0401/p07s02-woap.html.

Marsh, C., and J. Teufel Dreyer (eds.), *US–China Relations in the Twenty-first Century: Policies, Prospects and Possibilities*, New York: Rowman & Littlefield, 2003.

Martel, G., *The Origins of the First World War*, London: Longman, 1996.

Martin, J. R. (ed.), *Defeating Terrorism: Strategic Issue Analyses*, Carlisle, PA: US Army War College, 2002.

Martin, L., "Interests, Power, and Multilateralism," *International Organization* 46 (1992), pp. 765–92.

Mearsheimer, J., *The Tragedy of Great Power Politics*, New York: W. W. Norton, 2001.

Midlarsky, M. I., *On War: Political Violence in the International System*, New York: Free Press, 1975.

Miller, B., *When Opponents Cooperate: Great Power Conflict and Collaboration in World Politics*, Ann Arbor, MI: University of Michigan Press, 2003.

Modelski, G., *Long Cycles in World Politics*, London: Macmillan, 1987.

Modelski, G., and W. Thompson, *Leading Sectors and World Powers*, Columbia, SC: University of South Carolina Press, 1996.

Monger, G., *The End of Isolation: British Foreign Policy 1900–1907*, London: T. Nelson, 1963.

Morgenthau, H., *Politics among Nations: The Struggle for Power and Peace*, New York: Alfred A. Knopf, 1948.

Moser, J. E., *Twisting the Lion's Tail: American Anglophobia between the World Wars*, New York: New York University Press, 1999.

Mufson, S., "In GOP, A Simmering Struggle on China Policy," *Washington Post*, 22 August 2000, p. A10.

Myers, R., M. Oksenberg, and D. Shambaugh (eds.), *Making China Policy: Lessons from the Bush and Clinton Administrations*, New York: Rowman and Littlefield, 2001.

Nathan, A. J., and R. S. Ross, *The Great Wall and the Empty Fortress: China's Search for Security*, New York: W. W. Norton, 1997.

Nevins, A. (ed.), *America Through British Eyes*, New York: Oxford University Press, 1948.

"New Leader Chosen in China," *Washington Post*, 15 November 2002, p. A1.

"New Pentagon Report Sees Rapid Buildup by China," *New York Times*, 13 July 2002.

Nicholas, H. G., *The United States and Britain*, Chicago: University of Chicago Press, 1975.

Niebuhr, R., "Awkward Imperialists," *Atlantic Monthly* 145 (June 1930), pp. 670–5.

——, "Perils of American Power," *Atlantic Monthly* 149 (January 1932), pp. 90–6.

Northedge, F. S., "Britain as a Second-Rank Power," *International Affairs* 46 (1970), p. 47–62.

Nye, J. S., Jr., *Bound to Lead: The Changing Nature of American Power*, New York: Basic Books, 1990.

Olson, M., *The Rise and Decline of Nations: Economic Growth, Stagflation, and Social Rigidities*, New Haven, CT: Yale University Press, 1982.

Oneal, J. R., and B. M. Russett, *Triangulating Peace: Democracy, Interdependence & International Organizations*, New York: W. W. Norton, 2001.

Organski, A. F. K., *World Politics*, New York: Alfred A. Knopf, 1958, 1968.

Organski, A. F. K., and J. Kugler, *The War Ledger*, Chicago: University of Chicago Press, 1980.

Ovendale, R., *Anglo-American Relations in the Twentieth Century*, New York: St. Martin's Press, 1998.

Padfield, P., *The Great Naval Race*, London: Hart-Davis, MacGibbon, 1974.

Papayoanou, P., *Power Ties: Economic Interdependence, Balancing, and War*, Ann Arbor, MI: University of Michigan Press, 1999.

Parmar, I., *Special Interests, the State and the Anglo-American Alliance 1939–1945*, London: Frank Cass, 1995.

"Pentagon to Renew Ties with China," *CNN News*, accessed online from www.cnn.com on 22 June 2002.

Perlez, J., "Asian Leaders Find China a More Cordial Neighbor," *New York Times*, 18 October 2003, accessed online from www.nytimes.com the same day.

Pillsbury, M., *China Debates the Future Security Environment*, Washington, DC: National Defense University, 2000.

Plate, T., "The Virtue of Keeping Mum on Taiwan," *Japan Times*, 29 April 2002, accessed online from http://www.japantimes.co.jp the same day.

Poggi, G., *The State: Its Nature, Development, and Prospects*, Stanford, CA: Stanford University Press, 1990.

"Poll: Australia Against Taiwan War," *CNN*, 28 March 2005.

Pomfret, J., "Beijing Signals New Flexibility on Taiwan," *Washington Post*, 5 January 2001, p. A1.

——, "China Sees Interests Tied to U.S.," *Washington Post*, 2 February 2002, p. A1.

——, "China Embraces More Moderate Foreign Policy," *Washington Post*, 24 October 2002, p. A23.

Powell, C. L., Remarks at Asia Society annual dinner, New York, 10 June 2002.

——, Remarks at the Elliott School of International Affairs, Washington, DC, 5 September 2003.

"Powell: I Can Call Chinese Foreign Minister Directly," *Lianhe Zaobao* (Singapore), 8 November 2003, accessed online the same day from http://www.zaobao.com.

Powell, R., "Uncertainty, Shifting Power, and Appeasement," *American Political Science Review* 90(4) (December 1996), pp. 749–64.

"Powell Speaks of China, Taiwan 'Reunification,'" *Reuters*, 25 October 2004.

"President: China Targets US\$4 Trillion GDP by 2020," *China Daily*, 16 May 2005, accessed online from www.chinadaily.com.cn/english the same day.

Puchala, D. J., "The History of the Future of International Relations," *Ethics & International Affairs* 8 (1994), pp. 177–202.

——, "Some Implications of China's Military Modernization," *Issues and Studies* 37(1) (January/February 2001), pp. 102–23.

Pumphrey, C. W. (ed.), *The Rise of China in Asia: Security Implications*, Carlisle, PA: Strategic Studies Institute, 2002.

Putnam, R. D., "Diplomacy and Domestic Politics: The Logic of Two-Level Games," *International Organization*, 42 (Summer 1988), pp. 427–60.

Pye, L. W., "China: Not Your Typical Superpower," *Problems of Post-Communism*, July/August 1996, pp. 3–15.

Rand Corporation, "The United States and a Rising China," Report MR-1082-AF, 1999, accessed online from www.rand.org/publications/MR/MR1082/.

Ray, J. L., "Status Inconsistency and War Involvement in Europe, 1816–1970," *Papers of the Peace Science Society (International)* 23 (1974), pp. 69–80.

——, *Democracy and International Conflict*, Columbia, SC: University of South Carolina Press, 1995.

——, "Does Interstate War Have a Future?," *Conflict Management and Peace Science* 19(1) (Spring 2002), pp. 53–80.

"Remarks by President Bush and Chinese President Hu Jintao After Bilateral Meeting," Hyatt Regency Hotel, Santiago, Chile, 20 November 2004. Released by the Office of the Press Secretary, the White House the same day.

Renouovin, P., "Britain and the Continent: The Lessons of History," *Foreign Affairs* 17 (October 1938), pp. 111–27.

Renshon, S. A., and D. W. Larson (eds.), *Good Judgment in Foreign Policy: Theory and Application*, Lanham, MD: Rowman & Littlefield, 2003.

Renwick, R., *Fighting with Allies: America and Britain in Peace and at War*, New York: Times Books, 1996.

Reynolds, D., *Britannia Overruled: British Policy and World Power in the Twentieth Century*, London: Longman, 1999.

Richter, S., "Repeating History: In Dealing With China, the United States Can Learn a Great Deal from British–German Relations in 1880," *Globalist*, 11 July 2000, accessed online from http://www.theglobalist.com/nor/news/2000/07-11-00.shtml.

Rieff, D., "A Second American Century? The Paradoxes of Power," *World Policy Journal*, Winter 1999/2000, pp. 7–14.

"A Rising China," editorial, *New York Times*, 6 May 2005, accessed online from http://www.nytimes.com the same day.

Rock, S. R., *Why Peace Breaks Out: Great Power Rapprochement in Historical Perspective*, Chapel Hill, NC: University of North Carolina Press, 1989.

Roosa, R. V., "Where is Britain Heading?" *Foreign Affairs* 46 (1968), pp. 503–19.

Rosecrance, R. (ed.), *Action and Reaction in World Politics: International Systems in Perspective*, Boston: Little and Brown, 1963.

——, *The Rise of the Trading State: Commerce and Conquest in the Modern World*, New York: Basic Books, 1986.

——, *The Rise of the Virtual State: Wealth and Power in the Coming Century*, New York: Basic Books, 1999.

——, *The New Great Power Coalition: Toward a World Concert of Nations*, Lanham, MD: Rowman & Littlefield, 2001.

Rosenau, J. N., *Turbulence in World Politics: A Theory of Change and Continuity*, Princeton, NJ: Princeton University Press, 1990.

Roy, J. S., "The Rise of China and the Outlook for US–China Relations," National Committee on United States–China Relations Notes, Winter/Spring 2005, pp. 14–17.

Rudman, W. B, "Homeland Defense: Issues and Challenges," Nixon Center, Washington, DC, 19 June 2002.

Ruggie, J. G., *Multilateralism Matters: The Theory and Praxis of an Institutional Form*, New York: Columbia University Press, 1993.

Russett, B. M., *Community and Contention: Britain and America in the Twentieth Century*, Cambridge, MA: MIT Press, 1963.

——, *Grasping the Democratic Peace: Principles for a Post Cold War World*, Princeton, NJ: Princeton University Press, 1993.

Samuelson, R. J., "Economics as Statecraft," *Newsweek*, 29 November 1999, p. 58.

Sanger, D. E., "Bush Outlines Doctrine of Striking Foes First," *New York Times*, 20 September 2002, p. A1.

——, "Bush Lauds China Leader 'Partner' in Diplomacy," *New York Times*, 10 December 2003, p. A6

Sarolea, C., *The Anglo-German Problem*, London: Thomas Nelson and Sons, 1912.

Schaller, M., *The United States and China: Into the Twenty-First Century*, Oxford: Oxford University Press, 2002.

Schell, O., "Prisoner of Its Past," *Salon Magazine*, 8 June 1999, accessed online from http://archive.salon.com/news/feature/1999/06/08/china/index.html.

Schmitt, B. E., *England and Germany 1740–1914*, Princeton, NJ: Princeton University Press, 1918.

Segal, G., "Tying China into the International System," *Survival* 37 (1995), pp. 60–73.

Shambaugh, D., "The United States and China: A New Cold War?," *Current History* 94 (1995), pp. 241–7.

——, "Containment or Engagement of China?" *International Security* 20(4) (1996), pp. 180–209.

——, "Beijing Charms Its Neighbors," *International Herald Tribune*, 14 May 2005, p. 8.

Shao, V., "Trojan Horse or Peace Bridge: Trade across the Taiwan Straits," *China Times*, 22 October 2002, accessed online from http://news.chinatimes.com the same day.

Shenkar, O., *The Chinese Century: The Rising Chinese Economy and Its Impact on the Global Economy, the Balance of Power, and Your Job*, Wharton School Publishing, 2004.

Singer, D., "The Level-of-Analysis Problem in International Relations," *World Politics* 14 (1961), pp. 77–92.

Singer, M., and A. Wildavsky, *The Real World Order: Zones of Peace/Zones of Turmoil*, Chatham, NJ: Chatham House, 1996.

Siverson, R. M., and M. P. Sullivan, "The Distribution of Power and the Onset of War," *Journal of Conflict Resolution* 27 (1983), pp. 473–94.

Snyder, G. H., *Deterrence and Defense: Toward a Theory of National Security*, Princeton, NJ: Princeton University Press, 1961.

Song Qiang *et al.*, *Zhongguo keyi shuo bu* (China Can Say No), Beijing: Chinese Indus-trial & Commercial Joint Publishing House, 1996.

Sontag, R. J., *Germany and England; Background of Conflict 1848–1898*, New York: D. Appleton-Century Company, 1938.

Special Report: U.S.–China Relations since the End of the Cold War, Washington, DC: Wood-row Wilson International Center for Scholars, August 2000.

Special Report: Theater Missile Defense and U.S. Foreign Policy Interests in Asia, Washington, DC: Woodrow Wilson International Center for Scholars, October 2000.

Spender, S., *Love-hate Relations: A Study of Anglo-American Sensibilities*, London: Hamil-ton, 1974.

Sprout, H., and M. Sprout, *The Ecological Perspective on Human Affairs*, Princeton, NJ: Princeton University Press, 1965.

Starr, H., "'Opportunity' and 'Willingness' as Ordering Concepts in the Study of War," *International Interactions* 4 (1978), pp. 363–87.

——, *Anarchy, Order, and Integration: How to Manage Interdependence*, Ann Arbor, MI: Uni-versity of Michigan Press, 1997.

Steiner, Z. S., *Britain and the Origins of the First World War*, London: Macmillan, 1977.

Stibbe, M., *German Anglophobia and the Great War, 1914–1918*, Cambridge: Cambridge University Press, 2001.

Suettinger, R., and R. Sutter, "The China Threat and Its Implications for U.S. Policy – A Briefing: Background and Rationale," talk at the Miller Center, University of Virginia, 2 April 2002.

Sutter, R. G., *U.S. Policy toward China: An Introduction to the Role of Interest Groups*, Lan-ham, MD: Rowman & Littlefield, 1998.

——, "The U.S. Congress: Personal, Partisan, Political," in R. H. Myers, *et al.* (eds.), *Making China Policy: Lessons from the Bush and Clinton Administration*, New York: Row-man & Littlefield, 2001.

Swaine, M. D., and A. J. Tellis, *Interpreting China's Grand Strategy: Past, Present, and Future*, Santa Monica, CA: RAND, 2000.

"Taiwan Independence Brings No Lasting Peace and Stability," *People's Daily*, 20 May 2004, p. 1.

Tammen, R. L., J. Kugler, *et al.*, *Power Transition: Strategies for the 21st Century*, New York: Seven Bridges Press, 2000.

Taylor, A. J. P., *The Struggle for Mastery in Europe: 1848–1918*, London: Oxford University Press, 1957.

Taylor, J., "Bush Scraps China Policy of Six Presidents," *Los Angeles Times*, 28 April 2002, accessed online from http://www.latimes.com the same day.

Taylor, P., *A Great Wall: Six Presidents and China*, New York: Public Affairs, 1999.

Thomas, M. S, and Zhao Mei (eds.), *China–United States Sustained Dialog 1986–2001*, New York: Kettering Foundation, 2001.

Thompson, W. R., *Great Power Rivalries*, Columbia, SC: University of South Carolina Press, 1998.

Thomson, J. A. K. (trans.), *The Ethics of Aristotle*, London: Penguin Books, 1976.

Thucydides, *History of the Peloponnesian War*, trans. Rex Warner, Harmondsworth: Pen-guin, 1954.

Tilly, C., *Coercion, Capital, and European States, AD 990–1990*, Cambridge: Basil Black-well, 1990.

Toll, J., *The Origins of the First World War*, London: Longman, 1992.

Torr, J. D. (ed.), *China: Opposing Viewpoints*, San Diego: Greenhaven Press, 2001.

Toynbee, A., *War and Civilization*, New York: Oxford University Press, 1950.

Tucker, N. B., "China and America: 1941–1991," *Foreign Affairs* 70(5) (Winter 1991/92), pp. 75–93.

——, "The Clinton Years: the Problem of Coherence" in Ramon H. Myers *et al.* (eds.), *Making China Policy: Lessons from Bush and Clinton Administrations*, New York: Rowman & Littlefield, 2001, pp. 45–78.

——, "If Taiwan Chooses Unification, Should the United States Care?," *Washington Quarterly*, Summer 2002, pp. 15–28.

Turner, A. C., *The Unique Partnership: Britain and the United States*, New York: Bobbs-Merrill, 1971.

"U.S.–China Flights to Increase," *USA Today*, 20 June 2004.

"US–China Relationship: Not Quite Friends or Enemies," *Christian Science Monitor*, 1 April 2002, p. 7.

"U.S.–China Ties Still Strong," *Associated Press*, 31 May 2001 at http://dailynews.yahoo.com/htx/ap/20010531/pl/us_china_life_goes_on_3.html.

"U.S. Nuclear Plan Sees New Weapons and New Targets," *New York Times*, 10 March 2002, p. 1.

"The US Reiterates It Does Not Support Taiwan Independence," *Lianhe Zaobao* (Singapore), 9 August 2002.

"US Willing to Cooperate with China in Many Fields: Rumsfeld," *Xinhua News*, 5 June 2004, accessed online from www.chinaview.cn the same day.

"U.S. Works Up Plan for Using Nuclear Arms," *Los Angeles Times*, 9 March 2002, p. 1.

Valladoao, A. G. A., *The Twenty-first Century Will be American*, London: Verso, 1996.

Van Evera, S., *Causes of War: Power and the Roots of Conflict*, Ithaca, NY: Cornell University Press, 1999.

Varg, P. A., *From Client State to World Power: Six Major Transitions in U.S. Foreign Relations*, Norman, OK: University of Oklahoma Press, 1991.

Vogel, E. F. (ed.), *Living with China: U.S.–China Relations in the Twenty-first Century*, New York: W. W. Norton, 1997.

Wallerstein, I., "The United States and the World 'Crisis,'" in Terry Boswell and Albert Bergesen (eds.), *America's Changing Role in the World System*, New York: Praeger, 1987, pp. 1–29.

——, "The Eagle Has Crash Landed," *Foreign Policy* (July/August 2002), pp. 60–8.

Walt, S. M., "Two Cheers for Clinton's Foreign Policy," *Foreign Affairs* 79 (March/April 2000), pp. 63–79.

Waltz, K. N., *Man, the State, and War*, New York: Columbia University Press, 1959.

——, *Theory of International Politics*, Reading, MA: Addison-Wesley, 1979.

——, "Globalization and American Power," *National Interest* 59 (Spring 2000), pp. 46–56.

Wang, J., "The Role of the United States as a Global and Pacific Power: A View from China," *Pacific Review* 10(1) (1997), pp. 1–18.

Ward, A., "China and America: Trouble Ahead?," *Survival* 45(3) (Autumn 2003), pp. 35–56.

Warner, G., "The Anglo-American Special Relationship," *Diplomatic History* 13(4) (Fall 1989), pp. 479–99.

Watt, D. C., *Succeeding John Bull: America in Britain's Place, 1900–1975*, Cambridge: Cambridge University Press, 1984.

"White Paper – The One-China Principle and the Taiwan Issue," Taiwan Affairs

Office and Information Office of the State Council, 21 February 2000, Beijing, available online at http://www.china-embassy.org/eng/c2865.html.

"White Paper – The Taiwan Question and Reunification of China," Taiwan Affairs Office and Information Office of the State Council, August 1993, Beijing, available online at http://www.china-embassy.org/eng/c2865.html.

Wills, G., "Bully of the Free World," *Foreign Affairs* 78(2) (March/April 1999), pp. 50–9.

Wolfowitz, P., talk at the Foreign Press Club, Washington, DC, 29 May 2002. News transcripts from the Department of Defense website at http://www.dod.gov/news/May2002/briefings.html.

Wright, Q., *The Causes of War and the Conditions of Peace*, London: Longmans, Green and Company, 1935.

——, *A Study of War*, Chicago: University of Chicago Press, 1942, 1965.

Wu, X., "Taipei Non-Negotiable," *South China Morning Post*, 19 November 2000, accessed online from http://www.scmp.com the same day.

Xie, X., and S. Ni, *Quzhe de licheng: Zhong Mei jianjiao ershi nian* (From normalization to renormalization: Twenty years of Sino-U.S. relations), Shanghai: Fudan University Press, 1999.

"Year after Spy Plane Crisis, China–US Ties Face New Uncertainty," *AFP News*, 31 March 2002, accessed online from http://sg.search.yahoo.com/search/news the same day.

Zhang, J., "U.S.–China Relations in the Post-Cold War Period: A Chinese Perspective," *Journal of Northeast Asian Studies* 14 (Summer 1995), pp. 47–61.

Zhang, Z., "US Containment Strategies Misled," *Beijing Review*, 16–22 October 1995, p. 4.

Zhang Zeqing, *America, Why Are You Powerful?*, Beijing: China City Publishing House, 1999.

"Zhu Advocates Continued Independent Foreign Policy of Peace in 2002," *Xinhua* news dispatch, 5 March 2002.

Zhu, Z., "To Support or Not to Support: the American Debate on China's WTO Membership," *Journal of Chinese Political Science* 6(2) (Fall 2000), pp. 77–101.

——, "Taiwan's Tragic Delusion," *Asia Times Online*, 10 December 2004, accessed online from www.atimes.com the same day.

Index

development of 27–8; expansionist
policies of 28–9, 41–2; indictment
of "British Imperialism" in 40;
industrialization of 33–4; "inferiority
complex" of society in 39; Jiaozhou,
seizure of 32; military forces of
(1872–1914) 44; naval power of
44–5; press hostility toward Britain
in 39–40; "preventive war" policy
of 35; revisionism of 163–4; rise in
power of 22; Triple Alliance (Austria,
Germany, Italy) 30; urbanization of
34; *Weltpolitik* of 31–2, 34–6, 41–2, 43,
135; *see also* British–German relations
(1871–1914); Prussia
Ghent, Treaty of 84
Gilpin, Robert 10, 11, 13
Gilpin's theory of "hegemonic war" 11,
13
Gladstone, William E. 57, 68
globalization 125; cooperative catalyst
92, 93; dynamic nature of 157;
inextricable links of 183–5; positive
aspect of 130; and power transition,
comparisons and contrasts 153–7;
US–China relations in era of 90–6
Globescan 152–3
Goschen, George Joachim 46
Grant, Ulysses S. 57
Great Britain 143, 165, 179; alliance
with Japan 61, 69, 82, 83;
apprehension in society, spiral of
38; balance of power in Europe and
29; bilateral trade with Germany
33; commercial domination of 27;
decline in global position of 146–7;
decline of (and rise of America) 54–6;
decline of (and the rise of Germany)
26–8; domestic politics in 36–8;
empire of 55; "financial Dunkirk"
post-World War II 64; "free traders'
and 'fair traders" in 36–7; industrial
pioneer 33; isolationist policy of
30–2; military forces of (1872–1914)
44; naval superiority, a "cardinal
principle" for 29; neutrality on Civil
War in US 57; opportunistic, ad
hoc diplomacy of 38; policy-making
elite of 69; political unrest in 36–7;
press hostility toward Germany in
39–40; rapprochement with US 58–9;
recognition of US great power status
21; traditional enemies, France and
Russia 28; Triple Entente (Russia,

France, Britain) 30–32; Venezuela
dispute 58; Washington Treaties
(1921–2) 60; *see also* British–German
relations (1871–1914)
Great Depression 69
The Great Illusion (Angell, N.) 162–3
Greece 67
Grey, Sir Edward 30, 32, 45, 68
Guam 74
Gulf War (1991) 95

Hamilton, Alexander 71
Hapsburg Empire 10
Hathaway, Robert 114
Hawaii 74
Hawthorne, Nathaniel 77
Helms, Jesse 98
hierarchical nature of world system 13
historical–structural analysis of power
transition 12
Hitler, Adolf 70, 161, 179
Hobbes, Thomas 155
Hohenlohe-Schillingsfurst, Chlodwig
Karl, Prince 43
Hollywood 75
Hong Kong 182
Hsu Hsin-liang 182
Hu Jintao 89, 93–4, 101, 104, 115, 129,
131, 139, 144, 158
hypotheses: challenging power, respect
of dominant for vital interests of
(hypothesis 3) 23; Anglo-American
relations (1865–1945) 86; British–
German relations (1871–1914) 51–2;
Sino-American relations (1990–2005)
127–8; dominant power, respect
of challenger for vital interests of
(hypothesis 2) 23; Anglo-American
relations (1865–1945) 86; British–
German relations (1871–1914) 51;
Sino-American relations (1990–2005)
126–7; general hypothesis 23; Anglo-
American relations (1865–1945)
87; British–German relations
(1871–1914) 52–3; Sino-American
relations (1990–2005) 129–31;
incorporation of rising powers
(hypothesis 1) 23; Anglo-American
relations (1865–1945) 85–6; British–
German relations (1871–1914) 51;
Sino-American relations (1990–2005)
126; leaders' commitment to stability
and constructiveness in relationship
(hypothesis 5) 23; Anglo-American